D1050022

FACING LIFE

By Oscar Handlin

Boston's Immigrants: A Study in Acculturation (1941)
This Was America (1949)
The Uprooted (1951)
Adventure in Freedom (1954)
Harvard Guide to American History (1954)
American People in the Twentieth Century (1954)
Chance or Destiny (1955)
Race and Nationality in American Life (1957)
Readings in American History (1957)
Al Smith and His America (1958)
Immigration as a Factor in American History (1959)
John Dewey's Challenge to American Education (1959)
The Newcomers: Negroes and Puerto Ricans in a Changing Metropolis (1959)
American Principles and Issues: The National Purpose (1961)
The Americans (1963)
Fire-Bell in the Night: The Crisis in Civil Rights (1964)

With Mary F. Handlin

Commonwealth: A Study of the Role of Government in American Economy (1947)
Dimensions of Liberty (1961)
Popular Sources of Political Authority (1966)
The American College and American Culture (1970)
Facing Life: Youth and the Family in American History (1971)

FACING LIFE

Youth and the Family in American History

by

OSCAR HANDLIN
and
MARY F. HANDLIN

An Atlantic Monthly Press Book

LITTLE, BROWN AND COMPANY · BOSTON · TORONTO

LIBRARY OF CONGRESS CATALOG CARD NO. 74-161852

FIRST EDITION

T10/71

ATLANTIC–LITTLE, BROWN BOOKS
ARE PUBLISHED BY
LITTLE, BROWN AND COMPANY
IN ASSOCIATION WITH
THE ATLANTIC MONTHLY PRESS

Published simultaneously in Canada
by Little, Brown & Company (Canada) Limited

PRINTED IN THE UNITED STATES OF AMERICA

PREFACE

WHY wish to be free?

Freedom carries with it obligations — for decisions, for choices and for unexpected experiences. It threatens routine and order, breeds change, conflict and insecurity. Yet some men and women seek it in preference to the comfort of unvarying habit, to the certainty of infallible authority, to the peace of a rigid system which admits no questions and holds each individual in place.

The human personality can grow in one direction or another. It can develop traits of character that reach toward liberty or toward stability as the social environment encourages it to unfold in one fashion or another. The relationship of the seed to the soil, of the individual personality to the society, is complex; but we believe that an important element in that relationship is the manner in which adults emerge from the dependence of childhood.

Through much of their past Americans preferred freedom, not only as a political philosophy but also as a style of life that emphasized risk, innovation, individuality, and impatience with social constraint. The inclination toward liberty had connections with the process of growing up which, in the United States, long required youths on the threshold of maturity to leave home. This book traces the changes in that process from the earliest colonial settlements to the present.

To describe the developing ways of leaving home called for an analysis of three vital but neglected aspects of the American past. The family into which the child was born and in which he lived part of his life was long the central institution of the society. The economic system that shaped opportunities for careers influenced the time and character of the departure. And the educational system supplied the channels of exit. Our account traces the reactions upon each other of parents, jobs and schools in the context of evolving social and cultural conditions.

We drew the material for this account partly from the records and histories of institutions such as colleges and academies and partly from the statements of contemporaries, argumentative, contemplative or imaginative. But to bring the story alive we also found it necessary to supply illustrations from the lives of the people who passed through the experience described. Some of the characters mentioned are famous, others obscure; both are necessary to a rounded portrayal. Some names will be known to every reader, others to only a few. Rather than load the text with a mass of identifying detail we have added a cast of characters at the end of the book in which we locate each person mentioned and supply brief references to some of the sources. We have used no material which came to us in confidence from students, colleagues, or parents. And we have shielded with pseudonyms some statements and actions which, though public, might later cause regret to their thoughtless young authors.

For the events of the past decade, we used the outpouring of sociological and psychological studies elicited by attention to the problems of youth. But having lived in close contact with some of those problems we utilized our direct observations also. We were aware of the danger of bias, growing not only out of personal observation and prejudice but also out of immersal in a particular type of community with a particular student body. We have tried to offset that danger by visits to scores of different colleges from Waterville, Maine, to Redlands, California, where we profited by the opportunity to talk with colleagues and students.

Those who read the pages that follow will learn that the crisis in which our youth are involved is neither novel nor unexpected; and it may run deeper than politicians and journalists suspect. From year to year it may wax or wane; but it will not disappear of itself. We can only hope that a longer perspective than they usually enjoy will help Americans understand it.

For more than a decade, we have profited from the opportunity to discuss the problems related to this subject with the Fellows first of the Center for the Study of History of Liberty in America and then of the Charles Warren Center for Studies in American History at Harvard University. We are grateful to them and to the Carnegie Corporation of New York which, for ten years, supported the first of those centers. In the preparation of this manuscript we had the assistance of Richard Gringeri and of Nancy Hair and, above all, of Alicia Zintl who cheerfully and efficiently imposed order upon our affairs and helped us around many difficulties that would otherwise have been time-consuming. For the opinions here expressed we are, of course, alone responsible.

OSCAR HANDLIN
MARY F. HANDLIN

CONTENTS

FACING LIFE

1

A WAY OF LIFE ON THE SOIL

Aloys clings soberly to the edge of the cart as it lurches along the rutted mountain path. The rough planks of the flat bed offer him no convenient grip and he must keep his dangling legs out of the way of the wheels. It would be an immense indignity for a boy of seven to fall off, or to suffer a scrape from the turning iron rims.

Nevertheless Aloys looks up as the cart passes us. His father who holds the reins up ahead has greeted us; and Aloys does too.

"Grüetzi, Miteinandt," says Aloys.

That is the proper way.

In the late afternoon the cart comes down, laden with logs. Now the boy is on foot as is his father. Again Aloys is in back, but this time he clutches the rust-flecked crank that applies the wooden brakes to the rear wheels. He watches his father who strides just to the left of the front wheels. At the steeper slopes, on the way to the village *holzlagerplatz,* the man swiftly twirls his crank and the boy follows his lead; they thus ease the burden on the old horse. When the road levels off, Aloys will again watch his father to know when to release the brake.

This is the first year that Aloys can help. He is seven and can do what he should. He remembers earlier times when he went up to the forest. But the flow of the path is not as familiar to him as it is to his father, who knows every twist and turn, every rise and ascent, and who can therefore anticipate what lies ahead. In time, of course, the boy too will learn the way and then will not only watch but know how to place the wedge and swing the axe and apply the brake. Some day indeed he will be in front.

That is how it should be.

The village maintains an elaborate pretense that nothing has changed. Down below there is a motor road and a railroad and some of the logs go off to a factory to be turned into pulp for unknown uses. Also there is a school where Aloys will learn to read and write. Now and then one of the boys will be singled out to go on to the *gymnasium,* twenty miles away, to become a clerk or engineer or teacher. But that is most unusual and it makes sense neither to Aloys nor to his father, for those who leave do not come back and thus lose their places. On the other hand, it might well make sense when Aloys is a little older to go off in the winter to work for a season in a hotel; for the youths who do so usually do come back in the spring with a little cash and do keep their places.

Place is important. The child acquires a claim to it through being born into a family which is itself situated in the village. The process of growing up is one of learning how to behave in a manner appropriate to the position manhood will bring. Some day Aloys will lead the way into the woods and youngsters of his own will follow him. To be a good father in the future he must be a good son now and, by watching carefully, acquire all the skills the head of a household must possess. Therefore he will do as the old man tells him to — in the fields as in the forest, in the marketplace as in the home, in the manner of dress as in the manner of speech.

That is how the place remains intact, from generation to generation.

Places such as that to which Aloys belongs survive in the twentieth century only in the remote corners of Europe. For hundreds of years, incessant changes in the ways goods were produced and distributed, the restless movements of peoples and the growth of cities undermined the stability the mountain village still struggles to preserve.

Yet the home in which Aloys grew up long was central to the social institutions of Europe. And its influence persisted in the memories, in the habits of behavior and in the emotional needs — fulfilled and unfulfilled — of the descendants of the Europeans who came to America.

Always the migrants left because they had to. Yet in moving away, they wished to retain, preserve and strengthen the values of home. Often resentment embittered the leaving: there was no place for them. At the thought of the barely known spaces of the outside, the heart sometimes leaped with hope, sometimes throbbed with dread. The motives that entered into each individual departure took a thousand different forms. Yet never was the break so complete, whether the wandering was a few miles to town or hundreds across the waters, that it did not leave the ache of emptiness. So that, wherever the son arrived, the need to re-create the place home had been became an overwhelming concern. At the journey's end, each man aspired to the father's role, his by right of birth, his despite the separation.

Life on earth had meaning in the completion of the cycle. The son was born to be a father, so that when he died there would be a son still to be a father. The son followed so that some day he could lead; he learned in order, in time, to be able to teach. Only through the family could the individual fulfill himself, for thus the generations succeeded one another.

For a long time, in the European setting, the conditions of rural life preserved the continuity of the family. The father directed the enterprise by which all lived. He was the breadwinner, the others helpers. Without his labor, all would perish and therefore all accepted his authority. Everyone else had tasks related to age and status. The years of infant idleness were brief indeed; there was work for the young children in the domain of the housewife and as the boys grew up each moved on to new duties commensurate with his strength and skill. The passing years thus demanded from the growing youth a steadily increasing amount of labor; but they also brought him closer to the goal of being his own master. It was thus, by helping the father, that he learned to sow the life-sustaining seeds and reap the grain, to cut the hay and dry it in stacks, and against the winter's cold and blasts of wind to lay in stocks of wood, to weight the roof with stones and in good time to replace the worn or rotting planks—all the techniques a man must know to be his own master. And the blade that shaped the board for the wall or a new leg for the stool, also found in the wood the same fanciful figures it had for the father, just as slowly, listening to the talk of elders, the boy acquired the wisdom of the man.

Growing, learning, doing were aspects of a single process by which the individual preserved a place in the home. He accepted the narrowness of the space prescribed for him, the constraints that forbade spontaneity or deviation from habit because he was who he was by virtue of the roles he performed — first the son of a father, later, father of a son. With remarkable consistency this conception endured in the Old World and survived in the transplantation of European culture to America.

The discrepancy between the ideal and the actuality created persistent problems. The recurrent cycle functioned when there was place enough for those involved in it. When the boy became a man he was ready to marry and to be head of his own household. That was the object of growth; the increase in physical strength and in knowledge brought the lad closer to the day when he crossed the line to adulthood with its burdens and duties but also with its opportunities to satisfy the bodily urges and emotional needs maturity also brought.

But there was always a lag. The hulking youth of fourteen might be as tall as his father and as strong. In the fields the two did the same work; and at home the same passions moved them. Generally by then some ritual had marked the passage from childhood, had confirmed the young man's responsibility for his own soul, and had charged him with the duty of distinguishing good from evil. Yet he could not at once act the man; often he had to wait until death made room and meanwhile he still owed deference and obedience to the household's head. As the years passed those who felt their energies wasting might rage with impatience at the father still in the way and might mingle with the guilt of willing him gone the dark competitive hatreds, so illicit they could only be suppressed.

The prospect of an end within view alone made tolerable the stress of those intervening years between the access to manly power and the ability to use it. The boy, having become a man possessed of a man's power and passions, held himself back knowing that with the passage of a few seasons more his time would yet come. Then in the sight of the village and the church he would take his own woman, have his own household and fulfill himself.

The prolongation of life in modern times posed for the peasant families a cruel problem. The dutiful son mourned the day when his parents passed promptly to their reward in the better world to come. That was as it should be and he inherited their place. But there were no attitudes proper for the situation in which the old people lived on and on while their successor waited impatiently. The responses varied. Sometimes, as in Ireland, the only solution was to postpone marriage; then the resentful son put off until he was in his thirties the moment when a wife would satisfy his manhood. Or else the son did marry, but then remained within the father's household, still subject to the elder's will, not yet fully his own master. These circumstances were always trying — two to make the decisions, two to share the proceeds — but they became ever more so with the lapse of time. The one, having passed his prime, had to recognize that his day was over and yield to the other pressing impatiently on his heels. If some old men withdrew contentedly to sit by in the corner or to help with little household tasks, others never ceased to grieve the loss of authority which was the measure of their loss of strength and of the waning of their earthly life. Meanwhile the one who, having entered upon the inheritance, had to shoulder responsiblity, learned the weight of decision made heavier by the anticipated criticism of the more experienced. And often by then a grandson was underfoot, a bumbling reminder that a further displacement was not far distant. Tension festered the more for the lack of means of expression.

The increase in the number of sons also disordered the family. The calculation was simple. One son could inherit a tract of the same size as his father's and thus expect to retain the same status and the same standard of living. The dowry acquired in marriage might provide for a younger brother. But several lads growing to maturity posed a dilemma; neither of the alternatives various communities recognized was desirable. With the holding divided, none of the sons was as well off as the father had been; alternatively, with the eldest inheriting all, then the rest either had to depart or lose the chance to be masters of their own households. The issue might involve the extensive farm of an independent proprietor or the meager acres of a tenant or a miserable cottier's hut; but always the stake was place and the son's ability to act as the father had.

For centuries in Europe, alternations of prosperous and disastrous years, of rises and falls in birth and death rates, along with internal shifts of population, evened out the imbalances. But a long-term and accelerating increase in population after 1600 persistently expanded the numbers at every level of society for whom there was no room. Thereafter, growing up often meant a loss of place. Those who arrived at man's estate without an estate, or without the prospect of one, could only leave home.

The deprivation damaged the peasants and their children most seriously. Some men commanded skills they could transfer from one locality to another. Younger sons of English noblemen took their swords eastward to battle the Turks and the journeyman from one town packed his tools to apply his craft wherever the need might be. But peasant skills had no value without some connection to the land; and concern about the lack of space darkened the youth of boys who felt the surge of their power as men, and feared the wasteful choking consequences of cramping and confining families.

The thousands who advanced beyond the age of fourteen with no inheritance, no succession, in sight moved toward a gloomy future. They could stay on indefinitely in the father's or brother's home, becoming dependent uncles to the children of others, or they could enter the service of strangers — in either case forfeiting the chance ever to become the heads of their own families. Or they could marry and seek space in the wretched expedients that the village economy allowed its less fortunate members, renting the sites for cabins, doing paid labor, or working the plots of others for shares, thus dooming themselves and their offspring to everlasting inferiority. Or they could go away to join the rogues and vagabonds who thronged the seventeenth- and eighteenth-century roads, or to find refuge in the dense anonymity of some London or Paris, or as many increasingly did, to seek in a New World the places the old no longer afforded them.

Young women faced a different problem. Girls had no

prospect of inheritance. Growing up prepared them for work in the household. Trained by the mother in the expectation that they would marry and become mistresses of their own families, they too approached maturity with some anxiety. In little communities, the small pool of potential husbands, the rules of consanguinity, and the considerations of dowry all limited the range of choice. Nevertheless the consequences of the lack of opportunity were not so serious for girls as for boys. The perils of childbearing made female mortality higher than that of males and created second chances for unmarried women. Above all, rural society provided means for lightening the penalties of spinsterhood. In Catholic lands, the church held open for them respectable careers of service and every household could make room for the extra pair of hands of a helpful aunt or servant.

The penalties of unfulfilled manhood were more drastic. He, for whom there was no space, forfeited his birthright — to the role in the community, to the wife, the children, the satisfactions of body and mind as master of the home. Without space, there was no continuity and both the preparation as a boy and the anticipations as a man were meaningless. Leaving home was one means of finding space to make a home.

The seventeenth-century settlers in America and their children experienced the dilemma which successive generations of later migrants also encountered. The men who came alone quickly sent for wives and children or married as soon as feasible; and many arrived as families seeking thus to forestall the dissolution that threatened them in Europe. Having left homes that had no place for them, they struggled, once arrived, to reconstruct the environment they had lost. Earlier and later, these efforts failed. The soil of the New World was uncongenial.

Settlement followed a variety of patterns in the seventeenth century: Virginia began as a commercial company, Maryland as a feudal barony, and Massachusetts and Pennsylvania as experiments in the creation of religious communities. Some places at first held land in common; elsewhere each man always received a holding of his own. Yet in time, every colony agreed that all people should live in family units.

On this point the Puritans were most explicit. Literate men, inclined by religion to introspection, they often put into words the assumptions upon which others acted without explicit verbal statement, perhaps even without conscious awareness. Massachusetts and Connecticut early used their power to strengthen family life. The little towns frowned upon those who wished to live alone; bachelors were taxed and ordered to join some stable household. Furthermore, the law upheld traditional authority within the home, sternly forbidding children to challenge parents; the stubborn and rebellious faced the wrath of the magistrates with death the penalty for flagrant disobedience, at least on the statute books. What had been customary and commonplace in Europe was to be restored in America, by force if necessary.

Fewer recorded sermons survived in the middle and southern colonies and the reasons men there gave for insisting that the family be the basic social unit generally remained unstated. Yet the actions of the legislatures and courts had the same goal as in the North, encouragement of the stability of the household and reinforcement of the familiar pattern of authority within it.

The experience of the Africans brought to labor in the New World reflected the same pervasive assumptions. In the very first decades of their appearance in the Chesapeake settlements, they were servants, whose status was similar in the eyes of the law to that of Irish and English bondsmen; all were members of the master's family and subject to his government. After 1660, subtle changes distinguished the white servant, held to labor for a limited number of years, from the black, whose servile condition became permanent, total and inherited. Among the advantages the planters expected from slavery was the ability to mobilize, manage and exploit the labor force in gangs, as in the ships that brought them across the ocean and in the rice and sugar fields of the West Indies. In the outcome, however, the plantation developed a different organization. By 1750 southern bondsmen lived in family units, although their owners long remained ambiguous about the binding nature of the ties of husbands and wives or parents and children among slaves. Despite abuses in practice, the family ideal was strong enough to extend to a depressed group with a totally strange cultural heritage.

Europeans and their descendants believed more strongly still that humans lived most appropriately in households within which the father and mother reared their children by transmitting the skills and ideas inherited from earlier generations and within which all together earned a common livelihood. Though departure across the ocean had severed old continuities, it was to establish new ones that the settlers had come to the wilderness; and the family was the means of doing so.

The colonists insisted upon constructing the social

order upon a familiar basis not simply out of habit or inertia, but because this long seemed to them the most practical expedient. Arrived in the vast emptiness of a world totally strange in its outward aspects and devoid of the familiar monuments of civilization, the Europeans huddled together for the warmth of each other's comradeship and for defense against the unknown perils of the forests. In the close confines of Jamestown or Plymouth or Boston, unyielding rules of behavior bound all persons; the community had enough force to punish the individual who deviated and possessed the additional sanction of expulsion. The dread of being abandoned, of being cast out to fend alone in the strange wilderness was itself sufficient compulsion to hold people in families.

The colonists knew no other means of training the young than through control by the parents who taught the children to accept the understandings and conventions that held the community together, persuading them by precept or force to obey the laws of God and man. Fathers and mothers also transmitted to sons and daughters the skills with which to earn a livelihood, find shelter against the elements and guard against the daily perils of life. A proper rearing in the home produced an obedient child and also one prepared in time to make a home of his own. Discipline, important enough in the Old World, seemed vital in America where savage forces scarce concealed in the wilderness rubbed away at the veneer of civilization. Unless the oncoming generations learned to resist, a relapse to barbarism would be the ironic outcome of the great adventure of migration. The well-regulated family was the staunchest defense. *Such as families are,* a Puritan fervently wrote, *so the church and commonwealth must be.*

However desperately the seventeenth-century settlers strove to strengthen and preserve it, the home was not an effective instrument of social control in the New World. The laws with monotonous regularity tried to shore up the institution; the preambles which described the need were a dejected commentary on the failure.

The pressure of time often explained the inability to devote appropriate attention to the young. Where necessity forced people to make everything from nothing — clear trees, build houses, mend clothing, tend beasts, till the soil — all through the desperate expenditure of labor, it was comprehensible, as a Massachusetts law of 1642 put it, that many parents neglected the training of their children in learning and labor. The feverish effort to survive, on the first frontier and at each successive advance, generally left fathers and mothers little energy or patience for the education of their offspring. And when conditions improved enough to grant the family a little security, then the nagging temptations of the New World's opportunities still diverted some men and women from their responsibility. The worm of avarice already made its presence felt in the seventeenth century even in that land of sober habits, Connecticut: those who had acres enough to sustain them and possessions in plenty wanted more and soon the need for acquisition consumed as much effort as the need for survival once had. People drawn by the lust for gain no more heeded the reiterated reminders — from the statute book, from the tithingmen, from the county officials and the ministers — of the obligations of proper family behavior than those driven by the fear of want.

Children in America also neglected their duty. Cut off from tradition, deprived of connections with the past, they knew no better; and injunctions to preserve fidelity to the home rang hollow, unpersuasive when voiced by elders who had themselves deserted the places of their birth. Then too the fathers, fumbling through the forests for paths they did not recognize, lost the ability to assure their sons of the way and thus also lost the authority to lead. The old wisdom did not hold in a land strange in soil and climate and devoid of the fixed monuments by which men located themselves in time and space. Often, a lad of fourteen reared in the wilderness and flush in the strength of approaching manhood knew himself more capable of dealing with the environment than his parents, still strangers exhausted by migration. Experience separated the generations — the older still formed by European faith and visions, by habits of behavior and speech and inextinguishable memories of sights their descendants would never see; the younger, products of a savage continent, superbly self-confident out of the ignorance of the lost heritage of the Old World, ready to fend for itself at once. Obedience then did not simply follow from enactment of a law.

There was more continuity to the skills of the kitchen than to those of the field, and girls generally stayed home until marriage.

The boys, however, tended to break away early. Families were large; the fruitful mother of William Phips, who bore twenty-six children, was exceptional, but a mother of six to ten was not. It was hardly worth waiting for the little there was to inherit when each hoped to make more through his own labor. The frontier, nowhere distant in seventeenth-century America, beckoned the sons as the ocean had beckoned the fathers. Even the New England towns which attempted to direct the flow of settlement had to yield to the young, impatient to be on their own; and elsewhere no effective restraints whatever checked the impulse to move off. The passage of the child to adulthood ceased to be a gradual progression through well-defined stages and became a single great leap away from home.

Economic and social conditions encouraged the precipitate assumption of responsibility and hasty departures. In some places, the absence of a network of relatives and of a strong enveloping community left each family to itself. Elsewhere, the death of a father, exhausted by work or a victim of the hazards of the wilderness, made a stripling head of the household; and remarriage of the widow gave the stepson an additional incentive to leave. Or if the father lived on to an advanced old age, as some did who survived the initial trials of settlement, then his impatient offspring were certain to clear out and go off on their own. Sometimes a well-to-do parent voluntarily gave a portion to his prospective heir: let him take the up-country acres and a pair of beasts and do for himself — there will be more room in the cramped little home for the others. At fourteen, the daughter not needed at her mother's side was available for marriage, mature enough to be a housewife in the wilderness.

Above all, there was space. Beyond the water's edge, through the forest, lay the endless West. No limits hemmed in those who did not fear either the wilderness or its isolation. The young men who learned to clear the woods, to drive away the scattered Indian occupants, to subsist off the game and fish the country afforded, and to do without contact with the amenities of town, could make homes for themselves as soon as they had the physical strength.

They had every incentive to do so, for always the lands

to the West seemed better than those already occupied. Partly, the appearance of superiority reflected an economic reality; American farmers who quickly exhausted the soil they hastily cleared and carelessly cultivated, preferred to shift to virgin plots rather than to invest labor and effort in preserving old ones. But the confidence in the superiority of what lay to the West also reflected the faith all too often doomed to disappointment — the faith of men on the edge of a continent who believed that the deficiencies of the present would vanish in the further future, the disappointment of those who having reached the future found it the same present and therefore could only continue to look ahead. The West, wherever it was, was best because the East never satisfied the quest initiated when the sons departed to make homes that would replace those they left.

By the eighteenth century, decades of experience had begun to reshape the character of American parents and children. The separations that pulled a family apart were still painful, but people habituated to the absence of continuity across the generations learned to expect and accept the wrench of departure. Living with the reality that the relationship between fathers and sons was transient produced a subtle change in personalities.

The father, having himself once gone off to make his way, could not object, indeed learned to approve, when his sons packed up. He retained authority at home over children while they were there, as over wife and servants, but the consciousness that his rule was temporary qualified his power, as did the dawning awareness that the proper rearing for boys was one that prepared them to go, not to stay. As for himself, the father understood that life's satisfactions were not patriarchal — the pleasure of knowing that an endless tribe would extend through time his own labors on the earth. Whatever joy life held in store was individual, the product of his own achievements.

The sons too acquired values that conformed to the situation. Emotion fashioned ties to mother or father, to brother or sister, ties in their nature temporary and not binding. Living with the certainty of separation, a year earlier or later, by ten miles or a hundred, a boy learned to act independently and to get along on his own resources. Self-sufficiency was the immediate goal and the sooner achieved the better, in earning a livelihood, in gaining affection, in gratifying the needs of the spirit. He who got quickly to stand alone fared best in the bruising day-to-day existence of the American countryside.

The early assumption of responsibility was therefore not only an unavoidable hazard where mortality was high; the salutary experience of shifting for himself forced a child to be a man in order to survive. The lad in his teens, left without a father, who took on the charge of a whole family, matured in a day as it were. Even in the absence of that drastic compulsion parents did well to hasten the moment at which the youth on his own completed his education through the practical encounter with life.

The necessity for standing alone became a preference. The precocious boys who knew the need for preparing to make their own way in life eagerly awaited the test; and, if it took too long in coming, precipitously hastened forth to meet it.

Haddam, Connecticut, in the 1720's — a place of small hard farms, its people much alike, steady, generations removed from the frontier rawness. A place nevertheless where youngsters grew restless, especially those whose imaginations reached toward the unknown future.

Terror strikes David Brainerd at the age of seven when he thinks of death, and his secret prayers in the years that follow do not erase the worry. When he is fourteen his mother dies after a wave of sickness hits the town and destroys all sense of *carnal security*. Then he determines to leave his father's house and for four years works on a farm in nearby East Haddam. So much for growing up. At nineteen, he takes up his own farm in Durham.

Two decades later, another intellectual, dreamy lad thinks of escape from Cornwall, not far away from Durham though closer to the edge of settlement. But the death of his father leaves sixteen-year-old Ethan Allen head of the family, responsible for running the farm. Three years later a few weeks' service in the Army takes him to Lake George and there he listens eagerly to tales of the richer lands in the North and the West; discontent sets in with the dullness of Cornwall and he then begins to plan the moves that will take him away.

The restlessness of such lads as Brainerd and Allen revealed the weakening of the inhibitions which held at home the youths in other societies. Attachment to a place — every landscape was equally acceptable to those whose minds fastened not on scenes of past childhood but on those of future success as a man. Respect for authority — a passing phase for those who quickly outgrew their fear of the father and drew confidence that they would outdo their predecessors. Learning that all ties were transient, the American boys of the eighteenth century learned also that home was not a place at which to remain but a point from which to depart. Davy Crockett, rented out by his father at the age of twelve, thereafter wandered and never came to rest. A few such lads became loners, passing through the frontier to lead the huntsman's or drover's or teamster's life or maintaining on the fringe of settlement a detached, unmarried, existence. There was less overt social hostility than formerly to the eccentricities of bachelorhood. But most men who left home intended in time to make new homes of their own, to be fathers of families, and they had only to find the clearing and the wife in order to do so. Yet they could not fail to realize that their sons in turn would extend the cycle of departure and re-creation.

The patterns of rural family life established before the Revolution endured through the nineteenth century. The line of settlement passed across the Alleghenies, then reached the Mississippi and, at last, the Pacific, opening in the process ever-fresh expanses of space. Young men whose eyes first beheld the roll of Yankee hills or the still flow of tidewater streams gazed incuriously at the virgin forest through which the wild Ohio rushed; they moved through the oak openings into the open prairies and, defying the hazards of mountains and deserts, penetrated the great valleys of Oregon and California. In each generation, the grandmothers cried unheeded: *Child, I will see you no more.* The children went forth. So long as the continent held out to each man the promise of a homestead of his own, the cycle of departure and quest continued.

Occasional communal efforts to hold the sons back rarely succeeded. Even before the Revolution the German sects in America had feared that children who strayed would lose faith, and the elders had tried inducement and compulsion to keep the boys at home. These groups and their counterparts from every part of Europe in the nineteenth century therefore preferred to live in close clusters, insulated from the temptations of the alien world about them, moving in unison, organized, intact. Little islands dotted the American landscape within which zealous men and women labored to fan alive in their offspring the spark of some Old World cause. But the pull of external space drew the young away even from such sheltered enclaves.

Some southern planters of the 1830's and 1840's also sought to staunch the flow. Their baronial dreams had a patriarchal tone; from the colonnaded castles of their imagination they surveyed estates tilled by the grateful servitors who were the subjects of their fatherly solicitude. A genealogical line extending into the future would validate the aristocratic pretensions, whatever the actualities of the past may have been. And indeed there was much to attract a boy in plantation life — horse racing, fox hunting, the play with weapons and the sports of the countryside, as well as the freedom from labor and the young lord's power to command the helpless slaves. Nevertheless, the rival frontier vision of golden discoveries glistened in the South too and lured into strenuous departures sons impatient with the vistaless ease of their fathers' verandas. In any case defeat in war and emancipation of the labor force made a lost cause of the plantation and dissolved the dreams of its former masters.

The cycle of departure to seek a new home on the soil drew to a stop only in the twentieth century when the farm ceased to be a setting for family life and became a rationalized productive enterprise. In the new order of agriculture, bulletins from the commodity exchanges, the costs of capital invested in land and machines, and the levels of government price support shaped the calculations of the managers. The vision, which had long entranced Americans, of each man on his own acres an individual nurtured by his labor on the soil, then dimmed and at last faded from sight. Through much of the history of the United States, it had supplied the great majority of the people with the meaning of the drama of their existence. Its disappearance would focus attention on other ways of growing up and leaving home, ways which formerly had served small, if influential, minorities.

Perhaps the difference originated in temperament or personal idiosyncracy, perhaps in a particular family situation — of being the oldest or youngest or in resentment of a father who was too lax or too rigid — however it happened, some boys did not follow the expected cycle. The impulse that led them away from home also persuaded them to abandon farming as a way of life.

Europe too had known such desertions; the folk tales were lurid with accounts of the fate of wanderers who fell in with gypsies or who ended their days as vagabonds, rogues or beggars. But the aberrant on one side of the ocean became usual on the other. The looseness of parental controls in America permitted youths who wished to go their own ways to do so. A land of few fences, where it was as easy to change a name as a shirt, put no effective restraints on the ability to move about so that an energetic lad could try his hand at any one of a number of things.

Thomas Jonathan Jackson of Clarksburg in backwoods Virginia shifted from one occupation to another before he knew what he wished to do. He was about ten in 1834, an orphan, living on his uncle's farm. With a brother two years older, Thomas took off down the Ohio to the Mississippi where he worked the summer on an island cutting wood for passing steamboats. The experience left him as poor as when he started and fever-stricken in the bargain. Back to the farm. He thought of keeping a store or doing some swapping, but had no capital. None was needed, however, for public office. At age seventeen he wangled himself an appointment as county constable. Then after two years he finally decided upon a military career.

Trade, public office, and the Army offered such boys as Winfield Scott and Abraham Lincoln a way of escape from farm life. The temptations were great, as were the hazards. These were roads away from the endless drudgery — the twice-daily milking, the dawn-to-dusk routine in the fields and the lonely struggle against an inclement climate. Fame and fortune were the destinations. But these roads also exposed travelers to capricious turnings and called for reserves of self-confidence, capital or influence.

However, there were also other paths away from home, better charted because they were the products of a long tradition, though one different from the life of the soil, a tradition which also had origins in Europe.

Aloys, like his predecessors, knows the stationmaster, the shopkeeper and the priest in the village and can point to the place where once a monastery stood. Nearby is a castle and a town where nobles and merchants and craftsmen go about their affairs, all brought to maturity by a process different from that of the farm.

Aloys knows that the life of such people is not for him. Even were he tempted to surrender his own place, he would hardly know how to go about edging into that of someone else.

In the New World, however, no walls contained the towns or the professions. Farm boys and others could find a way in. Increasingly they did so.

And by 1970, the paths they traced had become the usual thoroughfares by which American youth left home to face life.

2

BEYOND THE CLEARING, 1600–1770

At first in the wilderness each settlement is shut in on itself. Immense distance separates Boston from Plymouth.

In time, the regular passage of vessels and the trodden roads bring places together. The forests fall, the clearings spread toward one another.

The population thickens. There are about 200,000 colonists in 1660, about 2,000,000 a century later, and they have flowed out from the edge of the water to the Alleghenies. They live by agriculture, but they sustain vigorous cities. Philadelphia, Charlestown and Newport join Boston and New York as thriving centers of administration, trade and culture.

Expansion creates opportunity. There are never enough skilled hands to reckon the sums or write the letters, to caulk the ships or clapboard the houses, to make boots, coats, bread and candles, to fashion silver bowls and mahogany chests.

Expansion turns skill into wealth. The calculators and contrivers command a price and they accumulate a margin for investment. With good fortune the margin grows.

Others aspire to emulate the successful who become models for the most ambitious youth of the town and of the countryside. Meanwhile the fathers who have gained riches wish their sons to gain more, to rise still further in rank and prestige.

Experience in the colonies showed that the hope of climbing the social scale was realistic. Not all succeeded and some did better than others; but the prevalence of opportunity and the inability of privileged families or groups to shut out competitors gave almost everyone a chance at the New World's prizes. The Manigaults and Hancocks had started with little; in time they moved among the great men of the provinces.

The owners of vast landed estates in Rhode Island, New York or South Carolina were far above the yeomen, tenants, servants and slaves who made up the bulk of the population, as far as were the great merchants of Newport and Boston from the crowd of petty traders, craftsmen, apprentices and laborers who moved through the city streets. Yet though social differences deepened in the eighteenth century, the distances between ranks did not diminish the incentive to move up. The lowly, knowing that others had risen, aspired to do likewise; and since neither legal nor informal barriers blocked the way, all who wished were free to scramble for the best places.

Luck was always important. A ship went forth and, months later, either came back or not. The seasons favored the crops or they did not, and the tobacco and rice sent overseas brought high prices, or they did not. But the proper use of training, skill and capital enabled men to make the most of the good turns of fortune, mitigate the effects of the bad.

Hence the pressure on fathers to equip sons for the battle of life. As in the past girls would learn all they needed to know from their mothers and later, from their husbands. Some women, out of misfortune or exceptional energy, were the breadwinners in their own households. But even the widow who managed for herself or the wife who helped in the shop generally required no other learning than that acquired in the home. The ambitious boy, however, would leave sooner or later; better that the family prepare him so that the departure led upward rather than simply out.

Only the most fortunate households possessed the resources to endow the youths with capital while the parents still lived. But every good family could impart to its children the training in economy, self-control and industry that equipped them for the struggle. Not every family, however, could supply a boy with the specialized skills that would give him an advantage over rivals in getting ahead.

To acquire such skills it was often necessary to leave home; and long European practice had developed a traditional mode for doing so.

The Price of Skills

Some boys gained the skill to make or to buy and sell in the home. The son, standing at his father's side, watching the play of hammer on silver, observed the bowl take shape or, helping fit the leg in place, saw the mortised joint support the table top. The lads who wished to follow the craft that already occupied the family, learned to do so without leaving.

Most boys, however, sought skill away from home. Certainly those born on the farm who had no wish to follow the plow had to find instruction in a strange household. But even the children of craftsmen and merchants often prepared for life under the oversight of someone not related to them by kinship. There was always the consideration that only one heir could take over the enterprise; the brothers had to leave town to practice the same trade or else learn some other. In any case, many sons were unwilling to follow their fathers' calling, preferring in moving off to move off to something different, seeking in becoming men to assert their strength by not following their parents, thus testing and proving themselves. In the wish to quit the parental roof, the motives of doing better in life and of displaying individuality were intertwined.

The fathers generally approved. Departure would advance the son's welfare; it might also subject him to stricter discipline and more rigid training than the home provided; and it removed a source of running tension when those still young in years but growing in power competed with their elders.

For centuries apprenticeship had offered the means of transferring youths from the control of their fathers to that of appointed masters. In England, and elsewhere in Europe, the system had acquired a regular pattern through long years of development. Transplanted to the New World, apprenticeship remained a surprisingly vital, although altered, method for the upbringing of boys. Less regular in practice than in the Old World, indeed sometimes chaotic, it was nevertheless long the accepted way of leaving home to gain skill.

Apprenticeship in Europe meant life in a family of contract rather than of birth; ideally it remained so in

America. The master took the place of the blood father; the apprentice became a son for the duration of the agreement. The older man undertook to house, feed and clothe the youth, to train him for the chosen vocation, to supervise his behavior and guard his moral welfare and usually to teach him to read and write. The youngster became subject to family discipline and to the requirement to labor faithfully and obey all commands. A contract, consented to by the boy and signed by the natural and adoptive fathers, set out the terms in detail.

In Europe the system had operated within communities powerful enough to regulate and enforce such agreements. Often the municipal authorities registered the documents and passed judgment on the grievances of either masters or apprentices. It addition, in most parts of the continent the guilds retained enough power to establish general standards about length of service, quality of instruction and other mutual obligations. The law and the organized opinion of the townspeople often treated members who did not conform like outsiders, forbidding them to practice the crafts or engage in trade.

The communal controls did not long endure in America. The colonial towns, occupied with the necessities of surviving and growing, were too weak to maintain the old standards. Everything was new, nothing was firm enough to resist disruption from the constant going and coming of strangers. Moreover European customs did not always function well in an alien environment so that masters and boys fumbled through trial and error adjustments to take account of differences in tools, materials, and business methods. Yet no guilds developed to supply the guidance and supervision they had across the Atlantic. In the absence of any common authority, each man had to do as best he could. Contracts of apprenticeship lost their uniformity and the certainty of enforcement faded. Since each arrangement was therefore the product of individual negotiation, great variations were possible. The result was less a coherent system than a loose bundle of practices.

Above all, an expanding and mobile society suffered from a consistent shortage of skills. No one was eager to exclude outsiders or punctiliously to examine the credentials of plausible men who offered scarce goods or services. People grew accustomed to purchasing boots and medicine without regard to the antecedents or training of those who supplied them. The breakdown of communal control also permitted the master, pressed for help, to take on anyone willing to do a job and to treat his apprentices simply as extra hands. The clients who solicited his labor tempted the artisan to get as much work as possible out of everyone in his shop and not to waste precious time on instruction.

The temptation mounted when the apprentice mingled in the family with other kinds of dependent laborers. At a public auction, the head of the household could buy orphans or the children of the poor or incompetent, to be held until the age of twenty-one, or he could buy indentured servants for a term of years, or he could buy African or Irish slaves — they and their progeny to be his property forever. The confusion of rights and responsibilities deepened when these purchases jumbled together under the same crowded roof combinations of colonial, English, Welsh, Scottish, German, Irish and African, lads and maidens, men and women. Under such circumstances, rights and responsibilities blurred and the master was likely to skimp on his paternal obligations.

The ambitious apprentice could, of course, insist on receiving the proper training in craftsmanship and sometimes appealed to the law to secure it. Moreover, he possessed a powerful weapon for getting his due in skill as in food and other perquisites: he could refuse to work, or — worse — slack at his tasks, or — worst of all — spitefully spoil costly materials. Fear of these damaging tactics limited the master's tendency to negligence. But no lively boy was likely to protest when the old man for want of time skimped on family prayers or on the study of the Bible or on the oversight of the morals of his charges or even on the requirement that they be taught to read and write. A pious lad like David McClure of Boston could do little to guard his soul when bound to a dissipated, gay and profane shopkeeper. The familial aspects of apprenticeship receded to the background as Americans began to think of the relationship as a kind of employment and not primarily as a kind of education preparatory to a vocation.

Nor did the townspeople have the means to impose order. The master's discipline was not enough to assure the good behavior of those dependent upon them. The lads and wenches met when they wished, they drank rum at the taverns and they danced together till late in the night. Reproved, they threatened to burn the town down over the ears of the burghers. From time to time, disorderly gatherings and even open riots showed the limits of control. Apprentices were often among the active elements in the eighteenth-century mobs.

Again and again the law tried to maintain the expected standards. The enactment of a new statute and the judgment of a court had only limited effect. Like the exhortations of a sermon, the statements of the legislator and the judge expressed the intentions and aspirations of the society rather than described its actuality.

Nevertheless apprenticeship did not disappear or even decline in significance. It changed character as the advancing decades narrowed its familial functions. But even when the youth began to live apart from the master and came to the shop only for work, apprenticeship remained the most important means of transmitting skills from one generation to another. Learning was a matter of demonstration, imitation and experience. The novice watched how the task was done, he tried his own hand at it and then by repeated practice he acquired the ability to do the same.

The esteem accorded a skill depended on its rarity and the difficulty of mastering it. Teaching, therefore, ranked low in the opinion of the colonists. This was the one occupation which called for no specific preparation. Anyone who could himself read, write and cipher could demonstrate how to others, who would then imitate and in time acquire the same ability. It was enough therefore to staff what schools there were with transients, generally young men on the way to some genuine vocation who picked up the job for a season or so for the little income it provided.

By contrast, the callings which required specific skills, mysteries not known to everyone, could only be exercised by those prepared through a long period of training which gave them the opportunity to observe a master, to try their own hand at doing and to perfect themselves through practice.

Ben Franklin had the choice of an array of crafts in the Boston of the 1720's. At the age of twelve, he was clear in his own mind that he would not follow his father's calling as a soap chandler. Perhaps the two years he had already spent helping made him dislike the job. Perhaps the bookish taste which for a time led the family to believe he might aspire to the ministry pulled him in another direction. Perhaps he was just restless, itchy to be off like his brother Josiah, who had gone to sea. The threat implicit in that possibility was persuasive. His father took him on walks to see joiners, bricklayers, turners and braziers at work, hoping thus to settle his inclination on some trade on land. The parent knew that he could not hold the youngster at home; better to settle him in a desirable vocation than to lose him forever.

Fortunately there was another brother, well situated. James had recently acquired a press and set up as a printer. A formal contract of apprenticeship put Benjamin in his service for nine years. The position was as good as a reasonable youth could expect; the work was respectable, indeed prestigious and especially so when James began to put out a newspaper. Ben learned not only to clean up the place but also to handle accounts, not only to distribute the type but also to set it, not only to make up a page but also, when space required, to write a column. Nevertheless a brother's control was almost as irksome as a father's; soon endless bickering over the terms of the formal arrangement embittered relations between the siblings and matters grew worse after the troubles that followed upon James's venture into politics. One way or another Ben found an excuse to be off and sought the opportunity to do for himself in Philadelphia. He remained a printer through life, whatever the other activities in which he engaged.

In Philadelphia as in Boston, a multitude of other crafts engaged the artisans. A boy could learn the skills needed to outfit the vessels which connected the colonies with the outer world, to make sails and rope, to forge anchors and put together casks to carry the cargo. House carpenters, cabinetmakers, and gold- or silversmiths were on the lookout for lively lads to help equip the prosperous townsfolk who also provided custom for tailors, cordwainers and bakers. These needs opened opportunities for anyone who had mastered the techniques and possessed the tools; and apprenticeship offered many youngsters the means of gaining both.

Other boys found their chances in buying and selling, both in the city and the country. Matthew Lyon was also apprenticed to a printer but at the age of thirteen, a year older than Franklin. Matthew's shop, however, was in Dublin, which offered fewer avenues of escape than Boston. In 1765, at the age of fifteen he arranged with an American captain to serve as cabin boy in return for passage. Once across, the boy became apprenticed first to Jabez Bacon, a merchant in Woodbury, Connecticut, and then to Hugh Hannah of nearby Litchfield. Finally at the age of eighteen Matthew had learned enough about swapping for the produce of country people to set out for himself. At about the same time and at the same age, in the Valley of Virginia, John Sevier became a partner in his father's store, buying and selling whiskey or land, farming on the side. Later Lyon moved north to Vermont, Sevier west to Tennessee, each seeking fortune where he could.

Petty trade in the larger cities sometimes opened out into promising opportunities. Thomas Hancock, apprenticed to a bookseller in Boston at the age of thirteen, after seven years of service gained the freedom to open his own shop. Dabbling in related ventures (he had to sell the goods he often took in exchange for books), he built a small store of capital, to which he added substantially by marriage to an heiress. By then he was on the way to becoming one of the richest men in the colonies.

Well-established mercantile families developed a more regular pattern for their sons. The Crowninshields of Salem expected the boys who followed in their enterprises to go to sea at the age of fourteen. The long cruises brought experience in what it took to manage a vessel and a crew, to deal with foreign officials and strange merchants, and to adjust to the fluctuations of supply and demand in distant ports. A lad quickly became a man and might command his own ship before the age of twenty-one; then a few successful voyages would bring in the capital with which to set up in business. Moses Brown went into service with his uncle Obadiah in Providence, ran errands, copied letters, kept the ledgers and by the age of eighteen was capable of making independent transactions. The best families had resources, both of available money and of business and blood relations in various parts of the world, that could help a son in need. Small, tightly knit ethnic groups like the Quakers and Jews also passed their children along through a network of acquaintances who supervised their upbringing.

Such connections were helpful in getting a boy placed and in the assurance of support during crises. Still there were enough cases of young men who contrived their own means of getting ahead to show that anyone willing to take risks and able to accumulate the necessary savings could enter and practice the numerous trades that composed the urban economy.

The channels of access to some other callings were narrower than to the crafts or to trade. The men who exercised the select occupations of law, medicine and divinity claimed that the privilege ought to be available only through a controlled process of admission. They tried to make that claim good through licensing laws and through a monopoly of the skills passed on by apprenticeship.

At the beginnings of settlement, the rulers had improvised what justice was done in the colonies, drawing upon scraps of English law and upon the Bible and making rough and ready decisions about what was right and wrong. Characteristically the courts were at the same time legislative and executive as well as judicial bodies.

Eighteenth-century Americans, living in a more stable and more complex society, ceased to be content with unpredictable rule-of-thumb judgments. The protection of persons and property, the enforcement of contracts, the collection of debts and the assessment of taxes involved heavier stakes than formerly and called for the consideration of issues that were rarely clear-cut. In interpreting the statutes enacted by the assemblies, judges had to draw upon a knowledge of the acts of Parliament and of precedents in earlier cases both in England and in America. A dissatisfied party now could carry an appeal to superior courts in the provincial capital and even to London.

Trained lawyers gained steadily in importance as the law grew more formal and more technical. The Old World distinctions among barristers, solicitors and notaries did not survive in the New World. Americans resorted instead to an all-purpose advocate who could draw up a binding document, who knew for what writs to petition, and who could eloquently argue precedents with judge and adversary in their own technical language. The orthodox, for whom the word of the Bible was good enough, had serious doubts about the vocation; a respected adviser warned Benjamin Rush of Philadelphia that the practice of the law was full of temptations and by no means to think of entering it. Often, too, the plain people protested: the mysterious verbiage of the pettifoggers obscured right and wrong and provided a cloak for oppressive power; every man ought to plead for himself. Such intermittent protests nevertheless did not halt the trend toward putting control of the law in the hands of lawyers.

Admission to the bar called for some knowledge and for testimonials to the good character of the applicant. Apprenticeship of a sort was the means of gaining both. There was rarely a formal agreement and the youth did not always live in the home of the lawyer, who was therefore not fully the master. The prospective applicant helped with the routine work and learned by doing. He wrote out the motions, searched the books for precedents, observed the process of pleading and when he had the time and the inclination, read whatever treatises lay at hand. Just as important, he came to know the gentlemen of the bar on whose favor or influence he might some day depend, for personal connections were of the utmost significance in a small group thrown together in frequent contact in town and even more so when riding the circuit.

In medicine no one exercised control comparable to that which imposed order on the law. Of necessity, most colonists doctored themselves, drawing upon recollections of folk wisdom, upon the advice of anyone in the vicinity with a reputation as healer, and upon home-made nostrums compiled by trial and error out of available herbs and liquors. Bonesetters and barber-surgeons did what they could with injuries. The towns, however, supported a number of physicians who claimed that a superior kind of skill made their powders and ministrations effective and thus worth the fees they charged. Indeed, they argued, their craft was so far beyond the common reach, that only they themselves could judge their qualifications. While efforts to regulate the whole of medical practice through licensing were nowhere effective, in the larger places self-constituted groups were able to pass judgment on who was entitled to call himself Doctor.

The youth who wished to take up this calling entered the service of one of the established physicians as James Lloyd did. Sometimes visiting homes to help examine patients, sometimes pounding pills, and sometimes reading the books and studying the drawings, the boy learned how to guess the causes and prescribe the cures, how to reassure the ill and console the survivors, and how to behave in order to inspire the confidence that above all drew clients to the door.

The prestige of being a physician, trained by an established member of the profession, grew steadily in the eighteenth century. But control over practice was not as effective as in the case of law. Credulous sufferers from undefined ills welcomed every offer of cure or of relief from pain. Any rude fellow could gain a reputation as dispenser of nostrums, without passing through the appropriate apprenticeship; and while there was some agitation for licensing, only one colony, New Jersey, in 1772, actually limited by law the right of anyone to assume the title of Doctor.

The problem of standards gained importance when men trained by local procedures met the competition of rivals with European educations and credentials. The lawyer whose learning came from what books were available in the provinces was at a disadvantage when opposed to a man prepared in the London Inns of Court. The aristocratic William Byrd II of Virginia therefore went for his studies to the Middle Temple, rather than to the chamber of some neighborhood pleader. So too, Benjamin Rush, returning to Philadelphia in 1769 with a medical degree from the University of Edinburgh, aroused the curiosity of the whole town and the suspicion of his colleagues who had acquired their skills in the ordinary fashion.

The European ways of securing the ability to practice were unsettling. The prestige of a transatlantic education seemed to lessen the value of the colonial forms of preparation for the vocations of law and medicine. Moreover, the outsiders revealed that imitation and experience, the techniques of apprenticeship, were not the only means of gaining skill. The more general instruction of a school, in which pupils learned by listening to lectures or reading books, was another, and perhaps better, method. Physicians and lawyers reared through apprenticeship were uneasy, inclined to defend the good old ways which had made them what they were, yet hesitant to write off altogether the possibility that there might be something to the alternative technique. Before 1770, however, little was done to resolve the issue.

The question of whether experience or the school was a better preparation for a career was particularly important for young men whose vocation was religion. In the eighteenth century they faced a practical choice, not simply an abstract issue.

In almost all the American churches, the primary function of the minister was not that of the priest, administering a sacred rite through the authority of the bishop who ordained him. The role of the clergyman was rather that of teacher and preacher, and the call to the pulpit came from the congregation, as a matter of principle among the Puritans of New England and of practice almost everywhere else. The youth who aspired to a career in the church in effect, therefore, had to consider how best to prepare himself to shepherd a flock and how to acquire the qualifications that would persuade people to choose and to follow him as well as convince neighboring ministers to accept him in their fellowship.

These issues troubled David Brainerd of Haddam, Connecticut. At the age of twenty, tilling his own farm, he felt the wish to be a minister and knew that he had to respond to the call. He realized that he had to study in order to command the words he would address to others. But it was by no means clear what he need learn, for as a devout Puritan he was aware that men approached the all-important conversion experience, as he himself did, through solitary walkings that brought them a consciousness of their own sinfulness. The puzzle had concerned Puritans ever since the time of Anne Hutchinson in the very earliest days of settlement: did God speak through the learning of books or through the inner experience of the heart?

If the minister could feel the divine spirit directly then preoccupation with ancient philosophers and dead languages was a needless distraction; and the number of preachers who spoke without formal schooling grew, especially after the wave of revivals set off by the Great Awakening. Nevertheless Brainerd and men like him could not accept that simple solution; they recognized the Bible as the word of God and had to understand it, preferably in the tongue in which it had been set down, and they respected Calvin and the other doctors of the Reformation whose writings were guides to the comprehension of what the Scriptures revealed. Moreover Brainerd knew that he and others were prone to melancholy and dejection of spirit and therefore needed the assistance of doctrine to distinguish gloominess of mind, dark thoughts, and the promptings of Satan from a genuine religious experience and the bestowal of God's grace.

Brainerd at first saw a way out in a type of apprenticeship. He went to live with the pastor of the church at Haddam. There the young man could profit from the elder's wisdom, read with his guidance and yet acquire practical experience — learn how to compose sermons for various occasions, how to utilize the tricks of elocution, how to manage the cliques that might divide the parish, and how to cope with political and fiscal difficulties. Observation of the problems of dealing with a congregation would also exercise the religious faculties while leaving time for meditation. An increasing number of youths entered the ministry in this fashion in the eighteenth century.

But however pious, such men never advanced to the best pulpits. The thriving merchants and artisans in the growing towns sought a clergyman with more polish than a rustic education could bestow. Relieved from the pressure of the frontier struggle for existence such people had the leisure to read newspapers and journals; and listening in sermons for more than the reiteration of traditional truth, they wanted enlightening and entertaining commentaries on current issues. They respected therefore the broad general learning that a university might bestow and regarded the college degree as a credential certifying its possessor's qualifications. Attendance at Harvard thus brought John Wise, son of an indentured servant, to a respectable career in the ministry.

Sectarianism added to the value of formal schooling. In towns where several churches existed side by side, the members often vied with one another in the accomplishments of their ministers as in the fashion of their garments. Furthermore in a mobile, fluid society in which changes of allegiance were not difficult, each group tried to draw members from its rivals by proselytizing among them or by capturing the loyalty of families formed by intermarriage. A minister under those circumstances had to be well armed with arguments appropriate to polemic battles.

University graduates who could hurl about quotations in the original Hebrew and Greek and loftily demonstrate their superior familiarity with Scripture enjoyed a strategic advantage. As the eighteenth century advanced, and the number of contestants increased, the vigilant denominational champions had to be on guard against opponents trained in European as well as in colonial institutions. The Reverend Michael Schlatter, for instance, had studied with Professor Waegelin in his native Switzerland as well as in the Netherlands before coming to serve the Reformed Church in America. To deal with men like him on equal terms called for the kind of learning that came from books rather than from experience.

In religion, as in law and in medicine, however, the question of the function of a formal school in the preparation for a career was still unresolved in 1770. Apprenticeship remained the primary means of acquiring the skills to exercise those callings as it did to practice other vocations, because such schools as existed in the provinces as yet did not offer a significant number of youths the avenues for leaving home that they required.

Learning

The American colonists always considered schools useful, even necessary, ornaments of civil life. Almost from the first settlement the laws recognized the desirability of making some provision for transmitting learning to posterity. Otherwise the hearts of godly parents would have *vanished away with heaviness for their poor children, left in a desolate wilderness, destitute of the means of grace.* The Puritans were particularly conscious of the need for taking some action in order to remain a saintly people; but many others also wished to preserve and hand on to their children the knowledge accumulated by the civilization of the Old World. And indeed, in the seventeenth century a sprinkling of schools and a college struck roots in the young communities.

The environment was not propitious to growth, however. No matter how attractive the ideal, the effort to bridge the gap to reality was often beyond the will or resources of men hard pressed in the struggle for survival. A population that was overwhelmingly rural and perennially short of cash critically scrutinized any proposal that threatened to increase taxes. Who would teach, and what, and to whom and toward what purpose? Such questions echoed on through the eighteenth century, even when times were easier and there was some margin for elegance in life. Some of the larger New England towns boasted grammar schools, but the early aspirations remained unfulfilled. At the end of the seventeenth century, Plymouth was still seeking a schoolmaster to teach its children to read and write.

Americans withheld their support because they considered education a task primarily of the family and the church. Yankee children went to meeting as soon as they could walk and listened the sermon through whether they wished to or not. On Sunday evenings, the pious mother heard her youngsters repeat the catechism, and now and then the minister during a visit found an occasion to test their knowledge. The same obligation, to convey the rudiments of faith to their offspring, rested on parents elsewhere, although there were fewer opportunities for communal oversight in the middle and southern colonies. Everywhere boys and girls were expected to learn to read and write at home from their parents or from the master to whom they were apprenticed.

Arguments from tradition or from English precedent did not in themselves persuade Americans to hand over the fees or taxes to support schools; nor did the country have religious orders or foundations able to do so from their own endowments. Schools appeared in response to felt needs that arose either out of the shortcomings of existing arrangements for education in the family or out of the situation of dependent groups in the population.

The masters of apprentices and the parents of children, pressed by the other tasks of the household, often sought to transfer teaching obligations to a school. It was wasteful of time and effort for each laboriously to tutor his own charges, when any competent adult could instruct a whole group at once. The service was worth a moderate price. A wide variety of types of instruction arose as a response to the demand.

The dame school in many towns was no more than the corner of a kitchen to which toddlers came to rehearse their letters. The dame, often a widow or a housewife impoverished by misfortune, respectable, but with no particular qualifications, gladly undertook the task for the little extra income it brought. Standards were not rigid and she at least for some hours kept the very young away from home, out from under foot of those grown up enough to work.

In the cities, a steadily increasing number of evening schools catered to an older age group. Their promoters promised to teach whoever paid the fee the ability to read, write and cipher with ease. Among the clients were mechanics and journeymen who attended after the day's work was done in order to acquire or improve skills that would help them get on in life. But more often the students were apprentices sent by their masters after the shop was closed to imbibe the learning due by the terms of the contract.

Manifestly, education of this sort had a value in trade and its cost was an investment prudent parents would willingly make if they could. The reputation of the excellence of the hand he taught his pupils thus for many years drew a steady flow of students to Abiah Holbrook's writing school on the Boston Common. The ability to set down an impressive and legible letter or document was a valuable asset in a business community.

Institutions which provided instruction in the ancient languages and in other branches of traditional learning were fewer in number and less thronged with scholars. Of what use were they to boys who did not plan to be ministers? True, the ability to quote a Latin phrase was a sign of polish that might have some value to a lawyer eager to impress the bench. But only a small circle of colonial lads had such aspirations and intentions. Moreover, the ability to read and write was a requirement for admission and prolonged attendance was a financial drain on parental resources. Both circumstances limited the number of applicants. A literate boy could find something better to do than pore over forgotten texts. David McClure, for instance, who was eager to study, spent only two years at the Boston Latin Grammar School because his father, burdened with twelve children, could afford to keep him there no longer.

The patronage of Latin schools grew only with the increase in the number of leisured families. In the larger eighteenth-century cities parents with enough wealth to escape the anxieties of giving their children the necessities of life began to worry about providing the luxuries. The brick mansion replaced the clapboard cottage; the elegant new furniture simply cried out for a gentleman to grace the spacious rooms — if not in the generation which made the money, then in the next. The hope that a smattering of elegant learning would hasten the process sometimes kept a son in school.

Besides, as the cities grew and their society became more complex, it turned out that the quality of a boy's education might significantly influence his chances for a desirable career. In the expansive, ever-changing towns young people and their parents had to consider carefully the choices that determined who did well in life. The existence of a range of opportunities itself made selection necessary. The boy and his father had to consider which would be best: apprenticeship to a bookseller, a silversmith or a merchant. Having decided, they had also to determine to which master to turn, holding in mind not only the immediate conditions of lodgings and nurture but also the probable quality of training and the prospects for future advancement. And having come to a decision, they had then to go about persuading the man of their preference to take the lad on.

Every prospective master also took account of numerous factors in making his choice. Though conscious of the great need for labor, the prudent man knew that it was a serious matter to add a new member to the household. The ultimate decision often depended upon an appraisal of the boy's family not only because it was an index of upbringing and of the behavior to be expected in the future but also because it might establish a useful social link and create a reciprocal obligation. The master himself might well have a son whom he would one day wish to place. Personal connections, blood ties, and reputation meant much in communities in which people still knew one another and dealt with each other face to face.

But in addition, the prospective master favored the likely lad, the one who promised to do well, to render the best service in the years to be spent together. From that point of view the relevant questions were: did the boy write a good hand? how well could he read? could he do sums? That is, the state of a youth's previous preparation whether in a school or otherwise widened or narrowed his access to a desirable calling in life. The answers to questions of this sort might determine whether a young man found a place with a physician, lawyer or merchant or with a tallow chandler, ropemaker or carpenter.

Another characteristic of town life also lent importance to education. Thomas Hancock, for instance, started in a bookseller's shop and ended a great merchant. Unpredictable turns in a man's career were not uncommon because life was always full of hazards and opportunities, such as the chance to marry a rich widow. No one could count upon a lucky turn in fortune but everyone had to be ready to make the most of it, if it came. Society changed so swiftly that connections never had the time to harden or institutions to become rigid; and the advantage lay with the man capable of adapting to new conditions by breaking fixed habits of behavior.

While it was essential to master a trade, it was therefore also desirable to prepare to move out of it, or to seize unrelated opportunities for speculation or exchange if an occassion presented itself. And preparation of that sort was not to be found in the conventional training for any of the crafts. A boy could learn all there was to know about stitching boots or entering pleas or navigating a ship; those skills would not help him estimate the effect on the colonies of a battle in Europe or the potential value of a tract of western land, nor would they help him contrive new and unexpected ways of making, buying or selling things. The knowledge transmitted by parents from tradition had serious limitations in the New World.

Benjamin Franklin, settled in Philadelphia and thriving as a printer, never believed that he would remain a printer pure and simple. Always a contriver, he felt the need for self-improvement and, with his friends in the Junto, organized the means for further education through reading and discussion. The same reasons moved the Rhode Island merchants who organized the Providence Library in the 1750's. The books such men accumulated and studied were not narrowly focused on subjects related to their crafts; experience gave them what they needed for that. They read instead for a more general understanding of the world that lay before them, awaiting their use.

Franklin was aware of the inadequacies of existing educational institutions dominated as they were by religious influences which treated learning as a static heritage from the past. He believed that a school ought to transmit to youth the same kind of general knowledge that he himself sought, knowledge that would not ready a man for a specific calling but that would prepare him to seize the exciting possibilities of life, whatever they were. Franklin designed his scheme for an academy in Philadelphia with that purpose in view, although the institution which actually developed from the efforts he initiated turned out quite differently.

All these forms of learning left the pupils in their homes, that is, under the charge of their natural parents or masters. Colonial schools required students to leave the paternal household only under very exceptional circumstances. Boys from isolated families or from such as were incapable of providing an acceptable upbringing had to go away to secure an education.

Every now and then a farm boy like David Brainerd felt the desire to know. Often, but not necessarily, the impulse led to the ministry; but sometimes, as for Ethan Allen, it expressed just a general wonder about the universe beyond the clearing, a vague curiosity about the world of books and ideas waiting to be explored. The great plantation owners in the South could bring in tutors for their sons. But elsewhere a departure was the way to learning, particularly if, as in the case of Benjamin Rush's mother, a harried widow had no time to manage the rearing of her son. The likeliest destination was the home of a clergyman with the leisure and the ability to teach, who might be willing to take on an eager lad either for a fee or for work done or simply as a good deed. Some ministers such as the Reverend Samuel Finley in Maryland acquired a distinguished reputation for the training they gave.

The most perplexing of the families incapable of providing their children with an acceptable upbringing were the Indians. The intention of bringing Christianity to the redmen had been among the motives that most deeply moved the colonists, yet the work went but slowly, for conversion demanded not just acceptance of a ritual which the acquiescent tribesmen were usually only too willing to perform, but also a change in way of life and some understanding of doctrine, both of which required education. From time to time the colonists imagined that the task of spreading the gospel would go more speedily if the promising boys were drawn away from their pagan parents and savage environment and exposed to learning in a favorable setting. The Virginia Company in 1620 planned a college at Henrico for that purpose and similar schemes were common in the next 150 years, although rarely with any practical results.

In Lebanon, Connecticut, the intention of providing an education for boys who could not get it at home coincided with that of converting the Indians. Eleazar Wheelock, minister in the town, had taken pupils into his home for many years and had become known for the excellence of the training he gave them. In 1754, he conceived the idea of setting up a school for Indians; he had no doubt that he could teach one kind of boy as well as another. A year later, Colonel Joshua Moor, a local squire, provided the means to begin the experiment that would draw together youths of both races — the whites to prepare to go forth as missionaries, the Indians to learn at first hand the virtues of Christian civilization. Near forty of the children taken from the Six Nations to pass through the school in the years that followed became good readers and writers and a number of them advanced considerably in the knowledge of Greek and Latin. If they tended to relapse to their old ways upon the return to their families, that only emphasized the importance of the missionaries who carried the gospel to the tribes to counteract the wilderness influences.

To Lebanon David McClure came in 1763 at the age of fifteen, to find in Wheelock a father, patron and benefactor. The students lodged hard and lived on plain fare and there was much that was practical in their work; they were not spared the labor of the farm, for instance. Piety and the reading of books of solid worth occupied the rest of their time. For considerable intervals David was sent down to Yale to acquire what learning was not available in Lebanon and at the age of seventeen he went deep into the West to keep a school among the Oneida. Later, another spell of teaching followed before he was ordained and departed on his missionary labors.

Wheelock's institution was exceptional and even it recognized the necessity of combining learning from books with experience. The colonists did not regard the school as a replacement for, but rather as a supplement to, apprenticeship, which remained the common method of transmitting skills and leaving home. Nevertheless some uneasiness persisted about the proper place of abstract knowledge in education. By the time McClure was ordained, Wheelock's school had moved north to Hanover, New Hampshire, and had become Dartmouth College. It thus joined a handful of other little communities that struggled to advance learning and to provide some youths with an alternative means of setting out in life.

Colleges in the Wilderness

In 1770, Dartmouth was one of nine institutions of higher learning in the British colonies. Harvard, the oldest, had received its charter 134 years before, but remained small, awarding degrees to some four or five candidates a year in the seventeenth century. The number of its graduates grew after 1700 but never exceeded sixty. The newer places in Williamsburg, Virginia, in New Haven, Connecticut, in Princeton and New Brunswick, New Jersey, in New York City, in Hanover, New Hampshire, in Philadelphia, Pennsylvania, and in Providence, Rhode Island, were no larger. The total living alumni of all the colleges in 1770 amounted to less than 3,000. Yet this handful of graduates was influential beyond its numbers and symptomatic of a trend that would accelerate in the centuries to come.

Piety and pride were the motives behind the establishment of the colleges. Among the first settlers of Massachusetts were more than a hundred graduates of Cambridge and Oxford. The faith that drew them across the ocean also led them to make some provision to assure the colony a supply of learned ministers. Although it would have been simpler to send promising young men for training to Cambridge in England, the Massachusetts Puritans wanted a college of their own. Their mission in the New World was to create a city upon a hill that would light the way to redemption for all mankind. Harvard was a necessary ornament and, once established, it had to be sustained to demonstrate the success of the Holy Commonwealth as well as to produce proper ministers.

For the founders of Harvard as of other colonial colleges, higher education was primarily a means toward religious ends; the purpose was to train ministers, to convert the Indians and to shore up the faith of people remote from the centers of civilization. Yet bound in with these expectations was another, somewhat vaguer, motive. These institutions had symbolic importance and brought prestige to the communities in which they were situated. New Haven and Wethersfield battled fiercely over the possession of Yale as a token of their stability and permanence.

But pride, prestige and symbols did not bear a high cash value in the colonies, with the result that the institutions so hopefully founded never enjoyed adequate incomes. They satisfied an ideal aspiration rather than a need felt so deeply that society would make sacrifices for them. In England the gentry class had sent its sons to the university and had also provided the means of support. But colonial families with aristocratic pretensions, like the Byrds and Delanceys, were few in number, and, if interested in higher education, were as likely as not to ship boys off to the mother country. They would not carry the burden.

University funds were therefore meager. President Chauncy of Harvard complained in the 1660's that the wealthy of the province waxed fat yet refused to support learning. A century later, President Witherspoon of Princeton might well have echoed these sentiments, as he appealed to pulpits throughout the continent to help extinguish the college debt. By then the Great Awakening had increased the number of sectarian institutions competing for the limited resources available. Generous donors were rare and usually were Englishmen rather than Americans — John Harvard, for instance, or Elihu Yale, whose £550 was so extraordinary a gift that he was immortalized in the name of the college which benefited from it. In any case, there were no stable channels for investing whatever endowment came in response to pleas for help, so that the institutions always depended upon current income to meet expenses.

The hard-pressed college authorities often appealed for support to local and provincial governments, justifying the pleas for aid with the argument that higher education was a service to the state. The friends of Harvard in the 1660's thus reminded the authorities that the college had long supplied the province with educated gentlemen for the magistracy. A decade later, a commencement orator explained that without the university, Massachusetts would have been overwhelmed by lewd fellows who would govern by plebiscites, appeals to base passions and revolutionary rumblings. Promises that the college would fit youth for public employment in the civil state as well as in the church crept into statements at the founding of Yale, Columbia and Princeton as well as in efforts to spark life into William and Mary. Perhaps the most sweeping endorsement of the value of learning for government came from the pen of George III in 1762. Recommending aid for the colonial institutions, he pointed out that they guarded against ignorance a population drawn from different parts of the world and instilled into it a love of the constitution.

In response, legislatures sometimes handed over the cash for a building, more often granted the needy college a privilege—to operate a ferry, to conduct a lottery or to get the proceeds of special taxes. But the sums thus made available were far from munificent. The suggestion in 1762 that Massachusetts might charter a new school in Hampshire County threw Harvard into a panic. Competition, a committee of the Board of Overseers explained, would weaken both the old and the new institutions, cheapen the value of all degrees, and set back the cause of education in general. The committee really meant that there simply was not enough in the provincial coffers to do for two.

Justification by the promise to serve the state was, moreover, double-edged. Some legislators, listening to a commencement orator deplore the influence on the populace of mad nobodies and haranguers at street corners, snapped shut their purses. Members of the assemblies who had themselves never been to college were reluctant to vote public funds to support would-be gentlemen who, the word had it, dressed in gold or silver lace, brocades and silk nightgowns. The reluctance grew stronger in the eighteenth century when habits of deference to the gentry faded.

Hard-fisted farmers, calculating merchants, even aggressive, expansive planters responded a little more generously to a somewhat different justification: the college deserved support because of its practical utility. President Clap of Yale in the 1760's thus explained that his graduates had applied the principles of mechanical and experimental philosophy to the improvement of agriculture, and had been able to instruct their neighbors in the science, for the public good. The claim to usefulness was rarely that precise and was often acknowledged to be more potential than actual. Yet it subjected the college to the constant pressure of demonstrating its value.

In the last analysis, however, the universities depended for survival on student fees. Beacons of learning though they might be, the flame would flicker out unless their administrators could persuade such skeptical fathers as Benjamin Franklin's, with large families to provide for, that education was worth the price, especially when many of the graduates afterward obtained only a mean living.

The college degree was not a requisite for any calling, not even the ministry. Nevertheless fifteen-year-old John Adams, an ambitious boy, came to Harvard because the experience would raise him above the humble circumstances of his parents. He shared a widely held belief that study of the classics advanced scholars in all professions, helped them secure pulpits in the best churches or brought them success as physicians, lawyers and merchants or simply as gentlemen. Higher education was valuable, not for the specific skills it transmitted but for the cultural signs of superior status it fixed upon its products.

Adams's attitude was by no means crude or calculating; it consisted of multiple, scarcely conscious, values. The ability to quote a Greek maxim in a legal brief was not essential but helpful. More important was the prevailing conviction that minds sharpened on the complexities of Greek thought were better able as a result to deal with the day-to-day problems of trespass and contract. Most important was the awareness that colonial society rewarded people who displayed such signs of gentlemanly rank as command of the classics.

The concept that there was an order of learning apt for

a gentleman had originated in the Renaissance and had been elaborated in England by Sir Thomas Elyot, who argued also that mastery of that order ought to precede the study of medicine or law. Thence it came to the colonies. Although counterparts of the English gentry were rare in the New World, other families, which aspired to a rise in status, turned to the American universities for training in proper behavior, unrelated to vocational goals and gentle in quality. As was appropriate to seminaries, the chief purpose of which was the preparation of ministers, the emphasis was at first moral. President Dunster of Harvard directed his tutors to do what they could to advance learning but to take special care that the students' conduct be honorable and without blame. The charter of 1693 justified William and Mary not only by the training it offered clergymen but also by the pious education in good letters and manners it assured youth.

In the eighteenth century, the moralistic injunctions lost importance and the colleges stated the gentlemanly ideal more explicitly than formerly, although none ever followed Oxford and Cambridge in separating commoners from gentlemen or in distinguishing between earned and pass degrees. The charter of the College of Rhode Island (1764) explained that institutions for liberal education were highly beneficial to society because they transmitted virtue, knowledge and useful literature to the next generation and thus preserved in the community a succession of men qualified to discharge the offices of life with diligence and distinction. At somewhat the same time, Provost William Smith in Philadelphia argued that thinking, writing and acting well were the grand aims of a liberal education. The college provided a general foundation in all the branches of literature, which enabled young men to perfect themselves in those particular callings to which their talents afterwards led them.

Liberal education, training in proper manners of action and thought, had a clear — though not always perceived — link with gentlemanly ideals. The connection emerged in the fear expressed by one friend of universities lest learning become cheap and too common so that every man would be for giving his son an education. It was also perceived by a hostile critic, young Benjamin Franklin, who, in *The New England Courant,* accused Harvard of being a refuge of wealthy young men, where, for the lack of any other talent, they learned little more than how to carry themselves handsomely and enter a room genteely.

There was a very thin line between the desire of parents to send their sons off for a liberal education and the desire to send them off because it was inconvenient to keep them at home. The line was soon crossed.

In the seventeenth century, the word *college* referred as often to a lodging as to an educational institution. It was frequently used in the sense of hostel and so it served some Americans. Apprenticeship remained the most common form of getting a boy out of the home. Attendance at college became a variant for people with aspirations toward a social rank higher than that of the artisan. When the conditions of life in the colonies eased, some families could afford to provide their sons with an interval of study between childhood and adulthood.

Few men married before the age of twenty-six so that those who did not need to seek a livelihood as soon as possible had the time to spare for college. In large families, furthermore, the departure of one left more room for the others. The circumstances that determined who went varied. Sometimes the studious nature of the boy influenced the decision, as it did in the case of Jonathan Edwards, the fifth of his father's eleven children, who left for Yale at the age of thirteen. But there were also times when parents sent a lad off because they could not control him at home. The most prosperous households faced the sad dilemma that children relieved of the discipline of work grew unruly, particularly when the adults were reluctant to administer the punishment the society expected them to. Fathers, pulled on the one hand by affection and pride, and on the other by duty, eagerly grasped at the opportunity for transferring the obligation to control their offspring to an impersonal, religious institution.

Embarrassed parents early perceived Harvard's potential as an asylum for fourteen- or fifteen-year-old sons who were idle, disobedient or too much interested in plantation sports. In 1651, there were already complaints against those who sent their most *exorbitant* children to Cambridge. Yet the practice continued, indeed increased with the passage of time and, in the eighteenth century, was a significant component of the motives for which students left home for college.

Discipline therefore sometimes seemed to be the main business of these institutions. In the recollections of graduates, the images of warfare were more vivid than those of studious contemplation or religious observance. The president of Harvard, wrote a member of the class of 1642, was fitter to have been an officer in the Inquisition or master of a house of correction than an instructor of Christian youth. The president's role shaped his own character. To inculcate proper habits of behavior among his charges he had to enforce compulsory attendance at chapel, a daily routine which varied only on the Sabbath, and rigid regulations about dress. He also had to exercise strict oversight over meals in common, over general conduct, and over pastimes. His authority in dealing with a pupil was the same as that of a parent or master dealing with a son or apprentice.

The pattern of college life aimed to implicate the students themselves in enforcement of the rules. For instance, the custom that freshmen fagged, or ran errands for their seniors, gave a majority of the youths an interest in conformity and generated a desire among those who suffered in their first year to impose the same system upon their successors in the next three. The colleges, which in 1770 were still essentially clerical institutions, also brought religious sanctions to bear upon the young; appeals to piety mingled with threats of damnation for the blasphemy of disobedience. When none of these means of persuasion sufficed, the teachers resorted to floggings — at Harvard at least to 1718 — or to boxing the ears of offenders.

Disciplinary measures were necessary because the behavior of the fledgling scholars was much like that of apprentices, only less tempered by physical labor and by the immediate obligation of making a career. At the opening of the eighteenth century, a Harvard tutor deplored the drinking and card playing which, he said, *made the college stink.* Again and again, the lads were punished for intoxication and carousing, for shooting or stealing turkeys, geese and other fowl, for the atrocious crime of committing fornication, and for other varieties of abominable lasciviousness.

However pure the college kept itself, it could not altogether escape the contagious corruptions in the environment. Generally, the rural setting protected the institution from the worst aspects of city life; but the Devil planted opportunities for sin everywhere. Massachusetts law forbade innkeepers and others to entertain the students; but enterprising young men had no difficulty in securing adequate supplies of rum and girls. The scholars were difficult to control for they knew that, in town, the lads and wenches met to drink and dance and were altogether brazen about it. What was license for the louts was liberty for the gentry! The frequenting of alehouses, breaches of the Sabbath and vandalism were common. Sometimes disobedience flared out from pranks and broken windows into unrestrained riots.

As far back as 1656, Harvard had appealed to the civil authorities to deal with the unruly, for college criminals deserved to fare no better than similar offenders outside Parnassus. Public opinion supported endeavors to restore and maintain a due subordination in the society and condemned unlawful combinations of students to interpret the rules as they thought fit.

There was nevertheless an inclination toward indulgence, for outbreaks of violence had been characteristic of the history of universities since the Middle Ages. In the nature of the case, punishment for lesser offenses than rebellion was not severe — occasional blows from a tutor, fines, admonishment and, only as a last resort, expulsion. Even those dismissed generally earned forgiveness by public confession and a promise of better behavior in the future. In part the willingness to pardon offenders was due to the tolerance of teachers reluctant to damage the careers of their charges. But it also sprang from the pressure of parents who objected to having their sons—future gentlemen—flogged like beasts. The influence toward restraint was potent because the fathers paid the fees on which the college depended. Harvard in 1749 was so destitute that it seriously considered altering the mode of commencement in return for a gift from three parents of seniors. Two decades later, the same institution readmitted some other rioters it had expelled because benefactors condescended to intercede on their behalf. At about the same time similar pressures forced President Clap to resign from Yale. Later in life one of the freshmen who had joined the outcry against the poor man ruefully acknowledged that he had done so heedlessly, merely to go along with the other students. By then Clap was dead of chagrin.

The realities of dealing with a heterogeneous, and only partly interested, student body had more effect upon college life than idealistic aspirations toward learning. Presidents did not welcome disciplinary responsibilities; the desire to reduce the weight of these obligations lay behind Increase Mather's recommendation to the founders of Yale that students board in town under the guardianship of worthy families. But the burden was not so readily displaced; parents wished the college to bear it.

An etymological change which obliterated the distinction between university and college was evidence of that wish. In England the university was the degree-granting, examining, instructional body within which colleges housed communities of students and masters. The colonists persistently confused the terms university and college and, in the end, came to use them synonymously, incongruously uniting degree-granting academic attributes with quasi-parental functions.

The hazy goals of the American colleges created intricate problems. Founded for grandiloquent motives and inflated by community pride, these institutions nevertheless staggered along in abject poverty. The pursuit of learning remained a distant aspiration while the discipline of unruly boys consumed much energy; and the day-to-day dependence upon fees and gifts resulted in repeated, wearisome, exercises in self-justification.

Since its purpose was unclear, each seminary had to rest its case on the excellence of its teachers and curriculum. The recruitment of faculty was, however, haphazard. With rare exceptions such as Henry Flynt, who remained more than forty years at Harvard, the tutors were recent graduates who spent a few years in service before moving on to more desirable posts. They had to be vigorous enough to hold their own in discipline, bachelors to be able to live on the premises, and orthodox in religious views. These requirements hardly made the jobs attractive, and Yale on one occasion found itself without any staff at all.

The quality of the president was more important to parents, students and donors. He enjoyed continuity in office, prestige and some power. In most places there were no professors with fixed educational functions or salaries. Sometimes, indeed, the president was the only teacher. Always he was the source of discipline, the continuing force in setting instructional policy and the focus of the authority to dispose of the college's financial resources. The weight attached to that position induced Princeton to send to Scotland for a man competent to fill it.

The desire to attract support also led to changes in the curriculum and even more, to a gurgle of rhetoric about what should or might be taught. The seventeenth-century Harvard course of study, modeled upon that of the old Cambridge, had focused upon logic — the art of reasoning — and upon the languages — Latin, Greek and Hebrew — presumably helpful to future ministers. Any marked departure from that pattern might put off conscientious students. David Brainerd, who finally went to Yale, thus came afraid of the temptations of the place and wary lest the ambition to do well in irrelevant studies might take time away from God and dull the fervor of his faith. The college had to be traditional enough to satisfy him and yet innovative enough to attract other boys whose destination was not the pulpit and who came for the more liberal purpose of learning to think like scholars and to behave like gentlemen.

The adjustment to these contrary demands was sporadic and inconsistent. Occasional instructors in the eighteenth century began to draw upon ideas emanating from the Enlightenment, which was then transforming the world of the intellect. Thomas Clap's public lectures at Yale and President Witherspoon's course in mental science at Princeton were among such new departures. Elsewhere the claim of utility justified the introduction of subjects held to be more relevant to the lives of most Americans than the ancient languages. John Winthrop at Harvard and Ezra Stiles at Yale gave instruction in science. In Philadelphia William Smith, with Franklin's aid, put the emphasis on English, science and practical studies rather than on the classics, although he insisted that the students each day converse with one of the ancients who *at the same time that he charmed with the beauties of his language* illustrated the branches of knowledge to which the other hours were devoted. Yet it was after such changes that John Trumbull, tutor at Yale, in a poem entitled "Progress of Dullness" attacked the curriculum for its neglect of literature.

The criterion of practicality was not an effective guide to what to teach or learn. Apart from those destined for the ministry, the students had no clear idea of why they were in college; and prospective merchants, lawyers and landowners were no more easily persuaded of the future utility of French and chemistry than of Greek and logic. The vague promotional promises could not be fulfilled. What an assignment Columbia undertook when it announced that it would teach *everything* useful for the comfort, the convenience and elegance of life, *and also* the chief manufactures relating to any of these things *and also* the knowledge of God and man that would contribute to true happiness! The expectations thus nurtured were doomed to frustration.

The difficulties of the college exposed its anomalous condition in American life. The pride that entered into the foundation of seminaries of learning in the New World was not enough to sustain them for their own sake. To survive, they sought to provide a gentlemanly liberal education to young men in the awkward age between childhood and independence. Yet for the time being most Americans found alternative means of leaving home more attractive, so that the college, whatever its future importance, remained peripheral to colonial life.

3

SPACE FOR EXPANSION, 1770–1870

FEW European observers after 1770 failed to note and comment upon the boastfulness of Americans. Promoters described every muddy crossroad as the metropolis of the future, and the whole nation seemed committed to a grandiose vision of its destiny, a vision that grated upon the sensibilities of visitors from London and Paris who struggled through the wretched meals of a Washington or New York boarding house.

The fact that reality often outran the most fanciful predictions was also annoying. The colonists had announced that their cause was the cause of all mankind and that their example would diffuse liberty throughout the world. Events justified their confidence. They completed a successful revolution, gained their independence and established a government that endured even the agony of a fratricidal civil war. They professed to move at the forefront of man's effort to convert into reality the Enlightenment dream of progress toward perfection through the use of reason and knowledge; and by the middle of the nineteenth century they had launched a score of vigorous reform movements to redeem the vicious, to raise the dependent and to liberate the victims of disease, poverty and slavery. From the huddled settlements of the Atlantic coast they had pushed westward to the Pacific, knit the country together with canals and railroads, and funneled the products of its fields and mills through thriving cities to every part of the world. The United States had absorbed millions of newcomers while its own restless population remained ceaselessly in motion.

Here was opportunity for whoever wished to grasp it, and not only in the abundant land awaiting the farmer but also in the cities and towns. The politics of a democracy offered the ambitious endless chances for getting ahead; Jackson, Johnson, Webster, Lincoln — the great names and many lesser ones — were standing reminders of the heights of eminence to which a poor boy could rise. Scarcely less familiar were the names of the great merchant princes, Thomas H. Perkins or A. T. Stewart, who grasped the opportunities of expanding commerce. Or Horace Greeley the editor, or Samuel Gridley Howe the physician, or Joseph Story the jurist. All these models had in common one trait: they had not followed the careers of their fathers but had made their own way in life.

Lowly origins did not matter; achievement did. A story by a fourteen-year-old boy in a school newspaper of 1848 drew the moral. A pretentious girl despises the suitor who works with his hands. The mechanic never visits her again. He is now a wealthy man and has the best of women for his wife. The young lady who disliked the word mechanic is now the wife of a feckless fool — a regular vagrant about grog-shops — and she, poor miserable girl, is obliged to take in washing in order to support herself and her children. A man's standing depended on his achievement, and success was within the reach of all.

No one took it for granted that he would follow the career or reside in the community of his father. The expectations of parents and children often diverged. The father of Abijah Whiting was dismayed to discover his son's choice of law as a career; that profession, he believed, was not congenial to the practice of personal religion and probably was not really beneficial to society. The father of Marion Sims deplored the decision in favor of medicine, a profession for which he had the utmost contempt. There was no science in it; and the boy, *going around from house to house with a pill box in one hand and a squirt in the other,* would achieve no honor in it.

Each youth approaching adulthood had his own criteria. The judgment of the ages, according to a common saying, ranked the desirability of callings — heroes, legislators, orators and poets. So much for aspirations. In actuality most choices fell where opportunity lay in the services demanded by the expanding population of the great cities and of thousands of small towns. The shops, offices and mills needed armies of clerks, managers and entrepreneurs who, in turn, read newspapers, consulted lawyers and physicians and attended the numerous churches of their choice. The abundance of places thus made available gave every boy's dream some touch of reality.

But some youths were also aware of the somber aspects of a changing society. There were failures as well as successes. Light-Horse Harry Lee, a revolutionary hero and member of a great planter family, spent a term in jail in 1809 for debt and finally fled to the Barbados to escape his creditors. His son Robert, then six years old, later in life often thought back on the glamour and pathos of the fall. Nor could Stephen A. Douglas ever forget the reversal of family fortunes when the death of his father — a doctor and college graduate — forced his mother to eke out her living on a scrubby Vermont farm. Such strokes of disaster were sometimes social as well as personal; the panic of 1837 was said to have thrown out of work 40,000 clerks in New York City alone.

The open slopes that made both a steep ascent and a precipitous drop possible emphasized the importance of a proper family upbringing, which developed the traits and the habits of behavior to assure success and command confidence. Lorenzo Waugh, wandering without resources or destination, reached a turning point when the housewife who gave him a meal, after inquiring of his home and people, expressed her great pleasure in seeing him observe the Sabbath day and got him a job. A prospective employer could tell at a glance that a boy was honest from the family upbringing reflected in appearance and behavior.

The reverse was also true and visible: the least fortunate members of society were those whose family life was incomplete or in disorder — the slaves and the immigrant laborers. Nothing more condemned the South's peculiar system than the pangs of empathy stirred up by descriptions of the sale of children away from their parents in *Uncle Tom's Cabin.*

The major responsibility of parents was to provide their offspring with the home that would guard them against the adverse contingencies of life. Prudent men therefore still postponed marriage until after the age of twenty-five, by which time they would have advanced in their careers far enough to take on the burden. James

Colles waited until thirty-three, Stephen A. Douglas until thirty-four. The delays were wise, for the new husband understood all too well that he would soon have to provide for a numerous brood of children — six, even twelve, in an urban family were not uncommon, although the eighteen, of whom Joseph Story was one, were unusual. The arrival of the first baby generally ended the interval of boarding-house life through which the more cautious postponed the expenses of settlement.

To accommodate the expanding menage, the father needed the means to suppy the housing fit for family life, and that meant something specific to Americans before the Civil War. Neither the barracks of the Irish laborers in New York and Boston, nor the luxurious St. Clare mansion in New Orleans, built in an ancient Moorish fashion, was ideal. The proper setting for family life was the farmhouse or its urban equivalent, the row house, clean and orderly, with everything inside and outside in place — not a picket loose in the fence — and where all domestic arrangements moved with the exactness of the old clock in the corner. Here each individual had space enough if all respected their own obligations and honored the rights of others.

On the farm, and among some artisans, physicians and lawyers in the towns and cities, the home was still the location of the family's enterprise. But a growing number of Americans now separated the place of work from the place of residence. The father went off elsewhere to earn his livelihood. The home thus lost its economic functions and its activities narrowed to the purely domestic; it remained the focal point of discipline, religion and affection among its members, more necessary than ever in urban communities grown too large to oversee individual deportment. Furthermore the collapse of the belief in predestination put extraordinary weight on conduct as the key which opened the gates to heaven or hell. A Christian nurture which made *the good* attractive and *the wrong* odious was, the Congregationalist Horace Bushnell explained, the essential element in salvation; and correct personal behavior was the cardinal virtue in the teachings of the Presbyterian John Holt Rice. At home the youngster learned the first principles of faith, and many in later life ascribed their preservation from vice and crime to the moral and religious training they had received there as children. The well-ordered family twice daily prayed in its parlor together, and together on Sunday worshiped in its square high pew.

Religious precepts in turn sustained the ethic of work and manners taught in the home. For New Englanders such as Miss Ophelia, the sin of sins was *shiftlessness,* by which she meant an aimless drift, a waste of time while there was work to be done. It was a matter of course that children who had worked on the farm should take jobs in Samuel Slater's mill when their parents did. Employment in the factory or shop kept boys correct and moral; the father who brought his sons up in idleness, warned Freeman Hunt, might live to see them hang. Except where the presence of slaves complicated the household, the gospel of home and church emphasized the obligations of purposeful endeavor and self-discipline against all weaknesses of the flesh.

A child well reared also learned manners in the family. The ability properly to speak and be spoken to, the knowledge of how to respond to persons of different ages, sexes and quality, and the habit of acting in ways that would not offend others — these traits were increasingly important in the numerous encounters of a society which frequently brought strangers in contact with one another.

Above all, the family remained the ultimate emotional resource of the Americans. It was a strangely barren landscape through which these men and women moved, with few outlets for the passions. The immigrants who recalled European cities could make the comparison — the visual impact of ancient monuments, the lush ritual of recurrent holy days, the indulgence in seasons of carnival or *faschung,* the flash of uniforms, the blast of trumpets. The native born did not even know what they missed unless, like Abram Hewitt, they caught a glimpse of magnificence during a tour abroad. The austere sermon or Fourth-of-July oration, like the simple lines of their public buildings and statuary or the persistent didacticism of their reading matter demanded restraint and rationality. Respectable city folk lacked even the outlet of the occasional revival or the election whiskey keg through which the country people let go. Only well on in the nineteenth century, and then sparsely, did other less constricted forms of expression unfold. The natural wildness of mountains and falls, the gothic curlicues of cottages, churches and tombs, Fanny Elssler, Jenny Lind, balls, concerts, the New Orleans Mardi Gras, the circus, the minstrel show and vaudeville began to offer the American open occasions to laugh, to cry, to wonder — in moderation. But even then the family remained the source to which the individual drew for all the warmth his emotions required.

For the boy advancing to manhood, the parents were central to the family. Siblings, like friends, were allies or rivals moving in and out of consciousness and experience; and grandparents, cousins, aunts and uncles were remote though sometimes pleasant relations. Father and mother were immediate, vital presences in life.

More rarely now in the city did a son stand at the father's side, desirable as that might seem. Nevertheless the paternal role was still authoritative. The father was the breadwinner, though his work was at a distance from the home, less visible but perhaps therefore all the more impressive for the daily bread it provided. He was the man of power, the earthly representative as it were of a Heavenly Father, who rewarded virtue and punished transgressions and established the values that were the guides through life. His will was of iron, his industry indefatigable, Julius H. Pratt remembered. Self-command, one father informed his son, was the pivot upon which the character of mortals turned. A man was not only to be virtuous in reality but was always to appear so — moderate in eating, drinking, sleeping; truthful; and avoiding debts and frivolous and skeptical books. The vigilant parent applied the sanctions that held boys to this code. *Never darken my door again* was more than the music-hall line it later became.

The boy's mother also supplied his material wants and guided his behavior. In the city, as on the farm, she could not hate to do anything that needed to be done — prepare the daily food and churn the butter and dry the fruit, nurse the sick and stew medicine from the herbs, mend the clothes and neaten, clean. She was the kind fairy dispensing the good things the stomach and the heart craved. The child, impressed by her numerous competences, also learned from her the lessons of self-denial and self-control in all matters, lessons sometimes emphasized by force — *whip and pray and pray and whip,* a friend advised Ann Carter Lee — and sometimes by the desire to win the sustenance of her affection. To offend a being who was the embodiment of every grace was unthinkable. A New York merchant recalled that as a boy he read the Bible because he saw that it gave his mother pleasure. Often he slipped stealthily to her bedroom door to listen to her prayers; and if ever he forgot to repeat certain forms she taught him, he would arise in the dead of night and kneel at his bedside to do so.

Yet of all the certainties the boy came to accept, none was more fixed than that of the implacable extinction of the tender little flames that flickered briefly through life.

Death was always present.

It might be a younger brother or sister (it might even have been he) — and then he hears the painful anguish of father seeking consolation. It was better for the child, a lovely and charming flower, to be called by its heavenly Creator into His presence pure and innocent, unpolluted by sin and uncontaminated by the vices of the world (as he himself is, or will be).

It might be mother, or stepmother, often after a season of suffering as the words of encouragement and love grew still, gaiety faded, and a hushed withdrawal to her bedroom left the whole household in unaccustomed disorder. Then she yielded her soul to Him who gave it and escaped to a brighter world where sickness and sorrow; pain and death were felt and feared no more. *We would not wish her back,* the man said. (Would we not?)

And the father. Rarely did the boys know of the father's fear of being forgotten, of his concern for the family deprived of support by his departure, of the anxiety that embittered each illness: *God only knows how they will subsist — and the education of the children!* A sudden mysterious accident simply removed his presence from the home: it took six months for news of the death of a Virginian in Georgia in 1818 to reach his wife and children, and many a shipwreck left unexplained an emptiness in the household. At other times, the strength seeped away, the sure movements faltered and the towering figure tumbled in illness. Again an emptiness for all dependent on him. When her husband died, Nathaniel Hawthorne's mother moved back to her father's house and remained for forty years in the seclusion of an upstairs room. The boy watched.

The hymn made it clear:

O there'll be mourning, mourning, mourning
    at the judgment seat of Christ.
Parents and children there shall part!
Parents and children there shall part!
    Shall part to meet no more!

The home in America was a fragile structure. Within it the child looked for guidance to the father's power and the mother's competent solicitude. But it offered those who depended upon it for physical and emotional security only a flimsy shelter against the shock of separation.

Where the Boys Went

Ned was twelve in 1816 when he went off to live at school. Bravely he had boasted that he would not be homesick. But his brother Ralph, a year older, understood the pangs departure would bring and tried in letter after letter to bolster the absent boy's courage. Perhaps the new place did not look as pleasant as home to one not accustomed to the tumult of the voices of strangers. The teasing lines aimed to make Ned laugh.

Here is a reminder that home too had unsightly aspects. A description of the view from a window acquaints the absent brother with a domestic scene he may not have had the opportunity to take in before departing:

> The wide unbounded prospect lies before me.
> Imprimis then, a dirty yard
> By boards and dirt and rubbish marr'd
> Piled up aloft a mountain steep
> Of broken Chairs and beams a heap.

Their father, William Emerson, had died some years before, and their mother, who lived by taking in boarders, had not the time to devote to the upbringing of her sons. School was one of the ways the boys left home.

Apprenticeship was another.

At the age of fifteen Horace Greeley took leave of his family. They had seen hard times together and were fondly attached to one another. Now all the others in the family were moving to the West and he was entering an apprenticeship in Vermont. At the moment of separation he was tempted to go with them. A word from his mother might have overcome his resolution. But she did not speak it and he went his way. The twelve-mile walk to the new master's shop was the slowest and saddest of his life.

The wrench was hard upon the parents also, even under the best of circumstances. A flow of letters reassured the absent member that he was not forgotten. The father whose son went off to Yale in 1839 could not be reconciled to the empty place at the table and every morning half turned to call his name at the top of the stairs. Hardly a night passed but that mother wondered what the lad was up to. As age crept on and friends died off, it was to their children that Americans looked for the consolation that earth could give and it was no easy gesture to send them off.

Yet the partings were usual, except when the death of the father forced one of the sons to remain and take over the responsibility of supporting the family, as Robert M. LaFollette did at the age of sixteen. But in the absence of such obligations the boys were thrust out, however painful the separation. As soon as the young American approached manhood, a foreign observer wrote in 1840, the ties of filial obedience were relaxed day by day; master of his thought, he was soon master of his conduct. Having foreseen the limits of paternal authority long beforehand, the father was prepared to surrender it without a struggle when the time came. The same habits, the same principles, which impelled the one to assert his independence predisposed the other to consider that independence an incontestable right. Fathers, proud of their sons' abilities to find their own ways, were unwilling to erect restraining barriers that might limit the direction youth would take.

The parting was not as easy as Tocqueville supposed, however. Parents felt the emptiness the separation caused. The sons when in difficulty missed the support of an elder; and when prospering grieved to think of the old folk left behind and still working hard. Nor was the parting primarily a product of democracy, as Tocqueville thought. It was an inescapable circumstance of the approach to maturity in an unstable and expanding society.

You are entering *a stage of life full of danger,* the minister's letter warns the boy of twelve. *Its feelings are new, its temptations are strong and different from any you have ever encountered.* Remember the lessons of home, avoid the sin of pride, and exercise self-restraint.

Phillips Brooks, age fourteen, feels himself trembling on the verge of manhood. Regret mingles with hope in a school essay. He has left behind *the morning of life* and the world is about to cast around him its *fettering cares,* as he moves on his *solitary way.*

Jonathan Fisher of Holden, Massachusetts, falls into dark discouragement when he considers God's intention. Is a youth with *a propensity to impurity* fit for the ministry or had he better settle for a blacksmith's or cabinetmaker's or a clockmaker's trade? The concern seeps into secret verse:

> But my hard heart is prone to sin.
> What deep pollution reigns within!
> Meanwhile I tread with awful speed
> Those ways which to destruction lead.

What ways? A weakness for cards and a fondness for spirits and an uncle's servant girl whose shameless suggestions trouble Jonathan's soul.

As the boys grew older, gained physical strength and reached toward the powers of men, they became aware that the father was not only a model for emulation but also a rival to be surpassed. The discovery threw the youths into confusion — for a moment or for years. The crisis was often religious; where did the earthly son stand with the Heavenly Father? But the crisis sometimes also focused internally within the family. When Charles Francis Adams conceded that he would depart from the rule of eternal bachelorhood to which he had sworn himself, but only if he met a woman as pleasing as his mother, he measured himself as he usually did by a paternal standard.

Better that the youths with men's bodies should remove these broody feelings, these fears of temptation and these resentments of restraint away from the bruising emotional contacts of the homes in which they had been children! It was painful to send them forth but less painful than to hold them back. The family's task of preparation could not go on indefinitely and the conventions of society weighted the decision in favor of departure.

The attitudes of both fathers and sons were ambivalent toward the grand gestures of separation that occupied their imaginations. Everyone knew that a bad end threatened boys who ran away to sea, as John Haskins did to become cooper on a privateer, or Mark Fernald who had the skill of a carpenter; rum and the rowdy forecastle might lead them to ruin, destroy their bodies and endanger their souls. Yet Richard Henry Dana's decision in 1834 to leave school and go before the mast on a two-year voyage to California, was not outlandish; and contemporaries read his account of the experience with approval.

It was the same with enlisting in the Army or going West to trap or to dig for gold — all potential paths to damnation. The corruptions of camp life, the absence of the refining influence of women, the lack of churches and of the safeguards of home constituted a threat to morality more dangerous than the physical perils of the wilderness. Once exposed to evil habits, young men yielded to temptation and came to miserable ends in the prison and on the gallows. And yet — and yet the thought remained that men discovered their true temper through trial in the furnace of experience. Shielded from exposure to evil they could not reveal their capacity for virtue, and heroism was manifest only when there was an occasion for it. Daniel Boone, Davy Crockett, John Paul Jones, Oliver Perry went forth and were the better for it.

The extreme case was that of an orphan. None more than he was a potential victim of the corrupting influences of the world. Deprived of parents and home, of food and clothing, of a father's discipline, and of the lessons learned at a mother's knee, he was in total want, unprepared for the perils of getting along on his own. Hence the long-standing concern to insert him into a family through apprenticeship or servitude. When the supply of wage and slave labor in the nineteenth century increased to the point at which masters no longer found it attractive to take on the responsibility for the unattached child, then it seemed appropriate to rear the orphan in an institution through which society as a whole would compensate for the absence of parents.

The orphanage was, however, a place mistrusted, despite the praise lavished upon it by reform-minded sponsors. Bernard McQuaid, raised in the Prince Street Asylum, rose to be a bishop of the Catholic Church; but he and his vocation were both exceptional. In the judgment of most Americans the institution was without the love that tied fathers and mothers to their children, and the relationship that prevailed in the asylum was that between keepers and inmates, as in a prison. The boy in flight from such a place was a favorite figure of nineteenth-century fiction. His plight in escaping was analogous to that of the most sympathetic slave characters, the fugitives who ran away from home toward freedom.

In actuality, there was no consistent attempt to round up the army of homeless boys which wandered unattached through the alleys of the great cities. Jerry MacAuley came to New York from Ireland in 1850, at the age of thirteen. Life in the streets led him to theft, gambling and drink, and ultimately at the age of nineteen to Sing Sing — so ran his later lachrymose warnings to other youths who followed the same course. By the time he had landed in America the gangs of children were visible in the largest cities, although not all the citizens wished to look, for the society had lost the ability to police the whole community and was willing to tolerate enclaves where the law did not hold and where the homeless drifted about with little fear of being apprehended. In the countryside, too, unattached boys followed the roads without fixed destinations and lived by odd jobs on the way.

Yet the orphan was not doomed. Andrew Jackson had lost both his parents by the time he was fourteen and, left utterly alone, shuttled unwanted from family to family. Winfield Scott at five lost his father, at seventeen his mother, and floundered without help until he landed on his feet. Even Jerry MacAuley ultimately was saved. The perils which surrounded him elicited his heroic qualities, just as the wilderness, the field of battle and the sea did for the frontiersman, the soldier and the mariner. The dangers of the city subjected him to the trial of temptation, but innate goodness armed him to resist.

The city offered a taste of liberty even to Negro boys. For Frederick Douglass, going to live in Baltimore at the age of eight opened the gateway to all his subsequent prosperity. He remained a slave, but felt quite free; growing skill and self-confidence rewarded his toil. In town, the future was not utterly blank for black young people as it was on the plantation. They might even get to purchase their liberty as Denmark Vesey did and become skilled craftsmen.

A youth alone learned at an early age that life was a serious business; and that he who did not grasp whatever opportunity the currents of the times swept by would go under. But the strong ones also learned the maxim one of them set down in a notebook: *You can be what you resolve to be*. Henry Villard, arriving penniless and alone in New York in 1853 and lacking even a word of English, in time learned his lesson of America: *with a strong will and proper push* everything is possible. Boys who lacked external supports were also unhindered by external restraints and could make of themselves what they wished.

The hazardous freedom that misfortune imposed on orphans, other lads were encouraged to seek out. They left home with the approbation of the family to test and discover themselves and to prepare for the battles life held in store for all men. Morrison R. Waite, a Yale graduate, could have stayed comfortably in Lyme, Connecticut, to inherit his father's practice, but preferred to make a law career of his own in the West, unaided by family and ancestral prestige. James W. Austin, a Harvard Law School graduate in 1851, gave up a place at the Massachusetts bar for adventure in Hawaii. Stung by his father's offer of support, sixteen-year-old John D. Rockefeller left to prove he did not need it. The shield of faith and sober habits instilled by the family guarded these young men safe against evil; and in every community Christian spirits, such as those who organized the Boston Y.M.C.A.

in 1851, met the young stranger, took him to church and to Sabbath school, and threw around him good influences to counteract, though not eliminate, the moral dangers encountered in drifting alone from one boarding house to another.

There were no two ways about it. Risk was inescapable and was to be met boldly, with the family's benediction or without. Andrew Jackson in 1783, having spent what little he inherited, was down to the horse he rode and in debt. He bet the horse on a single cast of the dice, won, and imbued with new spirit as well as cash was ready to climb. Man's task was to convert obstacle into opportunity and to wrest achievement from difficulty.

Horace Greeley's mother could not utter the word that would keep her son with her. When the boy had been eight years old, one of the leading men of the vicinity had offered to send him to an academy and then to college, without expense to the family. Horace's parents had gratefully declined the proposal. It was better to struggle ahead without help. Grover Cleveland put it more strongly. At the age of seventeen he had refused a wealthy landowner's offer of support through college. The boy had already earned his way for two years as a clerk in a store and as a teacher. He would study law on his own. He *enjoyed his adversities*. They were good for him.

The forms of apprenticeship by which boys acquired training and left home were not quite as varied after 1770 as before. In those occupations in which the level of skill was relatively low, employers used wage labor, especially after immigration increased the supply of hands and the factory provided the techniques for managing large numbers. A succession of mechanical inventions made it cheaper to take on help by the hour, day or week rather than to get ensnared in the cumbersome apprenticeship arrangement. The trend somewhat narrowed the chances for the children of families without connections or financial resources.

Furthermore, in many callings the family aspects of the apprentice relationship faded away. Informal arrangements replaced the written contract or indenture, terms were rarely fixed or precise, and the youth often lived with his own parents or in a boarding house rather than with the master. In many cases, the labor and wages involved became more important to both parties than the discipline and instruction.

But boys eager to rise, and their parents, still had a wide range of choice for apprenticeship training among crafts in which skill remained important. Printers, for instance, long remained persons of consequence, among whom family connections counted in taking on a lad. Matthew Lyon thus sent his son James from Vermont to Philadelphia to learn the trade from Benjamin Franklin. It seemed a matter of course for Ellis Lewis to take a place at the presses when orphaned; his father had founded the first newspaper in Harrisburg, Pennsylvania. Ambitious outsiders could also break in; Horace Greeley served four years in East Poultney, Vermont, then tramped about the country as a journeyman, living as was fit in the homes of his masters, and at last came to New York City, which he entered friendless and with an unquestionable air of country greenness about him. Long after he had become famous as a publisher and editor Greeley concluded that he had received a better education than he would have in four years of college.

Other vocations also remained open to boys willing

to learn from the experience of apprenticeship, as when Andrew Jackson entered the service of a saddler or Stephen A. Douglas of a cabinetmaker. Carpenters, masons, stonecutters, bricklayers — indeed almost all the skilled participants in construction work — received their training thus, as did artisans occupied in making clothing and food; many boys in time by this means rose to be their own masters. Wherever apprenticeship remained important, unions appeared to regulate the conditions of entry into the trade and to protect its practitioners.

In vocations in which formal apprenticeship disappeared, experience remained decisive and youths who wished to succeed had to seek it out themselves.

There was no other entry to careers in commerce. It might be a business in pennies — as when the poverty of his father forced young Bronson Alcott to take to the road as a peddler. Or privateering, which brought wealth to Simon Forrester, an Irish indentured seaman who came penniless to Massachusetts at the age of nineteen. Or it might be overseas trade, as for Nathaniel Hawthorne (whose son would turn to the pen), who went to sea at fourteen and at twenty-one was captain of the *Perseverance* when she set sail from Salem to Batavia in 1796. Or William Sturgis or John Suter or Nathaniel Silsbee or John Boit, Jr., of Boston, who were the same age or younger when they took command of their own vessels after proving themselves before the mast. For great or small, practice was the teacher.

After 1820, the merchant ceased to accompany his goods or to own his vessels. Steam and improved overseas communications enabled him to conduct his affairs from his countinghouse desk. Other attributes then led to success in trade. The important abilities for the man who executed transactions at a distance, who kept his accounts in books rather than in his head, and who dealt in bits of paper rather than in the actual casks of goods and piles of gold, were those of calculation — of prices, insurance, interest rates — and negotiation — with banks, clients, customers, partners, employees and suppliers. These managerial skills too a boy acquired through practice.

Some youths brought their business training from abroad as did John Johnston, apprenticed at seventeen, who used the habits drilled into him in a Scottish countinghouse to good effect in his career as a New York merchant. But the opportunities to learn were abundant in the United States also, although less knotted into a system than in Europe. Indeed, the rapid pace of movement in the expanding New World gave scope to the boys who wished to be off by themselves.

In Philadelphia, seventeen-year-old Jay Cooke worked for a transport company but kept an eye out for a better place. He had left home at fourteen and worked at Sandusky, Ohio, and St. Louis before coming to the big city. After a year he moved to a broker's office where he kept the books, delivered messages and wrote fifteen to twenty letters a day, thus learning every aspect of the business. At twenty-one, he was a full partner in the firm. In Cleveland John D. Rockefeller was bookkeeper to a commission dealer when he decided to strike out on his own at the age of nineteen. In New York, George F. Peabody was an errand boy, and in Pittsburgh, Andrew Carnegie delivered telegrams. J. P. Morgan, who had an easier start, established his own firm at twenty-five. Alert youngsters, who kept their eyes open in the shop or office, absorbed the *method and system* of doing business. The majority spent the whole of their lives as clerks or salesmen while they waited for the turn of fortune that never came. But some — no matter how few — did rise; and that kept the hopes of all alive.

Boys on the move uncovered opportunity in other vocations also. Andrew Jackson did not remain a saddler, nor Stephen A. Douglas a cabinetmaker. Both found their way through the law to fortune and political eminence. Jackson read law in a North Carolina office for more than two years. Once admitted to the bar, he rode the circuit, made friends, struck up political alliances and, having moved to Tennessee, used the income from his practice to buy land. Douglas, conscious that his want of schooling might be a handicap in the East, moved west to Illinois where standards were vaguer and there became a giant in law and politics — all five feet, one hundred pounds, of him. Ellis Lewis took the same course and became Chief Justice of Pennsylvania's highest court.

No more formal education was necessary. John Marshall, who long dominated the Supreme Court, had followed no systematic legal studies when admitted to the bar in Virginia. Others learned as he had. Law schools sprouted in the nineteenth century and some aspiring attorneys, when convenient, attended lectures, as R. H. Dana did upon his return from California. But Dana's real training was in the office of Charles G. Loring; and a similar preparation sufficed for Robert Barnwell Rhett and other young men who made their marks in the profession.

True, John Bigelow had to serve years of drudgery as a copier before getting established in New York in the 1830's. But that was in a great city where the competition was keenest. Elsewhere the law remained an open avenue along which the ambitious could travel, however dismal their starting point. Hannibal Hamlin of Paris Hill, Maine, never gratified his longing for formal education. The failing health of a brother, the death of a father, the need to support a mother and sisters bound him to the sterile farm with only occasional breaks in the slow season to clerk in a fruit store, to help a surveyor, to teach in country schools — all for the sake of a little spare cash. At the age of twenty, he determined to be a lawyer and Blackstone became his constant companion after each day's work. He learned enough in the evenings to risk his savings on a stay in Portland in the office of General Fessenden. At the age of twenty-four Hamlin was back in Paris Hill, a member of the bar, ready to find a wife, make a home of his own and go on to national prominence.

There were ways of gaining entry by experience to all the professions, although some branches of medicine and some churches called for more formal educational qualifications. Still, the first of the doctors Mayo who came to America from England in 1845 held jobs as a chemist and tailor before he was apprenticed to a physician in Lafayette, Indiana. The growth in the number of practitioners of diverse backgrounds who acquired their training in the same fashion eased entry to the calling. Even a slave could become a physician, as did James Derham, who learned by helping his master. The multiplication of medical sects stimulated the increase in the number of doctors. Homeopaths, aliopaths, phrenologists and others, competing in the common market for cures, eagerly enlisted disciples.

Denominationalism had analogous consequences for the supply of clergymen. Each religious group set its own requirements for practice; but few insisted upon a defined pattern of recruiting their ministers. In most, experience was a recognized means of gaining skill. Thus the Methodist Lorenzo Waugh first tried his preaching voice as assistant to Ebenezer T. Webster on the Guyandott Circuit. Waugh then helped out Barnard Cassatt, the older man doing the strictly theological, scientific preaching, the younger one, the more miscellaneous, exhortational work. Moncure D. Conway's service as a *journeyman soul-saver* for the same sect was also eminently practical and effective. Jacob Young simply followed his brother into the Kentucky revival fields.

Occasional efforts to restrict access to the professions of law, medicine and the ministry had little effect. Popular hostility to monopolies, privileges and licenses of every sort put the right to practice within the reach of many who had only perfunctory training; and in these as in other callings, it was more and more often possible to bypass the irksome hurdles of the past. Somewhat sadly President Charles W. Eliot of Harvard noted in 1869 that Americans were accustomed to seeing men leap from farm or shop to courtroom or pulpit, believing as they did that *common men could safely use the seven league boots of genius.*

An orderly mind could not predict whom the boots of genius would fit.

In 1853, when Thomas Alva Edison was six, his father whipped him publicly in the village square; the dunce had burned down the barn just to see what would happen. The lad thereafter nursed a hatred for the old man and for the brutal teachers in school who thought him addled. At the age of twelve, when the railroad reached town, Thomas Alva took a job as newsboy in the cars, daily leaving Port Huron, Michigan, at 7:00 a.m., returning from Detroit at 9:30 p.m. That, he later recalled, was the happiest time of his life — away from home all day. He remained a rolling stone for a decade — baggage smasher, telegrapher, dispatcher — until his train came in.

An exuberantly expansive society tolerantly made room for the boys who went away the more quickly to achieve adulthood; and the plentitude of chances encouraged boys to take the risk of leaving and eased the parents' pangs at separation.

And the Girls

The numerous forms of apprenticeship that led the boys away from home were not open to their sisters. The girls needed no such exit; they could gain whatever training they required for the move from a father's to a husband's household right at the mother's side. Home was the place for *Little Women,* as Louisa May Alcott's story explained (1868).

So ran the dominant assumption which, however, had ceased to be in full accord with the facts of American life well before 1870.

A variety of feminine types inhabited the pages of a single popular novel just as in real life. Mrs. Bird was round — a timid, blushing little woman of about four feet in height, mild, gentle, sweet. Her husband and children were her entire world and she ruled by entreaty rather than command. She upheld the standards of purity as well as the family's moral and cultural values. Cruelty she could not stand.

Mrs. St. Clare's physical presence hinted at voluptuous,

sensuous qualities. Her concerns focused inward and she yielded readily to the feminine maladies of no discernible cause, for which petted indulgence was the only palliative. Her selfishness no doubt ruined her husband and killed her daughter. The parlors of the well-to-do contained many a lady of sensibility who, like the object of Charles Brockden Brown's love, wished to pattern herself on Clarissa Harlowe; or who, once married, remained sickly, pampered, idle through life, like Mrs. Robert E. Lee and Mrs. Abraham Lincoln.

Nothing need change in this century for women such as Mrs. Bird or Mrs. St. Clare. Home, whatever they make of it, is a total career. They wait patiently for the hour when the man asks for their heart and their hand, and give their answer in full awareness of its awesome import. *I reached out one hand to him,* writes Fanny Newell in retrospect, *and covered my eyes with the other; and in my heart said, O God, thou knowest that for thy sake I do this, and not for ease, honor, riches, or pleasure.*

But for other women, either out of choice or necessity, marriage was not a total career; the alterations in society created a grave problem for them.

In *Uncle Tom's Cabin,* Miss Ophelia was tall, square-formed and angular, her face thin and rather sharp, the lips usually compressed while the keen dark eyes appraised all about her. Spinsterhood was tolerable in a rural setting; on the farm the single woman could remain one of the children, even at the age of forty-five, or go to live helpfully in the household of a cousin or brother. There, where labor was scarce, even the servant was one of the family and supped at the same table with everyone else.

But in the cities there was less space, except in the

very wealthiest of families; and there servants remained apart, inferiors, either Negroes or immigrants. Where the mistress had little to do, a maiden relative was unneeded; and in more modest, crowded homes the unmarried cousin or aunt was underfoot and unwelcome.

Such girls therefore faced a dismal outlook, obliged to support themselves by their own labor yet barred from the openings that awaited their brothers. Dependent females had few resources, as Mary Ackley discovered when not yet thirty, a widow with four children to support. Now and then there was a post as teacher or perhaps occasional earnings from the pen, after the manner of Hannah Adams or Anne Royall — those were the paths to unremitting though genteel poverty.

Women who shed ladylike restraints were scarcely better off. After the Lowell mills set the precedent in 1820, there were jobs tending the machines, and a little later the larger shops in the city began to hire young women to stand behind their counters. Female wage earners also performed the immemorial drudgery that had occupied seamstresses, dressmakers and laundresses for generations; the increase in the number of ladies who did not do their own work raised the demand although not always the pay for these services. A no less ancient trade drew some girls to the streets, to the horror of the citizens worried about the growth of prostitution in the cities. None of these callings was dependable. None led to a desirable future.

Then again, some of those females were not satisfied with wifehood, a role less ample than formerly. With the loss of the household's economic function, the woman ceased to be a participant in the enterprise and became a dependent and her own duties shrank to a narrow domesticity. Steadily the distance widened between the home which was her domain and the shop or office where her husband won the family's bread; as a result she lost the ability to share in his toil and to participate in the decisions on which both his and her welfare hinged. Although the great majority of women were content or at least unquestioning, a few rebels made their protests heard. They were individuals too and deserved the opportunity to fulfill themselves as persons, not simply as helpmates. B. A. Owens-Adair, a native of Missouri reared on an Oregon farm, always regretted that she had not been born a boy and married at the age of fourteen to escape the drudgery of caring for the babies her mother produced with monotonous regularity. Marriage, however, proved only another form of servitude from which she escaped after five years by divorce. Better to be free of the shiftless brute, though it required her to support her child by teaching or taking in washing. Saving, scheming, she prospered as a milliner and dressmaker.

A variety of motives lay behind the insistence that a woman ought to be free not to marry and free also to have a career whether she married or not. Perhaps it was a fear of being rejected, perhaps a failure of the figure in the mirror to conform to the image in the novel, perhaps an assertion of the will not to play a predetermined part in life. The women who grew up pitying their mothers trapped in the cycle of childbirth and chores or those who resented the power of the father sometimes envied the greater freedom of their brothers.

The girls remained at a disadvantage. The family obligations that bound boys applied to them also; the child stayed home when the death or disability of a parent demanded it. Lucretia Mott Davidson did not resent the duties she assumed at her mother's illness any more than Robert LaFollette did the need for tending the farm. But the departure in advance of marriage was not for a woman the normal incident on the way to maturity that it was for a man, so that the desire to break away bred self-questioning anxiety. Ten-year-old Mary Richardson of Baldwin, Maine, in 1821 determined to be a missionary in a far country. She grew up nurturing the dream and refused to escape *the horrors of perpetual celibacy* by accepting as a husband *a mere farmer with little education and no refinement*. She sought the glory of God in teaching, but felt her heart remain barren, bearing no gracious fruit until a providential marriage of convenience in 1837 gave her the opportunity to go west to Oregon.

For a long time such women did not question the *dispensation of Heaven* which had *appointed to one sex the superior and to the other the subordinate part*. With Catharine Beecher, they disclaimed any prompting from ambition or thirst for power and wished simply to perform better their destined roles. But in the 1840's, some female requests for concessions became demands for rights. Reform which could strike the shackles of the slave, teach the blind to read, and cure the bodies and save the soul of drunkards, paupers and madmen could also relieve women of disabilities which had long gone unnoticed. WE WOULD HAVE EVERY ARBITRARY BARRIER THROWN DOWN. WE WOULD HAVE EVERY PATH LAID OPEN TO WOMAN AS FREELY AS TO MAN.

Margaret Fuller articulated a desire which had steadily gained force in the nineteenth century — to put an end to sexual discrimination in law and politics and to eliminate restrictions on access to education, to the practice of the professions and even to a place at the pulpit. For one reason or another girls increasingly determined not simply to make the transition from one kitchen stove to another. They sought a way to leave home — like the boys.

Their discontent was symptomatic. The old ways of leaving home were no longer adequate to meet the full needs of American society. An ever-larger number of men also were dissatisfied with the opportunities offered by apprenticeship and experience and wished to replace, or supplement the existing system with something else. Self-conscious *workingmen* in the 1820's and 1830's, usually artisans who feared that their skills might lose value and anxious about their children's future, demanded another kind of education — open to all and preparing its pupils to move upward to every occupation in order to preserve the social equality of the republic.

No one doubted that the boys had to leave home — and a few of the girls too — and the older pattern had adjusted enough to the shifting conditions of the century after 1770 so that it remained the most important means of making the break. But the passing decades heightened the desire among some groups to follow the route Ned Emerson had taken. Increasingly, a variety of schools offered American youth an alternative to work for a master and drew them away from home in a different fashion.

Training to Achieve

Ned's departure from the Emerson home relieved a busy mother of the responsibility for his supervision. It was also evidence of the persistent belief in the value of an education which consisted of general knowledge, unrelated to a specific vocational goal. Some subjects — there would be much discussion of which subjects — were worth learning because they would contribute to the student's development as a person. They could therefore be taught in schools, the pupils of which would go forth to a variety of different occupations.

And yet the education thus imparted was considered useful also. It would help its possessor advance in life. The outpouring of words that promoted the establishment and support of various schools rarely described specifically how the classroom equipped those who passed through it for the struggle to rise in the world. Generally the orators and pamphleteers simply assumed that the institutions they advocated would train young people for achievement. The school thus offered parents custodial service for children, to whom it imparted a broad education in behavior, ideas and skills; and it also tried to give instruction that would aid young people to locate themselves in advantageous callings.

The sporadically founded schools which aimed to perform these functions suffered from the severe strain of the effort to meet the needs of an expanding and changing society with the most limited intellectual and financial resources. It was not only that the population grew and spread across the continent and that burgeoning cities created unprecedented problems; it was not only that the very conception of a qualified teacher was lacking and that legislators and donors were parsimonious, however lavish they might be in rhetoric; as important, more was expected of the schools than ever before. These institutions were now to assume some of the duties the family had formerly discharged, those of providing the child with the rudiments of intellectual, social and economic equipment he would use through life.

Moreover those schools which depended on or sought government support grew lavish in promises of public service. Many an orator gave full range to his power of declamation in explaining the importance of education to a free society: a learned citizenry would know how to guarantee its own unity and liberty and the mere process of sharing a classroom would bring every section of the community into harmonious relations with the whole. There was not much forethought about the means of discharging these obligations. But, although the rhetoric did not make taxpayers generous, it did move municipalities more actively into the field of education than formerly, and it did diffuse the notion of the universal importance of schooling.

No central authority between 1770 and 1870 imposed order upon the designs which expressed the variety of American educational intentions; each state made its own laws and each locality implemented them in its own fashion and, in addition, any individual or group could put its own schemes into practice. The result of a century of development therefore was not a coherent system but rather an aggregation of unrelated institutions, overlapping in function and differing considerably from place to place. Confusing as the outcome was, it set a wide array of choices before parents and children. The aristocrat Hamilton Fish in 1858 sent his sons to Europe, but that was uncommon. A student could stay at home and attend a public or private school in preparation for departure, or he could work and study evenings, or he could live away at a college, academy or technical training institute.

No established sequence took him from one level to another, nor were the courses fixed in duration, nor was there a customary age for attendance. Each individual's decisions rested on his own appraisal of his needs rather than on the necessity of fitting into a formal framework.

A boy born in the 1780's, as William Ellery Channing was, still received his first instruction in a dame's school. A generation later Phillips Brooks began his learning in the same way. Soon thereafter in one city after another that ancient practice began to give way to common or primary public schools. Sectarian complications and the need for avoiding the odium of charity which tainted any free communal service delayed and complicated the process. But after 1830, Horace Mann's campaign in Massachusetts enlisted the power and the resources of the states to impose uniform standards upon the localities and to improve the quality of instruction at the elementary level. Nevertheless in 1870 the reformers were far from having achieved the objective of giving every child some instruction at government expense. And in 1870, except for the very earliest grades, there was neither consistency nor uniformity to the types of schools available in various parts of the country.

A complex and variegated pattern served young people who wished to learn more than the rudiments. As in the past, hungry or enterprising teachers in the cities organized classes to enable apprentices and youths who held jobs to study in their spare time for a small fee. Thus John Kelly's attendance at night school while he worked as an office boy for the New York *Herald* later helped him set up his own stonecutting business. The curriculum of such institutions was flexible and altogether responsive to the pressure of supply (by the teacher of information or skill) and demand (by the pupils for usable knowledge). By the 1850's some of the more ambitious or pretentious of such institutions called themselves commercial colleges. One of them was the refuge of Joseph Steffens, the last child of a worn-out mother, judged too weak for farm work and sent to town to clerk in a shop, who there acquired the training to prosper in business. The evident value of practical courses induced young artisans in many cities to participate in mechanics institutes which supplied the instruction they valued.

The effort to make skills available outside the apprenticeship system led to the appearance of the high school, the first of which opened in Boston in 1821. Patterned upon the European *hochschule,* it provided municipal support and direction for theretofore sporadic ventures and by the middle of the nineteenth century had begun to make some headway in the largest northern cities. But even in 1870, only 80,000 students, a tiny percentage of the country's youth, were enrolled in high schools. None of these institutions possessed residential facilities; the pupils usually lived at home or, in rare instances, boarded with neighboring families. Only large towns and cities contained a clientele ample enough to sustain such educational enterprises.

In rural districts, the search for schooling was more difficult, and especially in the South, which before the Civil War made no provision at all for public instruction.

The planters and rich merchants often hired tutors, some highly qualified like Eli Whitney and William Ellery Channing, who spent brief periods below the Mason-Dixon line. Other parents of the same era sent their boys north to live in Mr. Rogers's school in Newport or its counterparts in New York. A wealthy clan such as the Carters of Virginia maintained schools of their own in which the flocks of cousins lived and learned together.

The resources available to most rustic children — South or North — who wished to go beyond the mere ability to read and write were limited. For a long time the boys with ambitions for schooling had to leave home to lodge with and attend the classes of a minister willing to serve as master. John Marshall thus spent a few months with the Reverend Archibald Campbell; that was considered school in Virginia's Westmoreland County. A generation later, when Nathaniel Hawthorne lived in Raymond, Maine, he too had to seek scraps of learning from a country preacher. By their very nature as the individual businesses of assorted clerical and lay teachers, these enterprises existed in both town and village, for a year or two or for decades, but in endless variety. Their common feature was the unstinting exercise of parental discipline. In the school William Wells opened in Cambridge, Massachusetts, in 1830, there was never a half day without a good deal of flogging. Terror disheartened the boys slow to learn; and one such youngster spent weeks and weeks upon a few pages of Latin grammar which he blotted with tears and blackened with his fingers until they were hardly legible.

The academy provided a more formal though not a more uniform structure for these efforts at education. Occasionally the term "academy" merely affixed a somewhat more elegant title to a familiar establishment of the old sort. But more often the designation was a mark of recognition by the state through a charter of incorporation. The institution thus created sometimes was completely new, sometimes had antecedents in an earlier private school, but it now acquired the right to hold property and to receive, or hope to receive, endowments. A social commitment justified the privileges, actual and prospective. John Phillips, having profited from Samuel's previous experience at Andover, Massachusetts, stated the case in the preamble to the constitution of the academy at Exeter, New Hampshire, in 1781. Despite the improvements in both knowledge and virtue of which the grand design of the creation made the human mind capable, ignorance and vice, disorder and wickedness still prevailed and young minds were peculiarly susceptible to corrupting external impressions. Academies, Phillips hoped, would somehow supply a remedy by instructing youth not only in English and Latin grammar, writing, arithmetic and those sciences wherein they were commonly taught, but also and more especially by teaching the *great end* and *real business* of *living*. Somehow!

At Brandon, Vermont, and Canandaigua, New York, at Colchester, Connecticut, and Pittsfield, Massachusetts, at Adams, Ohio, and Alexandria, Virginia — indeed throughout the nation, innumerable little academies sprouted hopefully; in 1850, there were 6,000 of them by one count. Mostly they appeared in rural regions, not only because the need was greatest there and costs lower, but also because the environment was considered physically and morally healthier than that of the city. They accepted day students from the vicinity and boarders from a distance.

Parents sent their children to academies for a variety of reasons which made schooling seem more advantageous than apprenticeship or job experience. Sometimes it was simply inconvenient to keep a boy at home, as was the case with Ned Emerson, who at twelve seemed by no means too young to go off; Azro Hildreth was only nine when he left; and eight-year-old Samuel F. B. Morse was so homesick that he ran back to his family. Perhaps none was younger, however, than Josiah Quincy, who was only six — *noisy, heedless, and troublesome* — when he arrived at Andover. Sometimes a son was just not fit for farming and there was nothing else to do at home. Daniel Webster, too feeble to work and sick much of the time, came to Exeter at fourteen, a timid lad, physically incapable of standing up to speak before the school. In time he learned. So too did Henry Ward Beecher, who was too shy to *speak a piece* at Mount Pleasant. Sometimes again, the decision grew out of the inability to discipline an unruly youth at home, who might more readily be tamed away. Andover's Uncle Sam Taylor, who considered every boy guilty until proven innocent, consciously relied on terror as a means of pedagogy; and some schools were frankly organized as *military* academies.

Most academies well into the nineteenth century were flexible enough to make room for late starters. Jared Sparks, the illegitimate offspring of a Connecticut farmer, passed his youth shuttling among reluctant relatives; at the age of twenty he was a journeyman carpenter. For the work of shingling the pastor's barn he took payment in Latin and mathematics lessons, then did so well that he went in 1809 on a scholarship to Exeter. The same school in 1845 found a place for nineteen-year-old Christopher C. Langdell, a farm boy from New Boston, New Hampshire; at that age, Eli Whitney entered Leicester Academy; and thirty-year-old James Anderson sat beside little Josiah Quincy at Andover.

The academies like many private schools undertook among their other tasks to tame the behavior and polish the manners of urban as well as rural young people whose families, often newly risen to wealth, were not able to do so. Girls required this service as well as boys and might in the bargain learn something useful — domestic economy or how to teach, for example. Out of the Troy Female Seminary established by Emma Willard in 1821 came a whole generation of young women who went on to staff academies in every part of the country. Some good Protestant families moreover willingly sent their daughters off to Catholic convents which had traditionally educated gentle ladies. Academies in the West and South often accommodated both sexes; elsewhere, as at Andover, separate but neighboring schools took care of the male and female of the species. In the 1850's, Ashmun Institute in Pennsylvania and Wilberforce in Ohio began to provide comparable facilities for free Negroes.

There was a school for anyone who sought it, and a variety of learning to satisfy every taste. At the approach of the public examinations, a fever spread among the students who now had to exhibit their accomplishments not only to friends and teachers but also to the curious strangers who crowded the rooms to suffocation. The reports of how their sons and daughters acquitted themselves went home to anxious parents, to be treasured with the wrought samplers, the painted mourning pieces, the rickety cabinet work and the battered Latin books that were the evidences of education.

Increasingly in the nineteenth century too, the academies found themselves preparing their pupils for college. Not that the completion of such a course was essential for admission to degree-granting institutions, the entrance requirements of which were usually perfunctory. Rather, the schools tried to compensate for the deficiencies in earlier training by equipping students with skills advantageous in college, especially foreign languages. So, James Colles, Jr., of New Orleans, sent off for his education to New York City in the 1840's, was content with amiable teachers whose lessons were few and short. Then his father's letters galvanized him into getting on with preparation for college which was essential for a well-bred man in the existing state of society and better than riches which *often take wings and fly away. If you are determined to know and understand your lessons you cannot fail. It is with yourself to WILL and DO IT.* Urged on, the boy made Columbia and later thrived as a tea merchant. Parental pressure in the same direction also began to convert the urban high schools from institutions which completed the education of their students into ones which sent the best on for more. That had not been the original purpose either of the academy or the high school.

Some academies, however, did not lose sight of the professed objective of equipping young men with useful knowledge for the real business of living. The value set upon gentlemanly or ladylike accomplishments did not altogether obscure the importance of somehow advancing the pupil's career more effectively than apprenticeship. Indeed some academies devoted themselves specifically to vocational training.

The United States Military Academy fell into that pattern. Created in 1802, it remained small until after the War of 1812 demonstrated the need for its products. Oriented toward careers of public importance, its students had a professional interest in their work and accepted the rigorous standards to which the institution subjected them — strict admissions examinations, tight discipline that accounted for every minute, and nine to ten hours of study daily. The subjects taught had a plausible connection with future work — not only drill, horsemanship and gunnery but also mathematics, which inculcated habits of logical analysis, and physics, which was an approach to engineering. Graduates might therefore look forward to a wide choice of employments in the Army or in branches of industry that valued technical skill. George B. McClellan, who was twenty when he graduated from West Point, served, as might be expected, in the Mexican War. Then the Army sent him to Europe to study developments in the organization and transport of large numbers of men, horses and equipment; and that brought him information that helped make him chief engineer of the Illinois Central Railroad.

The Navy was slow to develop a counterpart to West Point because it long used the same techniques as the merchant marine for training officers through experience. Thomas Macdonough, for instance, the future commodore, received an appointment as midshipman in 1800 at the age of sixteen through the influence of the Senator from his state, and both learned and proved his worth in service. But the decline of the American merchant marine after 1830 and the growing technicality of operating the larger vessels equipped with steam rather than with sails in time provided the justification for an academy for this branch of the armed forces also.

The establishment of the school at Annapolis between 1845 and 1849 was part of a larger trend toward educating technicians to operate the industrial plant the United States began to construct in the second quarter of the nineteenth century. The men who built the earliest canals, turnpikes, railroads and factories had possessed no particular training or even experience for their tasks. Eli Whitney, Loammi Baldwin and Samuel Slater had hit upon the innovations that furthered output and eased communication almost by chance. How much greater would be the contributions of highly trained engineers! Nineteenth-century economists thoroughly agreed with the conclusion of Francis Wayland that intellectual advances led society to material prosperity and that the funds which supported schools were therefore investments rather than expenditures. And by the middle of the century European experience seemed to have corroborated that judgment.

The issue was far from abstract. When trades changed or when totally new problems appeared the experience of apprenticeship proved inadequate. The surveyor's techniques were not accurate when applied to laying out a railroad, nor a house carpenter's to building a trestle bridge. When estimates of construction costs turned out to be wildly inaccurate, when bridges collapsed, investors, shippers and travelers gained a practical awareness that artisans and managers needed scientific knowledge such as the technical schools of France and Germany imparted to their graduates.

In the 1850's Americans debated various proposals to create such institutions, but lacked any clear conception of how they were to function. At Troy, New York, B. Franklin Greene struggled to develop a civil engineering program in an institute the original purpose of which had been the application of science to farming. In Massachusetts in 1859 a group of citizens requested the legislature to charter a Conservatory of Arts and Science, more practical than Louis Agassiz's Museum of Natural History in Cambridge, but of the same species — a place for the collection and demonstration of equipment and techniques useful in production. The petition failed. Presented once more the next year, it made the purpose more explicit — creation of a complete system of industrial education such as the Central School of Arts and Manufactures offered in Paris or the Trades Institute in Berlin. Again a rejection. But in 1861, the legislature acquiesced and incorporated the Massachusetts Institute of Technology to sustain a society of arts, a museum of arts, and a school of industrial science. The charter of the Worcester Polytechnic Institute four years later was more explicit still: it would instruct youth in those branches of education not usually taught in the public schools but which were essential to train the young for practical life.

The possibility of using the schools for vocational purposes had by then also extended to the preparation of ministers, doctors and lawyers, some of whom had long recognized the utility of academic knowledge. Apprenticeship in 1870 still remained the chief mode of entry to these callings, but a significant minority of practitioners supplemented or replaced the conventional training with formal courses of instruction. Schools devoted to professional training might increase the supply in a period of high demand for skills and yet raise the status of their graduates.

The multiplication of sects and the expansion of population sharply increased the demand for clergymen. Every year newly founded towns added names to the map and every year the number and variety of churches in each place grew. Yet low salaries and declining social status held down the supply of pastors. Many bright young men trained for the career abandoned it; John L. Sibley preferred the scholarly life of a librarian and Jared Sparks chose to be a professor once he gave up his dream of African adventures as a missionary. And Ralph Waldo Emerson left a prestigious pulpit, primarily no doubt for the intellectual reasons he gave, but also perhaps because he could not forget that his father, who also served a good church, had from the age of twelve never been free of debt and had left his family in want when he died.

Each sect therefore eagerly sought to raise the output of available clergymen by multiplying facilities for the appropriate education. Some divinity schools emerged by splitting away from the older colleges, as at Harvard and Princeton. Others developed as adjuncts to, or in connection with, academies as at Andover, Massachusetts, or Hanover, Indiana. Still others were entirely new, as was the Presbyterian Lane Theological Seminary. Each institution was idiosyncratic in response to the immense variations in local conditions, financial and scholarly resources, and the estimate of the quality of the communicants its products would serve. There were places in plenty for boys who wished to enter upon this calling.

Professional schools appeared more slowly in medicine and law and did not yet replace apprenticeship as the primary means of training. Some Americans crossed the ocean for medical studies, as Robert Carter did in 1803 or Oliver Wendell Holmes a little later; and the advances in

France, Germany and Scotland sooner or later reached the United States. But the American medical schools, whether attached to universities or not, were generally set up by local doctors to supplement their own practice and raise their own prestige. Requirements for admission and graduation were lax or non-existent. Elizabeth Blackwell even found a country college willing to bestow the M.D. on a woman in 1849 and shortly thereafter female institutions appeared to cater to other enterprising ladies like Martha J. Flanders. In effect, any student taken on by a participating physician could acquire the degree upon payment of the fees. *The ignorance and general incompetence of the average graduate* was *horrible to contemplate.* That was the conclusion of a survey of medical education by President Charles W. Eliot in 1871.

For the law there was not even a model. The subject was not taught in professional schools in England, which was closest to the United States in its legal system; and on the continent of Europe where the universities did support law faculties the fundamental concepts and conditions of practice were so different as to offer no basis for imitation by Americans. The contrast shocked Gustave Koerner, who came to the United States in 1833 after having studied at Heidelberg and Munich. The first American law schools in Litchfield, Connecticut, and Northampton, Massachusetts, were the enterprises of local practitioners. In 1829, Harvard began the trend toward legal education under university auspices and other institutions followed its lead. But none as yet provided a complete, self-contained course of study that altogether eliminated the need for apprenticeship. Their lectures and exercises may have improved the skills of students; but they supplemented rather than replaced the older form of education.

Organized schools for the preparation of teachers appeared after 1820. The preponderant judgment remained that this vocation required no special training, being essentially transient and performed by young men willing to board around with families through the winter while they readied themselves for other callings. Azro Hildreth was teaching full time in Piermont, New Hampshire, at the age of sixteen and working between sessions on neighboring farms to make ends meet. Ralph Waldo Emerson was fifteen when he went to Waltham to help his uncle keep school. His father had taught in the Roxbury grammar school before entering the ministry and in addition had conducted classes for girls in the summer and for the employed in the evenings. Charles Brockden Brown, Hannibal Hamlin and Stephen A. Douglas were among the many who taught before attaining distinction in other spheres.

The recruitment of schoolmasters was more difficult in the South and in the sparsely settled West, so that it was often necessary to send for expensive full-time teachers. Furthermore, the shortage of males willing to stay at the job increasingly led to the use of women whose qualifications seemed less certain. In many communities unattached ladies like Catherine S. Lawrence found a mission in the classroom, which became the field in which to cure of bad habits the children of ignorant and illiterate natives — white, colored and aboriginal.

In 1823, Samuel Read Hall opened a school for teachers in Concord, Vermont, and seven years later came to Andover, Massachusetts, as principal of a department devoted to the same purpose. Thereafter, state boards of education, impatient with all these variations, began to demand higher and more uniform standards and encouraged the creation of normal schools seriously to prepare teachers for their tasks. Massachusetts after 1838 led the way in these efforts.

After the middle of the nineteenth century reformers also sounded the call for scientific instruction in agriculture and the practical arts; these too deserved professional status. Farmers continued to believe that a lesson in loading manure was a better introduction to a life on the soil than dabbling with chemicals in a laboratory, and artisans remained dubious about the book learning of fancy mechanics. Nevertheless, the growing faith in the power of abstract knowledge to ease all tasks induced a number of state legislatures to create agricultural and mechanical institutions and the Morrill Act of 1862 lent the resources of the federal government to the effort. The establishments thus supported in time blossomed into universities and offered to train men and women for various vocations.

Missionaries also continued to use schools as instruments for reforming the characters of dependent groups, the Indians within the country, Hawaiians overseas. The Civil War exposed the largest field for the demonstration of what education could do to redeem people long held in bondage. Before 1870 the Hampton Normal and Agricultural Institute of Virginia, as well as similar efforts at Fisk, Howard, Talladega and Atlanta, expressed the faith that schooling could compensate the freedmen for the inadequacies of their former family life.

That faith, or hope, was alone common to the immensely variegated and patchy pattern of American education in the century after 1770. The academies, institutes and professional schools appeared under a great variety of local circumstances. Some sheltered the children of well-to-do parents; others prepared for life youths with inadequate home environments; and still others were alternatives or supplements to apprenticeship. The weakness of the system lay in its lack of order or coherence, its strength in flexibility and the capacity to respond to immediate needs. It kept opportunities open so that individuals enjoyed not single, but multiple, chances to make good. Azro Hildreth and John M. Scribner could begin their serious schooling at the age of twenty; and pluck and determination could offset the disadvantages of a poor previous education as they did for Thomas J. (Stonewall) Jackson at West Point.

The wide and growing popularity of practical education tempted some colleges into the field; those poverty-stricken institutions were ever eager to serve the public and ever avid for the fees. They had long made the claim that the youth who invested his time in studies gained a career advantage over his peer who did not. From 1830 onward colleges ingenuously extended themselves to attract students into part-time or special vocational programs. J. W. Draper then dreamed of seeing mechanics throng to the university in the city of New York; Yale offered farmers a short course in agriculture; and Brown provided classes in chemistry to the printers, and on precious metals to the jewelry makers of Providence. Engineering, Spanish and Italian for the mercantile community at Maryland, commerce at Tulane, and teacher training at Lafayette were experiments with the same objective.

Oberlin's Ladies Course gave instruction in the *useful* branches taught in the best female seminaries. The desire to supply even women with practical training in the 1850's began to make the state universities co-educational. A committee of the Massachusetts legislature pointed the moral in 1850; it condemned Harvard's impracticality and recommended a shift to useful learning, with professors paid by the head. *Those only would succeed who taught in a manner acceptable to the public. That which was desired would be purchased and that which was not would be neglected.* The culmination was Ezra Cornell's vision of an institution where any person could find instruction in any subject.

For a time it seemed that the colleges would cease to be places of *literary leisure and intellectual indolence,* and would advance civilization by concentrating on the mechanical arts. It was all very well to revere Milton and Dante and Goethe, explained President Francis Wayland of Brown; but there was talent in a factory as well as in an epic. A great expenditure of mind was required to produce the spindles, looms and engines of a cotton mill; education could replenish the energy.

The efforts to turn the college toward a practical course bore few results. All the experiments fizzled out. An Alabama report of 1855 appraised the situation: *the farmer will be made in the field, the manufacturer in the shop, the merchant in the counting room, the civil engineer in the midst of the actual operation of his science;* the college was committed to a different function.

The nineteenth-century colleges bore many resemblances to the other schools through which young people left home; and to a considerable degree all these institutions competed for students among the same pool of parents with children between the ages of twelve and twenty. The unique attributes by which the college hoped to attract clients were few. As against the academies it offered the prestige of the degree; and as against the institutes that stressed practicality it offered a program that was not vocational, indeed that emphasized the worth of behavior and general ideas associated with its gentlemanly history, as the true preparation for life.

The Value of Moral Discipline

A paradox. In 1870, some five hundred institutions in the United States were awarding bachelor's degrees to aspiring scholars — a total larger than that in all of Europe. The phenomenal growth in the century after 1770 was not a response to clearly perceived needs; nor did it utilize abundant scholarly resources; nor did it even accommodate hordes of students clamoring for admission. Indeed the fledgling colleges often had as much difficulty in finding students as teachers and in explaining to both the purpose that drew them together.

The increase in the number of institutions was a product of rhetoric, of inflated ambition and of sectarian bickering.

The Revolution stimulated expansion. A bill to reform William and Mary in 1779 explained that the college was now to endow with science and virtue those who were to be the future guardians of the rights and liberties of their country; and Thomas Jefferson envisaged the university as the capstone of a complete educational system which would train each man for a role in society appropriate to his ability.

Americans also wished to justify the Republic in culture as well as in politics, to create great seats of learning as well as great literature and great art. Dependence on Europe was irksome. George Washington left part of his estate for the establishment of a national university. The state of Georgia penalized students who went abroad, and made its own provisions for higher education at its own Athens — as did Ohio. Belief in a connection between learning and economic prosperity often justified the new charters. The government of a republic which abjured despotic or mercantilist methods could excite men to profitable exertions by furnishing colleges with the means for instruction, investigation and discovery.

The democratic implications of independence continued to unfold in the nineteenth century and hastened the rise in numbers. The diffusion of political power reinforced the earlier popular hostility to privilege or to tokens of exclusive status. Opportunities were to be available to all, in schooling as in enterprise. If magistrates were to be educated, and if any man was inherently capable of becoming a magistrate, then all men were entitled to the opportunity of becoming educated. Anyone who wished to do so was therefore to be able to attend a college. Part of the design of Oberlin was the education of the *common people* with the higher classes in such a manner as suited the nature of republican institutions. The founders of Kenyon hoped to help the children of the poor rise by merit into stations theretofore occupied by the rich. The new institutions were willing to receive women; a few even admitted Negroes.

The same hostility to privilege that made college attendance a right also put the charter within the reach of any applicant. Every group was as free to found a university as a bank or any other corporation. Furthermore, the federalism of the American political system encouraged the diffusion of institutions of higher education. Congress never did provide for the national university; but beginning with the Northwest Ordinance of 1787, it repeatedly appropriated lands to aid state activities.

The limits on the expansive capacity of the old established institutions encouraged the appearance of new ones. None was then able to accommodate more than a few hundred students. None possessed the capital to erect the necessary buildings; and the logistic problem of housing and managing larger numbers remained unsolved until well after the Civil War. Colleges therefore multiplied without effective opposition from those already in existence.

Exuberant boosters who wished to adorn their communities with universities found eager listeners. The promoters argued plausibly that schools, like other public institutions, contributed to the town's economic growth. The value of all real estate would rise, worthy mechanics would earn good wages building the plant, and the professors and students who were purely consumers would spend outside money in places where cash was always short. Political pressure thus forced South Carolina in the 1790's to establish five colleges in various parts of the state, all stillborn or sickly. Many towns out of local pride encouraged their academies to blossom into universities, transforming fledgling headmasters into full-feathered presidents.

Above all, sectarianism stimulated proliferation. Again and again Americans reminded themselves of the obligations to propagate the faith among the aborigines, to further piety and guard doctrinal purity along the frontiers, and to hold old communicants and gain new ones.

The increase in the number of institutions of higher education therefore mirrored the increase in the number of denominations.

The soil in which colleges sprouted so easily did not however contain the elements to sustain any of them adequately. Nationalism covered up a boastful provincialism and a parochial resentment of European connections that the new nation could ill afford in view of its own limited intellectual resources. Rhetoric was often a substitute for performance. Furthermore, democracy created problems for institutions with pretensions to training an elite group, problems generally evaded by the assumption that anyone who willed it could be a member of such a group. The result was a consistent undervaluation of qualitative personal differences. There followed the drastic conclusion: if anyone ought to be able to go to college, then college ought to be such that it could teach everyone.

The hastily established institutions had no money. After the flurry of excitement at the first founding, interest subsided and the supply of cash with it. The colleges were poor for much the same reasons as before 1770. Endowments were pathetically low; the University of Pennsylvania, for instance, added not a dollar to its total in more than eighty years. In 1862, Hanover College had an endowment of about $122,000, which however included $36,000 in unproductive real estate, $46,000 in unpaid pledges and $34,000 already consumed for current expenses. Furthermore, in the absence of reliable channels of investment, the little stores of capital brought meager returns and were periodically diluted by inflation. Gifts were few and small: the $50,000 Abbott Lawrence gave Harvard was unusually generous; $10,000 in 1865 was enough to set Princeton to building an observatory; and Colonel Henry Rutgers in 1825 had a university named for him for half that sum. Some institutions began to organize their alumni in the 1820's. But former students who became ministers were rarely in a position to make contributions, and more opulent graduates preferred to dispose of their benefactions otherwise.

As a result the college unhappily and hazardously depended on current income from students. Yet the marginal value of education left the market for its services uncertain and subject to violent fluctuations. Since admissions came at the very start of the school year and since transfers from one institution to another were easy and frequent, administrators never knew in advance the size of enrollments and had to budget parsimoniously. When the number of students fell, salary cuts hit the faculty and also the president.

Unremitting financial stringency forced the colleges into an endless routine of self-justification to draw students through their gates and to persuade parents to pay the fees. The cash-value argument was a staple, whether it squared with experience or not. The expectation that a few years of study would prepare a youth for a well-paying job and bring the reward of a rise in status excited some poor boys. Little Daniel Webster grew dizzy when his father first mentioned the possibility of college. The old man then said that he lived only for his children and that if the son would do all he could for himself the family would make the necessary sacrifice.

President Francis Wayland of Brown noted the willingness of some parents to bear toil patiently to render the lives of their children less irksome. Poor families pushed forward lads of talent so that the son and brother could dress in such clothes as they never wore, eat from a table such as they could not spread, devote himself to quiet study while they were exhausted with labor, and enter a sphere of professional eminence where they knew that they could never follow.

Some men thus encouraged made the most of opportunity. Harvey W. Wiley, a farm boy in homespun clothing and cowhide shoes, walked four miles to a midwestern college town, feeling miserable all the way at the thought of going into the presence of cultured people — well-groomed students and learned and urbane professors. He lived four years on corn meal mush and sorghum, graduated at the head of his class and became a physician. At Oberlin, Bowdoin and Harvard a few Negroes pursued the same goal of success.

But the argument from utility was often ineffective. Those who responded generally came for a year and then left, as Winfield Scott did at William and Mary. Most students interested in getting on with careers did not find the university necessary or helpful. In the scrabble for customers the colleges competed not only with one another but also with better, or at least more direct, avenues into vocations — apprenticeship, the academies, the professional schools and the institutes. The college had to promise its clients something more than its rivals purveyed.

The degree awarded the graduate stood for scholarship, which conveyed unique powers to those exposed to it. Look at Germany! The invitation resounded through the nineteenth century, voiced by ambitious presidents like Philip Lindsley of the University of Nashville, who wished to outdo Europe in science. President Henry P.

Tappan of Michigan gave the case its most persuasive statement. The university did not offer a mere professional and technical education which led directly to practice but rather a large and generous view of all the knowledge and all the agencies which entered into the well-being and progress of society and which fitted the individual ultimately for any calling.

Frequent efforts to revise the curriculum demonstrated that the university was alive to its responsibility for providing its students with proper intellectual nourishment. Abandonment of the heathen classics was an easy first step. No man of untainted morals could read the bare and despicable ancient pagan writings with patience, wrote Charles Brockden Brown. Nor was it difficult to ordain that original lectures by qualified professors replace the dull system of rote recitation. Excellent scholars held appointments to chairs of natural philosophy, of divinity, of oratory or of exact science. Rarely, however, could they teach their specialties. Princeton brought the distinguished chemist John Maclean from Glasgow, but asked him also to do mathematics, natural history, and natural philosophy. Benjamin Silliman, about to enter the practice of law, accepted a chair at Yale and, after two years of study, began to lecture on chemistry, mineralogy, and geology. The founder of American mineralogy taught mathematics and philosophy at Bowdoin; and such combinations as rhetoric, logic, theology, philosophy and political economy were not unusual in an instructional load. Caprice, accident and poverty played too large a role in these institutions to permit an overall view of their educational task.

The elective principle offered a tempting solution: the professors could teach what they wished and the students would choose freely among the offerings set before them. But President Jared Sparks of Harvard reported after a brief trial that the elective system, attractive as it was in theory, did not come up to expectations and soon fell into disfavor.

The unhappy fate of another Harvard effort to give scholarship a central place in the curriculum demonstrated the difficulty of using the German universities as models for colleges which in America sheltered young gentlemen away from home. The faculty which had proposed the scheme in 1846 had reasoned that many students left college so young that they could devote a year or two more to advanced studies in any one of the branches of learning, literary as well as scientific. The teachers were ready but, alas, the pupils did not present themselves. Within a few years, the school created at Harvard for specialized, scholarly instruction was giving an elementary practical course, called scientific, along with, and generally considered inferior to, the usual classical one. In a few years more, a speaker announced that everyone in the college was a student of science. The definition of science stretched to fit history, literature, political economy and ethics — in fact whatever the faculty wished to offer under that label.

The college generally did not seem an appropriate setting for serious scholarship. Books were available to those who wished to use them, of course. Robert Finley, who entered Princeton at the age of eleven in 1783, was already studious, a protégé of the president, and destined for the Presbyterian ministry. Earnest young men, like George Perkins Marsh, learned what they wished; and those who lived with a professorial family, as Richard M'Ilwaine did, were often surrounded by intelligent, kind, unselfish people who felt and manifested an interest in their lodgers. But these exceptional youths were not numerous or influential enough to create an environment congenial to learning. Science remained a pursuit of the devoted amateur or autodidact affiliated, if at all, with an autonomous learned society or institute.

The dominant influence upon the college was the function it served in providing certain boys with an exit from the family. George Shelby at the age of fourteen was not bad, just willful; it was natural that he should be and his parents did not wish his spirits crushed, simply directed into desirable channels. On the other hand, some youths of the same age were still babies emotionally. *I was afraid to be a man,* wrote one of them who was small in stature and tormented by self-doubts. *I was afraid to assume responsibilities and thought that I did not have sense enough to go into the rough world making a living as other men had to do.* Still others eagerly sought the opportunity to break away from home, as did Nathaniel Hawthorne, who went to Bowdoin to be free of an uncle's control (and who let seven years go by without seeing his mother).

Such youths were aimless and haphazard in the choice of a career; college was an interlude for indecision, sometimes entered to relieve parents of anxiety, sometimes to escape the need for making up one's mind. In this refuge, young men who could afford it separated themselves from their fathers with communal approbation and began to chart independent courses through life. No place provided safer shelter during the critical passage from boyhood to manhood, Charles W. Eliot insisted.

The college in effect assumed the task of disciplining

young men with whom the family could not cope at home. Francis Scott Key conceded in 1827 that no father could oversee his son's morals, direct his judgment, restrain his passions and guide his pursuits with the same effectiveness as a well-conducted college. President Wayland of Brown recalled parents without number who informed him of the peculiarities of sons entering as freshmen — their dispositions were excellent if they were only governed in some particular manner. Of course, he soon learned that those peculiar young men were in fact, in almost every case, spoiled children who would make more than the usual trouble. *The most vicious boys* came to Louisiana State recommended with *all the virtues of saints.* The college replaced the parents and it had the advantage over academies and military schools of the degree it awarded and the polish it bestowed.

A Yale report of 1828 stated the function of the college simply. It was to train the future leaders of the nation. From its halls would emerge men of large and liberal views, having acquired the solid and elegant attainments which raised them to a higher distinction than the mere possession of property could give and which enabled them to move in intelligent circles with dignity. The graduates would be able to use their wealth in a manner honorable to themselves and beneficial to their country.

Education thus conceived was not practical or vocational but gentlemanly, aimed at equipping students with a general style of life rather than preparing them for a specific career. The Notre Dame catalogue of 1863 candidly explained that its pupils would gain even if they learned nothing more than to converse and behave with dignity and propriety. Hundreds of institutions throughout the democracy made the same promise: anyone in the Republic could become a man of distinction by acquiring elitist knowledge and manners.

Higher education in the United States, while borrowing what was best from Europe, would not however suffer from the ills of the Old World. The transatlantic universities, founded for the training of the medieval clergy, had been subject to the pressure of an all-powerful aristocracy and were therefore rich, conservative and illiberal. A moral purpose shielded the colleges of the New World from those failings. The American institutions would counter the excessive commercial spirit of a country dominated by the manufacturer, the merchant and the gold digger. Armed to do battle for the right, the colleges would offset the chicanery and selfishness of the rest of society, proclaimed President Henry P. Tappan of the University of Michigan.

This task was eminently acceptable to fathers more worried about their boys' perdition in the next world than about academic excellence in this life. *Preserve your morals pure and let your scholarship be as it pleases heaven,* wrote John Quincy Adams to his son. To these parents the religious administration of the college guaranteed the purity of the environment. The president was therefore almost invariably a clergyman. The professor of mathematics appointed to head Yale in 1817 prudently was ordained the day he took office.

The president and the faculty knew that their first obligation was to inculcate moral discipline. The classroom was a means of sopping up energy, whether through the old-fashioned rote recitation or through the mental calisthenics advocated by reformers who argued that the subject studied really did not matter so long as students exercised their brains through precise analysis and open discussion. Experiments with manual training in many places had the same purpose; carpentry shops and gardens not only enabled the youths to earn while learning and thus gave them the strength which resulted from the proud consciousness of self support; they also developed *firmness of muscle and elasticity of nerve* to sustain the operations of intellect.

The college, alas, needed every aid it could muster to maintain good behavior. Its sanctions were feeble, for it no longer ruled by thrashings as the academy still did, and it could not impede a student's career by dismissal as the professional school could. The experience of the University of North Carolina in 1851 was therefore not unusual — 282 cases of the infraction of rules among a total student body of 230 — and the faculty records of a small Presbyterian college in Indiana read much like the blotter of a police court.

Rebelliousness sometimes expressed the fear of homesick boys shipped away from their families for reasons that were unclear or confused. One of them entering Brown at the age of fifteen dreaded the revelation of his shameful weakness. He was terrified to sleep alone in the dark; the moment he got into bed and blew out the candle he shut his eyes, put his head under the bedclothes and kept it there. Determined to conquer the terror before college exposed it, he rose at midnight night after night and forced himself to walk through the pitch-dark house. Thirteen-year-old Felix Brunot had *perhaps forever left his own parental home* for Jefferson College. *Oh, yes!* the strangers say *in accents bland, "Thy bark is on a friendly shore!*" Still the first night away, the poem admits:

> At thoughts like these, why starts the tear?
> 'Tis that I feel too much alone.

Often such lads, indulged and petted at home, were sent off by their mothers *with tears and blessings.* They arrived at college, in the judgment of a professor at Davidson in 1855, undisciplined and uncultivated, yet with exalted ideas of personal dignity and a scowling contempt for lawful authority and wholesome restraint.

Rich youngsters squandered their money in eating and drinking. They were to be watched, borne with, and if possible saved to the world and their families. Others were also subject to the temptations of youth, though mostly petty ones. Teachers had to be alert to habits which might harden into vices — prevarication, pilfering, tippling, playing billiards or cards and cursing. Unchecked, such practices led to outlandish debts at the oyster house, to duels, to pranks on the professors, to uproar in the refectory, and, sometimes, to a general reign of lawlessness which spread contagiously from campus to campus.

Some upheavals, while painful, quickly subsided. The Harvard students of 1791 protested against an innovation requiring examinations at the end of the year. Some thought it unjust to disgrace them *ex post facto* for negligence they had been guilty of before the law was enacted. Others claimed that the procedure was unfair, for it penalized the underprivileged who had come to college unprepared. Windows were broken, the examiners were received with shouting and hissing, and the proceedings came to an abrupt halt when the tutors and more than a hundred undergraduates fell simultaneously sick of an emetic someone had thrown in the breakfast water. *Diverting would have been the scene,* wrote an observer, *were it not of too serious a nature to be sported with,* to see such a number of students, whose minds had just been crammed with elevated thoughts, *now hanging their heads and puking about the yard.*

An incident at the University of Virginia was more serious, but not unrepresentative. Fear of student violence had long kept the faculty on edge. But in 1836 the boys organized an independent military company and announced that they would resist the tyrannical order to remove all arms from the campus. The teachers out of desperation or boldness then voted a substantial number of expulsions. Two days of rioting ended in compromise: the appearance of the militia upheld the majesty of the law and the retreat of the faculty readmitted the offending students. Ironically, four years later a student shot to death the professor who had engineered the compromise.

Neither threats of damnation nor appeals to the sense of honor and the love of knowledge kept the boys under control. Presidents who began with a romantic view of the inherent goodness of man reverted to a belief in natural depravity when they observed the outcome of efforts to govern by the rule of inward principle rather than of outward fear and restraint. As a result, most colleges had to manage their charges by enforcing detailed codes of behavior. A schedule which began with compulsory chapel at 6:00 a.m. and spread recitations through the day, along with periodic unannounced room inspections, left neither the time nor the privacy for evil. Class rankings and prizes kept the students competitive and daily marks were the basis for term grades that would let parents know how their progeny were getting on. Misconduct lowered a student's academic standing as Henry Adams discovered to his sorrow when he paid a heavy price in demerits for absences from recitations and from prayers. Vigilant professors supervised the feeding in the refectory and counted the heads in church. *Mein Gott!!* Francis Lieber is said to have exclaimed, *All dis for two tousand dollars.*

Compulsion made for an uneasy peace. President Green of Princeton observed with dismay the fixed, irreconcilable and deadly hostility of the boys to the college's system of diligent study, of guarded moral conduct, and of reasonable attention to religious duty. And President Barnard of Columbia sadly concluded in 1870 that no situation in the world left an individual more completely removed from all effectual restraint, whether of direct authority or of public opinion, than that within the walls of an American college. Years after the event an alumnus of Hampden-Sydney recalled that as a freshman he had, instinctively, taken the side of the students in a college disturbance. Boys were very like sheep. *Let one of them jump a fence, and over goes the flock.*

Misbehavior earned no social opprobrium. Rustication did not injure the career of Richard H. Dana, nor expulsion that of Thomas Hart Benton. When the chips were down, the parents who wished their sons tamed rarely sustained the punishment meted out to the rule breakers. The plea for *another chance* was almost always effective. In the eyes of a father, said President Lindsley of the University of Nashville in 1848, each lad was a high-minded, honorable, brave, generous, good-hearted young gentleman who scorned subterfuge, meanness and, above all, lying, while the faculty were paltry pedants, bigots, charlatans — without feeling, spirit, kindness, honesty or common sense. Few Americans dissented from such judgments and there was a widespread tendency to wink at college pranks, no matter how outrageous.

In the running battle to maintain some semblance of orderly behavior, the presidents and professors resisted any trend that might loosen their control. That doughty liberal Thomas Cooper exclaimed, *Republicanism is good: but the "rights of boys and girls" are the offspring of Democracy gone mad.* Lest unsupervised youths have the leisure for subversive plots, Princeton urged all its students to spend their vacations at home or *elsewhere than in Princeton.* The university knew that young persons collected together without regular occupation or study could not resist the temptations to idleness and dissipation. For the same reason, colleges did not wish to erect dormitory buildings where most of the troubles of the faculty had their origin. President Hitchcock of Amherst in 1863, after his retirement, noted that parents believed it safer to the morals of students to have them congregated in large dormitories than scattered through the community. But the experience of many years had taught him that young men were in greatest danger when they were isolated from public inspection among fellows for whom it was a point of honor not to reveal each other's delinquencies and immoralities.

The ability of students to organize autonomously, which their teachers feared, did grow although not in a form anyone anticipated. Occasional efforts to induce students to discipline themselves through their own courts or legislatures were not notably successful, for these devices were too obviously contrived by the faculty. For the great majority of young men who passed through it, the college was a social experience, shaped not by their elders or by the subject matter of instruction, but by contact with their peers, the *chums* whose constant friendship brought *a sweet relief to every pain.* That was why all efforts to classify students by proficiency in courses rather than by length of time in attendance failed. The primary unit was the class, the group that entered together, together suffered as freshmen from water poured under the door or window panes broken in winter, then as sophomores together inflicted the same torments on others, and then at last together celebrated the commencement of their other lives.

Everywhere the common experiences of the class supplied the organizing elements of student life free to a considerable degree of the oversight of elders. Peers replaced parents and enforced a conformity more rigid than that of home. Fits of enthusiasm carried the youths along. The political interests of the revolutionary era sustained radical fervor down to the end of the eighteenth century. Boys read Tom Paine, burned the Bible and toyed with atheism. There followed a turn to religion. The Society of Brethren at Williams was the first of some hundred missionary clubs that had appeared by 1850. Periodic revivals then swept through the campuses and wild boys broke down, and sobbing, begged their fellows to pray for them.

Sooner or later, within each college narrower circles of students associated, either to pursue common interests or to achieve a sense of identity by virtue of passage through a selection process. The literary societies, the first of which had been founded at Yale in 1753, served both purposes. Their debates, libraries and publications were often more effective modes of learning than the formal academic exercises; and their ability to exclude some students was gratifying recognition of the distinction of those admitted.

The longing for fraternity and for autonomously created order in time justified association even without an intellectual content. The literary societies in some colleges evolved into convivial organizations with codes of behavior internally set. Elsewhere, the old groups lost ground after 1825 to the Greek-letter fraternities, which provided living quarters, an election process and a ritual relatively free of faculty control. The criterion for admitting a new member in 1836 — *Would you want your sister to marry him?* — showed the relationship students desired. They sought a surrogate family, that intimate group out of which would grow lifelong friendships to which they could revert in after years. Fraternal intimacy created a sense of mutual support as well as an atmosphere in which boys valued personal responsibility and the performance of duty. *We live in a perfectly independent way, choose our own associates and our own mode of life,* wrote a member of the Brown class of 1858 to his mother. The spread of these associations in the colleges ran parallel to the spread of Masonic and other secret fraternal orders in American society at large and was due to much the same reason — the desire for comradeship of isolated individuals in loosely organized and mobile communities.

The presidents perceived the advantages of the fraternities, which took the college out of the lodging business, freed capital for other uses and spared the faculty the tasks of supervision. Yet they could neither shirk entirely the disciplinary duties expected of them nor run the risk of hostile conspiracies. Most compromised. They set up stringent general rules of behavior and absolutely forbade membership in secret societies; but, they learned to interpret those regulations with a good deal of leniency.

Tolerance of the fraternities and of other activities in which students organized their lives without interference took the edge off the conflict between the generations. The faculties quietly recognized the importance of the learning outside the classroom.

A college party in the 1850's. The guests enter to take seats on the chairs lined along the wall. The bolder youths advance and engage the more interesting girls in conversation; both sexes exert themselves to be alert in repartee. To make an impression it is necessary to have read and thought, *to have something to talk about.* A boy who does not get over his shyness has *a pretty dull time, standing around;* and even the most solicitous hostess is hard put to rescue the tongue-tied feminine *Wall Flowers.* An abundant buffet eases the strain on the young people. But the essential element in the *good time* is the possession or acquisition of verbal skills; and the party is thus a festive counterpart of the disputations and debates, the long yarns and letters on which this generation sharpens its wits.

The growing interest in athletics also had unexpected results. Professors like Charles Follen had introduced physical training and gymnastics in the 1820's to *work the devil out of the students.* The motto of the Amherst gymnasium expressed its intention: *Keep thyself pure: the body is the temple of the Holy Ghost.* But in the

1850's the emphasis began to shift to team sports and to intercollegiate competition; and the increasing popularity of baseball in the 1860's completed the transition. The faculty and its intentions had little influence upon these contests which provided the boys not exercise but identification with a side. The mass of students became spectators rather than participants, the games became fiercely competitive and, in the process some youthful aggressiveness was displaced from the professors at home to the rivals at other colleges.

President Francis Wayland of Brown understood the dilemma of American higher education. The rowdyism through which he had suffered taught him that the government of impulsive, thoughtless young men differed from that of adults and had of necessity to be *kind, conciliatory, persuasive, or, in a word, parental.* He had had to balance his belief in the value of learning against the need to satisfy parents, against his respect for state law, and against his obligation to help students enter practical life by providing them with an intermediate place between the family and society.

No president achieved more than a tolerable equilibrium among those elements because Americans did not admit to themselves, but concealed with inflated rhetoric, the purpose the college served — to control their sons. As a result, Wayland sadly concluded, the institutions which obeyed the suggestions of the public failed to find themselves sustained. The means which, it was supposed, would increase the number of students in fact diminished it; and after every experiment conditions reverted to their original character. *And thus have we been taught that the public does not always know what it wants and that it is not always wise to take it at its word.*

The five hundred colleges of 1870 had come into existence for a variety of reasons and in some respects differed markedly — in resources, quality of faculty, religious orientation, regional characteristics, relationship to government, age and social level of their students. The similarities in style of life sprang from the unrecognized and scarcely articulated function all performed. Beneath the grandiloquent talk of republican culture and democratic education lay a simple need of many families. Whatever else the college aspired to be, its first responsibility was to supply some youths with the training for life in society that parents were unable or unwilling to impart directly. Its duty was to inculcate traditional morality in a fortunate minority too old to be any longer subject to a father's discipline and not yet within reach of the controls of society. This way of leaving home protected the outside world against disruption by reckless young people whom it thereby absolved from the necessity of as yet assuming full responsibility for their actions.

4

FINDING PLACES, 1870–1930

AFTER 1870, the society in which Lincoln, Jackson and Jefferson had passed their youth receded ever farther in the memory of Americans. Totally new conditions of life shaped the homes in which boys and girls matured and the careers upon which men and women embarked. Rapid intellectual and economic change left many with a sense of disorientation; especially for the young people, the beliefs of a former generation — religious, social and personal — did not seem appropriate to the situation of the last quarter of the nineteenth century.

Traditional morality grounded on religion no longer provided adequate sanctions for the rules of behavior. In the decade after the publication of *The Origin of Species,* Darwinism made subtle inroads upon American thought. Its impact was greatest among the best educated, but its influence seeped through the whole population. The erosion of the familiar Christian view of the creation and the destiny of the universe cut the ground out from beneath the belief in the uniqueness of man's role as the central actor in a divine drama. He was but a creature shaped by the environment, one who struggled, like other creatures, for survival and did so for a quite unknowable purpose.

Significant social influences added to the intellectual pressure toward change in attitudes about morality. The codes derived from ancestral wisdom did not seem pertinent to a milieu of which large organizations, heavy industry and metropolitan cities were the most prominent features. The faith in the old fundamentals remained vital in the rural regions least subject to change. But in the dynamic, urban sectors of the United States even occasional outbursts of evangelical fervor could not bring the old-time religion to life or turn it into a reliable guide to personal or social conduct.

Science became the potent rival of religion. The hopes of the Enlightenment seemed now to have blossomed: reason applied objectively to evidence assembled through research or experiment yielded knowledge more dependable than that derived from revelation or tradition. Scholarship after 1870 gained steadily in prestige and the claims for its validity quickly spread from the physical and natural realms to the social and personal ones which had formerly been the exclusive domain of religion. The systematic development of sociology, economics, law, politics and psychology created new standards which sometimes replaced the older ethical norms for Americans who were receptive to any novelty to which they attached the designation, science.

Without guidelines, unmoored from traditional faith, society was at the mercy of quacks and impostors. The astrologer who was a rare personage in the Middle Ages now advertised in the public newspapers and flourished as never before. Men and women of all classes, lamented President Charles W. Eliot of Harvard, sought advice from clairvoyants, seers, Christian Scientists, mind-cure practitioners and fortune tellers. The ship of state barely escaped from *one cyclone of popular folly, like the fiat-money delusion or the granger legislation, when another blast of ill-informed opinion came down on it, like the legislation which compelled the buying and storing of silver by Government.*

Their faith in the familiar doctrines severely shaken, Americans were often at a loss about how to raise their children, or how to regulate their homes. The sense of perplexity was worrisome in itself; and the transformation of the world outside the family through industrialization and urbanization intensified the concern.

The economy shifted rapidly from a rural, agricultural base to an urban, factory-oriented one. The new system of production functioned on a national scale through large complex organizations and it depended upon the labor of an industrial proletariat, much of it foreign-born. Its goods moved through complex channels of distribution, the flow directed by an intricate network of financial institutions. Parents who wished their offspring to find desirable places in the new order could not simply rely upon the earlier methods of launching a career. From the orators like Chauncey M. Depew came the tirelessly repeated assurance: given the right to rise and equal opportunity, all problems of labor and capital, of property and poverty, would solve themselves. But families found small comfort in the rhetoric when they approached the decisions that determined the future station of youth in this society.

The stories of the new men of great wealth were certainly familiar to Americans of the gilded age. Henry

Ford—the farm-boy tinkerer, nothing special about him — was the plain man become millionaire.

The stories of the new poor were equally familiar though not so frequently discussed. The bankrupt merchant, the foreclosed farmer, the clerk thrown out of work by depression, the tramps who crowded the country roads or urban lodging houses milled ominously in the background of men's consciousness. Failure could overwhelm anyone, as it did Dwight Eisenhower's father, whose dreams of becoming a merchant led only to a marginal night-watchman's job. Through life George C. Marshall remembered the *black spot* on his boyhood, the painful and humiliating experience of the reversal of family fortunes in the 1890's.

The rewards of success were fabulous and the penalties of failure disastrous. The widening gap between the two possible outcomes increased the hazards of competition in a dynamic and therefore unstable society. Young people had to prepare fully to meet the opportunities and to avoid the dangers industrialization created. A heightened tension now charged the process of leaving home.

Those Americans whose situation was either totally insecure so that they had nothing to lose or totally secure against the threat of loss were at least spared the anxiety of decision. Choices about the future of their children did not torture the great mass of immigrant and Negro workers. Tradition still had great weight and folk wisdom was still a guide to life among the depressed people whose position in society was relatively static. Boys could well follow the occupations of their fathers and the sooner the better; girls could take jobs as domestics, in factories, or, if they were lucky, in shops; the family could use the additional income of all their wages. The poor were long since inured to the age-old tragic eventuality that some of their children might slip into criminality or prostitution.

Social workers and reformers in their gingerly contact with these groups often expressed dismay at the low value placed upon schooling. Parents seemed callous in the insistence that children go out to work as soon as possible and in the insistence that years of additional study were only worth it to the exceptional youth willing to earn them for himself. *If you want an education,* his Mennonite mother told ten-year-old Dwight Eisenhower, *go out and get it.* That attitude was not simply the product of a realistic appraisal of family resources. It also grew out of limited aspirations. People who labored in the farms, factories or mines hoped that their sons would rise to less wearying, more remunerative jobs as foremen, perhaps even as managers or proprietors of businesses. The way to attain such posts was not by sitting in a classroom but by acquiring experience and savings through work. The banker's or the doctor's office was simply not in their line of vision; and they feared the moral hazards of unfamiliar callings. *I'd rather follow you to the graveyard than hear you had become a musician,* his father told W. C. Handy, who was not content to be a plasterer or carpenter. The prospect of moving into careers which called for prolonged preparation was so remote that the extraordinary lad with such ambitions — a Booker T. Washington or Michael Pupin — could be left to succeed or fail by his own efforts.

Generational conflicts over vocational decisions within these families therefore took an ethnic form. The old people were foreigners or former slaves; the sons were Americans or born free. It was not surprising that they failed to understand each other and that differences of behavior, habits and ideas separated parents and children and led to bitter emotional clashes. But that strife did not involve a sense of personal rejection. The young ones knew they could expect no help, the old that they could give none. The margin for choice was narrow; each did what he could.

Those Americans whose margin of choice was so wide that mistakes were no threat also escaped the anxiety of decision. Any career or none was within reach of the possessors of great fortunes and their heirs. The boys could, but need not, move into the family enterprises or they could prepare at home or abroad for whatever vocation they fancied. The girls, having finished at St. Timothy's, Miss Hall's, or Madeira, could make a proper debut and then marry dukes, millionaires or politicians; or, they could seek the further education to remain active in later life in community affairs, the arts or the professions. Above all such youngsters had the time and means to change their minds; they could start in one direction, redefine their objective and move in another.

The problems of parents of great wealth arose from the desire to stabilize their position and that of their children. The United States lacked the hereditary aristocracy which set the norms in Europe—there were not even the peerages or medals and decorations which were elsewhere precious symbols of status. Other means were necessary to demonstrate the importance of family connections, to develop in the next generation an awareness of the distinctive privileges and duties that accompanied the possession of riches, and to guard the young against the temptations of a confusing and changing world. Withdrawal and the exclusion of outsiders were the only tactics feasible in a democracy. Within a closed circle of activities and associations, the Four Hundred of New York, the Brahmins of Boston, the Main Line of Philadelphia and counterparts and affiliates elsewhere sought an identity they could transmit to their offspring. Boys and girls who went to the proper schools and belonged to the appropriate churches passed along to the correct clubs and learned a pattern of behavior and dress as close to that of good society in London as the absence of royalty permitted. They would then choose the right partners in marriage and transmit their heritage intact to still another generation.

Outsiders, however, insisted on attempting to pass into the loosely guarded circles. Men who had worked their lives through to establish great enterprises somehow wished to have the memory of their achievements survive after their deaths, and not simply in the name applied to pickles or oil. Increasingly they emulated the families already established and wistfully sought affiliation with them. The standards and tastes set in the great eastern cities subtly influenced aspiring people everywhere. Charles Perrin Smith, a man of moderate wealth, decked out his palatial home in Trenton, New Jersey, with expensive statuary, mirrors, silk curtains and ornate candelabra. Lavish receptions, trips to Europe, and an interest in his genealogy helped him forget how recent was his rise.

If not the generation which had earned the riches, then at least the next might enjoy the rewards! Silas Lapham, whose money came from paint, found a model in the Coreys, who had inherited wealth and who demonstrated the superiority of their breeding in their home, manners and conversation. A good upbringing was necessary to enable Lapham's children to meet them as equals. An observer at the end of the century noted the avidity with which parents who had acquired riches rapidly sought *social consideration* for their boys by sending them to schools where they would meet the proper friends and learn the habits appropriate to gentlemen. Edward H. Harriman had gone to work at fourteen; his boys went to Groton and Yale. H. J. Heinz had made his own way but sent the son who would succeed him to Yale; the John D. Rockefeller children attended Brown and Vassar; and Scott Fitzgerald left home on the fringe of St. Paul's good district for prep school and Princeton to become the Amory Blaine he later described.

Hostile critics charged that the wealthy hoped to establish a sort of tyranny over the social life of the people, as the aristocracy of Europe did, and supported their accusations with lurid tales of the wastefulness of high life. The actual danger of domination was slight, however. Society in the United States was fluid, unstable and subject to capricious changes in fortune. No system of exclusive association and education could here consolidate the control of the rich — old or new — or supply them with family continuity. But abundant financial resources eased the anxieties of parents and children at this level of society and gave each individual the freedom leisurely to find his own goals.

Far deeper was the concern among the middling elements of the population — those with enough means to perceive the heights to which their offspring might rise, but still with not enough to feel secure against the danger of a fall to the depths. Not so hard driven by necessity as the laborers, they could make choices; but their choices were critical because they were limited by lack of the reserves which cushioned the wealthy against disaster.

In every town, some skilled craftsmen continued to hold respectable positions which they could pass on to their sons, particularly in trades to which apprenticeship was the accepted mode of entry and in which unions controlled the admission of new members. The best paid places in construction, printing, and railroading fell into this category. Nevertheless a craft was a means of standing still, not of getting ahead and some boys aspired to other, better employment. The fathers did not deny them the chance, for their pride in their own callings could not offset the awareness, which had long troubled American artisans, that occupations which depended upon manual skill were sooner or later doomed in competition with the factory machine.

Businessmen also felt concern about the preparation of their children for desirable occupations. Entrepreneurial families were always on the edge of success. Many a shopkeeper dreamed of taking on a new line, adding a branch store, expanding into wholesaling or manufacturing; the opportunities existed if only one could grasp them. Many a salesman tinkered nights in his dreary hotel room with the invention that traveled with him and that someday, perfected, would draw the world to his door. Capital was what these people needed, just the bit of margin to let them spread out. They were drawn to speculation, the little flyers, the one chance, that might somehow put the big stake in their hands. Consequently, apart from those who acquired truly great fortunes, they were frequently short of cash when it came to the education of their children in which they nevertheless fervently believed. Robert

H. Goddard, the future rocket physicist, got little help in a family that made do with a bookkeeper's salary; the tuition that sent him to Worcester Polytechnic came from a grocer's loan to his grandmother.

The homes of professional people were more stable. A few lawyers and an even smaller number of physicians earned fees large enough to lift them into the ranks of the wealthy. Most of their colleagues were not that fortunate; nor were clergymen, teachers, engineers and military officers who worked for fixed salaries. But the incomes of such people were at least dependable and, down to the First World War, while prices fell and the costs of housing and servants were low, made possible a decent style of life.

But not a life-style readily passed on to the children. The necessity of maintaining a respectable appearance, the moves that called for adjustment to new neighborhoods and the constant scrutiny of communities ready to be critical prevented the accumulation of a surplus to pass on to the next generation. What could Stephen Crane inherit, born in 1871, the fourteenth child of a Methodist minister who died in 1880?

A son could not simply step into a father's profession. No doubt there were hopes in the family that Stephen Vincent Benét would hold a commission in the Army as his father and grandfather had. But the timid, fattish and very spectacled boy was not cut out for a military command. Personal preferences still pulled youth in directions not determined by ancestry. Opportunities were within reach, but the avenues to them were different from those used by earlier generations.

In the last three decades of the nineteenth century, those parents anxious to help their children climb upward or at least to guard them against the plunge downward, realized that inheritance no longer controlled the vital sectors of the economy. Few secure places passed along within the family. Nor were occupations open, as in the old frontier days, to any would-be entrant. The activities which had once been organized about the household or the family shrank in importance. Land ownership and agriculture ceased to be significant channels for advance or even means for retaining a high status in society. In trade and industry, the impersonal corporation replaced the family firm.

Increasingly the best places seemed to be the professions, to which aspirants gained access by formal education. The expectation gradually spread that entry to the practice of law, medicine and engineering and into large areas of corporate enterprise would come not by inheritance or apprenticeship, but rather by passage through a defined course of instruction in an institution of higher learning. A combination of needs fed that expectation. In a complex society, large organizations found dependable credentials such as degrees useful in recruiting and identifying talent for very specialized tasks. A B.S. from Tech meant something to the corporate personnel manager. Individual consumers of technical services also learned to trust the same standards; an M.D. from Hopkins or an LL.B. from Harvard had value to patients and clients. Purely pragmatic judgments of competence seemed less dependable than certification by an institution, just as experience seemed less instructive than science.

Since the middle of the nineteenth century, physicians and lawyers, architects and pharmacists had sought recognition of their distinctive status through professional associations which defined the qualifications, duties and rights of practitioners. Sometimes state licensing boards enforced these criteria; sometimes the sanctions were informal and voluntary. But with the support of the state or without it, the professional groups struggled to set standards that would protect the public and that would, at the same time, limit the access of outsiders to the field.

Preparation by apprenticeship was inadequate for these purposes; any practitioner could churn out followers guided only by his own tastes and prejudices and by the inadequate controls of licensing examinations which varied markedly from place to place. Schools were less idiosyncratic and therefore more dependable; they established prescribed courses identical for all students who passed through at a fixed pace and whose quality was consequently subject to uniform rating, as were the products of any other massive, mechanical institution. Hence the growing emphasis upon education by attendance at a professional school.

The antecedents of such faculties reached back to the early nineteenth century, but they had then been only loosely connected to universities and they had not been the usual mode of entry to any calling. Both circumstances changed after 1870; professional schools became integral parts of universities and they became the common means of acquiring certain vocations. Increasingly the important element in a legal or medical career was admission to such a course of training.

The rapid multiplication of professional faculties tended, however, to diminish the value of the credentials they awarded. Well into the twentieth century, the M.D. and LL.B. remained as easy to come by, and as uncertain in value, as admission to practice had been earlier. The institutions able to raise their standards and thereby to enhance the value of their degrees among discriminating consumers did so, on the one hand, by improving the quality of instruction and, on the other, by stiffening admission requirements, often hinging them on the previous completion of a collegiate program.

By 1900, ambitious young men understood that, while there were many ways of becoming a physician or lawyer, places on the staffs of the best hospitals and firms went to graduates of a few professional schools which in turn demanded a good bachelor's degree for admission. A popular handbook advised youths to attend *well-known and prosperous* institutions, for the same reasons that made strong business houses or professional firms attractive as employers — so that *the college will carry you instead of you carrying the college.*

The Consequences of Opportunity

Parents and children with some range of choice and with aspirations for getting ahead suffered from disquieting anxieties after 1870. Gone were the days when a boy left home at fourteen to make his way as best he could. Great opportunities still existed and the impersonal institutions which selected, trained and evaluated candidates for success were, in some ways, less restrictive, less dependent on connections and kinship than apprenticeship had been. But they demanded conformity to fixed standards of judgment and few families were certain about how best to ready their offspring for the test.

The dilemma deepened as changes in the social context undermined the stability of the home. Steadily the rural background dimmed; a study of children's minds in 1883 revealed no trace of a cow. Increasingly the city was the environment for growing up and the city had ceased to be the small comprehensible community that Boston had been earlier in the century, or even New York. The scale was totally different, measured in millions of population rather than in thousands. The endless streets no longer ran out into the countryside. The men and women, the boys and girls spun away through the day to jobs or schools and their residences provided them no more than common lodgings. Flight to the suburbs eased the menace of the *dangerous classes* who clogged the slum alleys. But the greater danger was internal — the dissolution of the family ties that had once provided affectionate discipline to all the members and education to the child. At the opening of the twentieth century observers described the change in clear, drastic and exaggerated terms. The home had once been the center of industry as well as of social life. It had produced nearly all the food consumed in it and had done much of the work later carried on in the factory. It had thus given the child the major part of his training for facing life. What would take its place in the urban economy?

Many contemporaries commented on the issue, but few understood its full complexity. The problem existed in the city. But it was not solely an urban problem. Nor was it altogether novel.

Red Lewis grew up in a small town, one of those half-rural communities idyllically described in the glossy magazines — the son of a doctor, nice house, respected family, active in Christian Endeavor. He felt stifled by comfort, which he equated with the dullness of life. Like the character in the novel he would later write he was always groping for something he was not capable of attaining, always dissatisfied, always restlessly straining to see what lay hidden just over the horizon. Intolerant of his surroundings and determined to escape, he nevertheless had no clearly defined vision of what he really wanted to do or be. An old American character — as old as Ethan Allen.

In 1870, the American family was already vulnerable, tense with the long-standing and pervasive ambiguities of a relationship which reared a child so that he would wish to leave. The break had always been painful — between dependence and independence, between the warm affections of home and the cold controlled dealings of the world. Now external dangers and internal readjustments also threatened the stability of the family. The after-effects of war, the gigantic fortunes in the hands of new men, the attenuation of neighborly responsibilities, and the weakening of supernatural religious beliefs, as well as the growth of factory and city, deprived parents of the guidance of reliable standards and persuaded them to keep their young sheltered longer than formerly. Furthermore, fathers and mothers were less certain than before about the adult roles for which they prepared their children. Increasingly girls aspired to the same careers as boys. Did that mean that the two sexes matured in the same way and at the same pace and therefore required the same education? The questions remained unanswered.

It was necessary for youths to get away. But not too soon. A little postponement would prepare them better for the struggle of life. Perhaps a job at fourteen or sixteen or eighteen was too early; boys and girls at that age were not equipped to do well under the new competitive conditions and once involved might never acquire the skill later to succeed at their callings or as citizens and parents. The risk was too great.

Such trepidations never entirely displaced the deep

popular faith in the value of departure. The orphan remained somehow an enviable figure — at least in fiction. Unencumbered, he could show his mettle, as in *Barriers Burned Away* (1872) by E. P. Roe, an account of a boy's virtuous triumph over Chicago which held untold readers through hundreds of pages dense with syrupy prose. Benny Brown escapes from the circus, Toby Tyler to it; the goodness of both remains intact. In a long succession of popular novels, Horatio Alger, Jr., names the desirable attributes: *Luck and Pluck*; *Rough and Ready*; *Sink or Swim*; *Strong and Steady*; *Slow and Sure*; *Try and Trust.*

Youth ought to wander lest sheltered, it become effete. There was more danger to church and state, a minister wrote in 1908, *from milksops and lickspittles than from bullies and braggarts.* Both were undesirable and the way to eliminate them was to train the young to be *kind and deferential but at the same time manly and courageous against all odds and opposition.* Charles Francis Adams, Jr., writing in 1891, explained that young men who grew up encumbered by family traditions could not cope with the vulgar people against whom they had to struggle for prizes. Somewhat wistfully (as if wishing the chance had been his), he explained that the forecastle experience — years full of danger which led to nothing practical — *took the nonsense out* of Richard H. Dana, left him *purged and strengthened* and brought out his manhood. Alas, the sailing ships were gone and the frontier was fading, although some could still exert themselves in the strenuous life of the ranch. War remained. The experience of battle had touched Oliver Wendell Holmes, Jr., with fire and had brought Henry Fleming to manhood; and the youth of 1898 and 1917 welcomed the trial of combat. If some were disappointed, it was less by the encounter with death than by the fumbling regimentation modern armies imposed on the individual.

Ultimately, Americans could not condemn the wild ones; the dreamers who acted out visions were too intimate a part of the national history. The lone gunman — cowboy, sheriff, bandit, urban detective, it did not matter — gripped the imagination. Buffalo Bill, Jesse James, Nick Carter peopled the fantasies of millions. In *Cup of Gold,* a novel of 1929, the boy runaway is captured by pirates, sold as a servant, seizes power, conquers city, then: gore, gold, beautiful women, orgies, and the wise man's prediction — *you will become a great man — if only you remain a little child. All the world's great men have been little boys who wanted the moon.*

Popular literature portrayed the boy-hero in constant rebellion against the civilizing efforts of parents. Dan, who *hated restraint of any sort,* every now and then had to burst out somehow. *I want to run straight ahead somewhere, to smash something, or pitch into somebody. Don't know why, but I do.* Huck Finn, in flight from the supervision of family, responded to a longing many others felt. The bad boys who did not take the whole risk — George Peck's, or Booth Tarkington's Penrod or Buster Brown of the funny papers — in their more restrained naughtiness expressed also the defiant will to be themselves, not copies of a model others had made. A psychologist in 1911 compared young people to animals in captivity. *They long intensely for the utter abandon of a wilder life,* frequently *discarding foot and head dress and even garments in the blind instinct to realize the conditions of primitive man.*

Often now, a word described the interim state between childhood and adulthood. President G. Stanley Hall of Clark University gave it widespread currency in a book,

Adolescence (1904). The term recognized the existence in the United States of a phenomenon that had previously been associated with the aristocracy of Europe — a provisional stage in life, years during which people with men's powers, relieved by wealth of the need to work or indeed, of the need to prepare to work, suffered the tedium of waiting for a role to be vacated. At fourteen, sixteen, eighteen, twenty, American youth were no longer mischievous boys whose loafing had a tolerable charm. Adolescence was a dangerous age, *when the very worst and best impulses in the human soul struggled against each other for its possession.* The family responsible for those who did not immediately enter the world had to find means for harnessing their energy constructively, for taming their spirits so that they would not damage themselves or others, and for preparing them to move ahead when life became serious.

Something useful to do between the ages of twelve and eighteen?

Some adults considered boys' clubs the answer—badges for distributing charity, good conduct and heroism. *Look up, and not down; look forward and not back; look out, and not in; lend a hand.* The fellow who might be reluctant to join The Princely Knights of Character Castle could imbibe the same principles of endurance, love, purity and patriotism with a frontier flavor in the Boy Scouts. Benevolence carried similar, though not the same, clubs to the slums. Important as these activities were, they consumed only small intervals at the edge of the youth's time.

Girls, as well as boys, passed through the adolescent stage of life. But well into the twentieth century American parents could not decide whether the condition of the two sexes was identical at this age or whether the same treatment was appropriate to both. Girl Scouts were the counterparts of the Boy Scouts, in a way; and there was adventure — of a sort — in stories of nurses and exploration. The term "tomboy" was not unflattering, nor was feminine interest in athletics outlandish. Yet girls could not learn to defend themselves by experience as their brothers did and therefore could not safely leave home to strike out on their own.

Hence the attractiveness of the activity that became central to adolescent life after 1870. Schools provided a setting in which boys and girls could safely occupy themselves. Whether they should do so in an identical fashion remained uncertain; but in practice the similarities grew steadily.

In 1870, the model of universal attendance already existed, although in a fragmentary and incoherent form. In the decades that followed, the belief that adolescence was the time for all to study hardened into absolute certainty. A properly organized system of schools would prepare all youth for life, compensate for the deficiencies of the family and fill up the interval before independence.

The most vigorous proponents of this point of view were professional educators. Teaching after 1870 ceased to be an expedient and became a career, calling for precise qualifications to which devoted men and women gave their whole lives. The time was past when parents, informally or through an elected board, hired and fired and determined what was to be learned. Effective control began to pass to a self-constituting bureaucracy with its own standards and aspirations.

The challenge that stirred the imagination of educators was the possibility that the schools could cure the evils of society. Teachers, principals and superintendents, themselves reared under the influence of the optimistic faith in reform, saw their roles as pivotal; a generation earlier, many of them would have been ministers. Now, they stifled their resentment at the unwillingness of others to accord them the same prestige and financial rewards as other professionals and found satisfaction in the determination to mold in the classroom a new and better world.

The Jeffersonian image of a pyramidal system profoundly attracted educators; it was democratic and egalitarian in intention and it gave them the role of selecting the nation's future leaders. The schools were steps upward, each narrower than that beneath it. The whole population mounted the lowest but only the most qualified could rise to the ones above. Opportunity was available to all and the whole society gained as the judgment of ability steered each individual to an appropriate station in life.

The pressure from parents unable or unwilling to guide their offspring to maturity without assistance meshed in with the desire of educators to widen their own role. Since tradition was no longer reliable, direction had to come from the experts with a claim to scientific knowledge. The result was to load upon the schools the responsibility for almost the whole process of training the young, which had formerly been shared with the church, the home and the shop. Indeed Americans now, for the first time, began to use the word "education" as if its meaning were identical with schooling.

The belief that the school was the nation's only educational institution explained the anxiety, which professional social workers shared with teachers, about the lot of children who worked in the mills or at home. The youngsters who earned their three dollars a week could not acquire the schooling necessary to make them decent citizens, to guard them from crime and vice and *to arm them properly for the competition of life*. Even part-time classes held in the factory were inadequate as well as undemocratic because, Carroll D. Wright explained, all education had to be administered through a single public system which treated all who entered it equally and offered all the same chance to advance.

Increasingly Americans divided the life of the person not yet an adult into fixed time spans, correlated with the stages of schooling. Infancy was a period of pure play and of such preparation for what would follow as a kindergarten might give; and childhood between the ages of six or eight and twelve or fourteen was the time of formal learning at the elementary level. There was general agreement that until this point every boy and girl passed through the same development and therefore that all should have identical *common* schooling. By 1900 more than half the states had enacted compulsory attendance laws to ensure to everyone the opportunity to study and therefore to arrive at desirable careers.

Fourteen had formerly been the usual age for leaving home. Now, however, families reluctant to cast adolescents adrift at that age faced an important choice. Parents who could afford the burden of continued support and of the loss of potential earnings could send their children on to further schooling rather than allowing them to take unpromising jobs.

Every prudential consideration seemed weighted in favor of further education. A Supreme Court decision of 1872 upheld the expenditure of public funds for secondary schools, which thereafter spread rapidly. Here youths who lived at home could attend to the age of eighteen, gain additional skills or prepare for college or professional institutions. If nothing more, the high school provided an interval in which career decisions could be postponed. It was true that those who followed this course also postponed the age of leaving home and thereby created profound new emotional tensions within it. But the alternative was worse. Changes in the economy progressively closed off the other avenues which had formerly led to desirable careers. A study early in the twentieth century of 25,000 Massachusetts children who did not continue their education after the age of fourteen showed them doomed to the *dead end* of unskilled labor and the years previously spent in school therefore *wasted*. The inference was that American society was on the way to stratification into classes similar to that long characteristic of Europe, unless the educational system made place for youth well beyond the age of fourteen.

Parents who did not send their children on in effect condemned them to the lowliest ranks of the occupational order. The ideal of independence and separation was no longer powerful enough to stifle the impulse to shelter sons and daughters for that little while more that would permit attendance at high school and enlargement of the chances for a rise in later life.

The function of that institution was however unclear, for it attempted to provide something to do for a heterogeneous student body. No doubt the regularity of schoolwork was itself a valuable moralizing agent. But G. Stanley Hall, among others, warned that to collect and cram masses of children with the same unassimilable facts would not absorb the energy of adolescents or lessen their incorrigibility or save them from vice and crime. He urged a wider spread of industrial education, purposeful because it would arm youth for the struggle of life. The pupils in institutions for Negroes, Indians and juvenile delinquents which stressed practical skills, he argued, received the best of trainings, measured by the growth in mind, morals, health and knowledge. The same methods would *regenerate in body and spirit many flabby, underdeveloped, anemic, easy-living city youth.*

By the twentieth century, however, the high school was developing in a direction not anticipated by its founders. Increasingly, it assumed the task not merely of completing the education of its students but of preparing some of them to go on to college. Hall noted with regret the rapid rise in the 1890's in the number which offered Latin as an index of the change in the high school's function.

Some parents by then expected the schooling of their offspring to continue well beyond the age of eighteen. The middle and upper social groups of the United States regarded people of that age not as adults, able to enter life fully, but rather as postulants readying themselves for careers. Furthermore, for a good many of them the years after eighteen were still a period not for occupational training, but for further preparation before arriving at a decision about future vocation. Their education extended well into the twenties.

Prolongation of the schooling process, to eighteen in high school, to twenty-two in college, and beyond in professional institutes, was a consequence of the novel conditions under which people found places in American society after 1870. Postponement of the age for leaving home and alterations in the form of departure were responses to the hazards and opportunities of the world into which youth then went forth.

A tightly articulated formal educational system replaced the loosely patterned arrangements of earlier times. A single track led from the right elementary and secondary school to the right college and professional school. To reach the destination it seemed necessary to stay on the rails.

The switching points were at ages fourteen and eighteen, with decisions about work, school and departure from home. An occasional crossover was feasible, but the transfer grew increasingly difficult as the youth moved toward his career. An early choice was exceedingly important.

Many Americans resented the pressure of decision even as they valued the opportunities upon which it opened. For years they read with nostalgic approval the idyllic description of another, older, kind of schooling in Louisa May Alcott's *Little Men* (1871). In those pages, each child was different and each found his own way to self-knowledge, self-help and self-control in a free environment where each loved and taught the others. There were no tracks in Plumfield.

Some two decades later a philosopher studying the ways of knowing and learning concluded that education had taken a wrong turning since his own Vermont schooldays. It had lost sight of its moral purpose, of the aim of making each person a worthy member of society. John Dewey's experimental school at the University of Chicago (1896) was the starting point of a progressive movement which gained force after the turn of the century in protest against the increasing rigidity which was the dominant tendency of the time.

The problem was not simply one of the schools however, but of the modes of grasping the opportunities social change offered. Calculations about career chances and views about the age at which the dependence upon home ended influenced the tracks followed within the educational system.

In families without margin, work fully occupied the time of each member as soon as the law permitted. But families that could afford a choice sought to put a long distance between the age fourteen and the time of standing alone as an adult. As earlier, the hope of upward social mobility was an inducement for postponement of the obligations attendant upon marriage. The desire to achieve offset the fear of spinsterhood or bachelorhood and, in extreme cases, delayed the venture into matrimony long beyond the period of formal schooling. Frances Perkins married at the age of thirty-one, after she had gotten her start. Bernard Baruch cautiously waited until twenty-seven and John Hay until thirty-eight, by which time they had accumulated the capital for establishment at an appropriate station. On the other hand, Henry Ford married too early, even though he was twenty-five, for he had not arrived at a position in which he could support a wife and still devote himself fully to the machines with which his future lay.

But even the family which did not anticipate for its offspring so long a wait before marriage felt the need to delay the moment at which children faced life alone. Increasingly parents used the schools to fill some part at least of the interval between adolescence and independent adulthood.

The usual age for entering college advanced to eighteen, and soon postgraduate classes lay beyond the first four years of higher education. Anxiety about fitting the youth to speed along the correct track to success deepened with doubts about the best age for leaving home. The young man or woman who stayed with his family saved the cost of self-support and minimized the risk of error. But caution also reduced the hope of dramatic gains.

The ability to choose among increasingly formal paths to careers was the painful consequence of opportunity. The exhilarating freedom to move away left the boy or girl without restraints, but also without supports. And the family which made the decision — whether to let go or to hold back — long suffered in anticipation the need for making it.

Neither parents nor children understood the subtle alteration in relationship caused by the prolongation of dependence.

A pronounced decline in the size of families, particularly among the middle classes, reflected the pressure of higher survival rates and of the need to keep space available for those who did not leave. Home was more crowded with four offspring who stayed than it had been for eight, each of whom moved out promptly. Then too it was necessary to worry more than formerly about making a provision, at least for the boys, to pay tuition or provide a stake in business. Mothers and fathers owed it to children to limit numbers; yet since birth control techniques were scarcely known, rarely discussed, and crude at best, abstinence and restraint seemed the unavoidable price parents paid for the welfare of the sons and daughters they had already begotten.

Emotions narrowed down, intensified. The decline of infant mortality wiped away the old torment of knowing that some offspring would die and that attachments were in the nature of life transient. The certainty grew that every baby would mature and with it the expectation of permanence in the relationship to its father and mother. Then too births now came within a relatively short span of the years of marriage and absorbed the concentrated attention of the family. As a result energies focused on the child's growth, not as a process of separation but rather as an extension of the parents' presence through another generation.

Mama set up and supervised a system of *good housekeeping* which the maids executed. Freed from chores and spared the recurrence of pregnancy (deprived therefore of the outlet of sexuality), she herself retained primarily the function of supervising the offspring. Heeding the warning that the unhealthy life of urban society might stifle the capacity for good motherhood, she hovered solicitously over her brood to fend away threats. Mrs. MacArthur in 1899 took lodgings in West Point to be nearby when nineteen-year-old Douglas entered the Academy. A mother's affection confined to one channel flowed over and was returned, as Robert Lee Williams remembered, *in full measure, pressed down and running over.* In the child's imagining no disaster was more dreadful than her loss.

Father too was solicitous, but a stern judge. When he was present and impinged closely on the lives of his children, holding one up for comparison as against another, he dominated their emotions, particularly of youths as sensitive as Henry James. But papa was often absent, away from home the day through, sometimes longer; and then he was a remote figure, supporting the family in ways not visible, yet also somehow an ever-threatening presence to whom mama appealed for sanctions. The ultimate humiliation of physical punishment came from his arm and the very thought of his displeasure was so awesome that the actual blow was rarely necessary. Alice Foote MacDougall never forgot how her mother forced her to sit and look at the photograph of Father then away in Europe, saying, *See how sad he is, with a naughty daughter.* And indeed the face grew sadder and sadder till the tears filled his eyes and ran down his cheeks and Alice herself was reduced to weeping and bitter lamentation.

Terror dominated my youth, wrote William Carlos Williams. The forms were various. Boys and girls kept dependent far into their teens could not afford the guilt of *being bad* and suffered the tensions of the efforts to be the parents' image of good; or they misbehaved and felt the sting of disapproval. Maladies not subject to medical diagnosis struck youths at moments of emotional crisis, as they did Robert H. Goddard or Robert Frost. By the end of the nineteenth century the abused children of neglectful parents and scenes of the death of boys who asserted the claim to live were familiar in American fiction. After the turn of the century, Randolph Bourne and others described the family as the deadly enemy of individual will and freedom.

In an earlier era, and for a time still in rural regions, boys had gone off at thirteen or fourteen either to work or to study and separation was a normal incident in the relations of one generation to another. But when eighteen became the usual age of entry to college, an earlier departure from a well-to-do home became exceptional. The father and mother who made the conscious choice of sending off a son or daughter accepted the premature loss only because it was presumably for the good of the child to do so. Attendance at a proper private boarding school which put a youth on the right track for future life was the ideal solution for it justified what was now the sacrifice of parting.

Yet what could a parent tell by just looking around a school, all polished and orderly on a visitors' day? The orators talked about Wellington and the playing fields of Eton—the grand imprint of character, duty, diligence, strength, patience, not simply the lessons learned from books. Fine! In the stories of Ralph Henry Barbour the lads were all the better for the experience; and had fun too. Better to believe that than the description in a novel of 1921 of a teacher with the *restraint of a hanging judge and the ingenuity in small cruelties of a Jesuit Inquisitor.* Reality lay somewhere between the extremes.

The soft, sensitive ones wilted. Exeter bewildered Gifford Pinchot, a boy coddled by doting parents, the kind of boy who worried about whether servants should call him by his first name. *How will I keep my manners what they should be, when there is no one to caution me when I go wrong?* he wrote Mama. No football for him, or pistol shooting. He suffered unenthusiastically through the course.

The tough ones thrived. Stephen Crane was glad to get away to the Claverack College and Hudson River Institute in 1888 at the age of sixteen. At this boarding school for boys and girls the minister's son hit it off with a gang of incorrigible *Indians,* learned to smoke and gamble and acquired a taste for liquor. There he adopted the motto: *do what is forbidden.*

The majority developed a tolerance for boarding school, not resenting it enough to rebel, not finding much stimulus to exercise their powers, passively obedient while they paused at an obscure way station on the road of life.

The kids who left had always felt the pangs of homesickness even when it was an expected and necessary event, as for Ned Emerson. Now for those emotionally unprepared for a break with the family, departure was cruel, intense — even violent. When *going back to school,* Stephen Vincent Benét nostalgically drifted to

> the great room,
> Curled in a chair with all of them beside
> And the whole world a rush of happy voices,
> With laughter bearing in a clamorous tide. . . .

and thought ahead to the *big boy's arm* and the twist of *shattering pain along his tortured wrist.* In and out of both images pulsed the remembered ecstasy of *a book of knights and bloody shields* read in bed.

The boy also saw *blurts of crimson light* splashing the *white grains like blood,* where *pirates sat and diced.* Only then he dreamed, of having sobbed, of having closed his eyes and of having crawled into bed, *after the whipping.*

At this age it was painful to leave and painful to stay.

Even later, for those off to college, going away was a wrench in its abrupt termination of what had theretofore been a permanent relationship. The very opportunities for which they left, however attractive, had altered the home so that leaving it was painful. The creed of competition, according to which all places were open, deepened the dependence of youths on the family, where they were readied for battle. So compelling were the ties that departure, whenever it came, was a shock.

The alternative was to slip onto the wrong track with all the penalties that seemed to entail.

On the Wrong Tracks

The right track, which called for departure from home somewhere between the ages of fourteen and eighteen, led those able to follow it from the good school to the good college to a professional course and on to a prestigious occupation. Increasingly the progression won the esteem of the whole society, so that the other tracks which branched away in various wrong directions were less desirable.

Most of the young people on the wrong tracks — that is, most Americans — did not consider themselves doomed by the inability to join the favored few who were *real college men*. The majority felt the pressure of a simpler imperative, that of preparing for a job that would earn them a livelihood as soon as possible; the detour through a college without a clear vocational purpose was beyond the means of boys and girls who had to scramble for a place and an income early in life. Some found employment promptly after completing the span of formal education the law required or circumstances permitted, learning then by experience or by whatever instruction was available in their spare time. Others, as earlier, moved about in pursuit of an elusive fortune, clinging still to the faith in self-made success. Still others enrolled in institutions which promised them specific training in a vocational skill. To take the chosen path they could either leave home or remain under the parental roof until they were established and married.

There was no single destination. A multitude of heroes and heroines inspired the boys and girls who selected among a variety of goals the one toward which to strive. Dreams of military glory, of exploration and of the West still stirred some lads, although not as deeply as formerly, for the career army was now an institution entered through school, ease of communication had taken some of the thrill out of travel, and there was less adventure than earlier in a subdued frontier. Still John Paul Jones and Daniel Boone kept their places in the pantheon of youthful minds, joined however by new figures — athletes and actors, the man of daring on the trapeze or in the detective's disguise, and the big dealer who rose to riches. Every youth who knew of Jackson and Lincoln was eligible for the presidency; some fixed their sights on the banker's big desk; and a few even slogged away in their rooms at the great American novel. The stock of feminine figures was less ample although the teacher, nurse and movie star now joined the wife and mother.

There was no single track to achievement; say, Babe Ruth or Douglas Fairbanks or Alexander Botts, the big tractor seller, all got there after the lucky break and often when everything seemed at its toughest. Since there was no predictable pattern to these careers, youths whose ambitions turned in such directions did not need to measure their progress by milestones fixed along the way, for an unexpected turning or rise in the road might come just after the point where the going was rockiest. Only pluck and luck counted — pluck to keep trying no matter what, and luck to turn up the great chance.

Dreams kept hope alive, but only rarely shaped the decisions by which careers were made. In real life most young men and women were more often driven by necessity than drawn by inspiration. Work was inescapable; they took what they could get and made the best of it.

Most often, the jobs they found kept people at home. Al Smith spent the whole of his youth in New York City within walking distance of the place of his birth, lived with his mother Catherine until his marriage at the age of twenty-seven and then spent the rest of his life with his wife Catherine, and was the same person, animated by the same belief in his future when he chased trucks or clerked in the fish market as he would be when climbing to political prominence.

The numbers shocked reformers when they learned that 100,000 children worked in New York factories in 1873; and the reality was harsh indeed — long hours, meager pay, no play, little to learn. But the kids who dragged their grimy bodies up the tenement steps each night came back to a home and the labor that exhausted them had a prideful and comprehensible purpose — to bring bread to the family. So long as they could dream, a good many were willing to hang on waiting for a break.

Toward the close of the nineteenth century Americans began to condemn the very idea that young people should work. Jacob A. Riis spoke from experience. He had himself known the necessity of hard labor, but understood the difference between the tasks of the farm and those of the factory or slum sweatshop. His *The Children of the Poor* (1892) movingly portrayed exploited youngsters, deprived of their birthright — play and education — by bondage to a job. Other journalists, social workers, and reformers took up the campaign. Compulsory education laws were not enough; a ban on child labor was also necessary and the minimum age crept steadily ahead from ten to twelve to fourteen and sixteen. *The finer the type the longer the period needed for its maturing,* wrote an advocate of child labor legislation in 1905; for members of the American nation competent to carry on its great traditions and help solve its tremendous problems, the period of preparation could not be less than sixteen years. By the 1920's in most parts of the country, the state forbade the employment of boys and girls in industry and insisted that they attend a school of some sort. It thus began to end early experience at work which for many generations had served Americans as a mode of discipline and a way of entering careers.

Until then some youths in search of employment chose departure from home. Any one of numerous causes sent them forth — a misfortune, such as the loss of parents; or an assertion of will, such as the refusal to stay in school as the family desired.

In one fashion or another wandering boys took to the streets or the roads; and the running-away fantasy became real for thousands of youth. In the country they joined the army of tramps; in the city they fell in with prowling gangs of street arabs, nomads — working, begging, pilfering. There were more than 10,000 of them in New York City alone in the 1870's. The communities through which they drifted sought to lock them up, reform and educate them, at least get them out of the way. Industrial schools, camps, clubs, missions, reformatories, newsboys' homes and farm placement systems multiplied after 1870 with the support of concerned citizens willing to vote taxes or contribute voluntarily for such benevolent purposes. The asylums could not be built fast enough.

New York's model House of Refuge could be staffed to hold 700 delinquents; where would the others go? As long as they dodged the truant officer and the cop, where they wished.

The restlessness that pulled them away from their families impelled other youths to struggle for decent jobs. They would never get anywhere at home and sight of a father's drudgery whether at the desk or the machine was a reminder of how the passing years closed off opportunities and left a chap bogged down in remorseless obligations. They had to cut loose, break out. Eugene Debs, one of ten children, was fifteen when he went to work in a railroad shop and he could have advanced to fireman or perhaps engineer. But though he never lost sympathy for those with whom he worked, he refused to accept the routine and escaped to be a grocery clerk and editor. Others moved about in an endless search for the means of rising. Al O'Flaherty, a traveling salesman, wistfully sought the big deal, not quite believing that he would make it, not quite willing ever to surrender the hope. The characters in O. Henry's stories, sharpers, confidence men — drummers all — play their games zestfully but keep moving lest life catch up with them. And William Sidney Porter modeled them on himself; he left home at fifteen for his first job as a drugstore clerk, shuffled around, did a little time in jail and never got his feet down to the ground.

The implausibility of the career matched the extravagance of the name! Billy Sunday was his *real name* — no William to it. An orphan, always on his own, he scratched about at menial tasks to keep alive. *Work never hurt anybody*. There was a spell of learning in Nevada High School while he was janitor there, but he did not graduate because there was a good opening in a furniture store. From tossing the ball around with the boys it followed that he landed a position with the pros and for a while flashed across American League infields. Then the spirit of God got to him, he mounted the pulpit and soared in the great cities as revivalist.

Now the girls too are restless. Marriage and motherhood are the common norms. Some of the sisters aspire to achievement outside the home as the brothers long had. Aimee Semple McPherson, Billy Sunday's counterpart, at seventeen leaves home to speak God's word and blossoms at Los Angeles in the adoration of delighted followers. Fanny Brice, having quit whatever schools did not expel her, learns the art of acting by pilfering and begging as a child and walks onto the stage at thirteen. Shirley Booth's chance in a stock company comes at about the same age and she never does finish P.S. 152 in New York City. Norma Shearer is just a little older when she comes down from Canada for her first film parts. Ora Henrietta Snyder stays with her family in Chicago; married and a mother, she wishes to do more, markets her homemade candies and becomes president of a big business. And Amelia Earhart yields to the aviation enthusiasm of the 1920's; her schooling is incomplete, she lacks the patience for teaching or social work, she takes wings.

Other spirits moved other youths — the desire to create, for instance. John Steinbeck could have gotten on the right track at Stanford but preferred to live by odd jobs as a hired hand on ranches and as a common laborer until 1925, when he went across the country to New York to be an author. So also, Janet Flanner, too rebellious to finish at the University of Chicago, wandered to Paris, to write as Genêt. Discontent with Ohio State brought

Berenice Abbott to Paris and to a career as photographer. James T. Farrell, by contrast, had never been on the right track and left Chicago for New York to be a novelist. On the other hand, Richard Wright, a black boy from the deep South, came up to Chicago for the opportunity lacking at home as Paul Laurence Dunbar had a generation earlier, fearful of the great wicked city yet thrilled by its challenge.

Apprenticeship still served some young people as preparation for a number of trades. Russell H. Conwell explained to willing listeners that extreme overemphasis on the advantages of schools had propagated the erroneous belief that all knowledge worth having was available only in some highly endowed university. Not at all. *Experience was still the very best teacher and always would be.*

Plenty of cases proved it. Henry Ford, for instance, left the farm at fifteen, after his mother died, to serve an apprenticeship in various Detroit machine shops. To make ends meet he worked nights in a jewelry store. He also occasionally attended sessions at Goldsmith, Bryant & Stratton Business University. He enjoyed it all and had plenty of energy. In time, despite personal adversities, he put together to his own advantage the mechanical experience in the shop with the selling experience in the store and the little knowledge of bookkeeping from the school. Any office boy might learn from doing errands, taking invoices to the consular agents, copying outgoing mail and indexing letterbooks.

Enterprising youths pulled themselves into the professions in the old way, although not into the best places. Bourke Cockran was seventeen in 1871 when he arrived from Ireland all brassy with self-confidence. Off the street in New York he walked into a parochial school for young ladies and talked himself into being a teacher. Two years later he qualified for the post of principal in the high school of suburban Tuckahoe, by demonstrating the ability to beat up the biggest, toughest boys. A success he was, so that Judge Abraham B. Tappan offered him the use of a library in which he could imbibe what there was to know about the law. At the age of twenty-two, without the benefit of law school, Cockran was a member of the New York bar. Even women now could take the same route — Marilla Marks, for instance, who was forty-two and a widow when admitted to the bar after reading with a good firm in Washington, D.C.

Despite the growing formality of the dominant educational system, the seekers of opportunity found means of learning even while they worked. Ambitious New Yorkers studied stenography at Pratt Institute or engineering at Cooper Union in whatever time they had. Private business colleges dotted the country and in the larger cities evening classes for adults gave a belated chance to immigrants. The determined youth could usually find a proprietary medical or law school with schedules flexible enough to permit him to study while holding a job.

The woman bold and determined enough could do the same. A borrowed anatomy book persuaded the divorced Mrs. Owens-Adair at the age of thirty to become a physician. She put her son into school, found a manager for the millinery shop, and took the stagecoach out of Oregon; then a fast course at Philadelphia's Eclectic School of Medicine readied her for practice. *You don't know how much nicer it is,* she wrote, *than selling goods and working night and day.* And it agreed with her too; she looked better — so much so that at the age of forty-four when she earned $7,000 a year, she remarried and three years later, gave birth once more. At about the same time in Boston Emily Bruce, a widow, earned the right to practice, and elsewhere Mary S. Danforth, Anna B. Taylor-Cole and Rebecca W. Wiley also made their way into medicine with similar determination.

The long-standing American desire to make education useful now sustained institutions with a frankly vocational purpose. Courses in the manual and mercantile arts multiplied. It was the duty of the state, educators argued, to establish urban schools preparatory to manufacturing for the purpose of assuring the efficient application of science to the productive system. Andrew Carnegie in 1907 added the forceful opinion that technical instruction was essential to replace the old pattern of apprenticeship. Full-time study of this kind would equip with valuable skills the young men and women who delayed their entry into the labor force for a while. The qualifications for admission were flexible — sometimes an elementary or secondary school diploma, sometimes no more than an expression of interest.

Some general high schools offered vocational training. Special trade schools taught printing or nursing, textile design or dressmaking. Or boys and girls could learn to teach in normal schools.

Callings close to the professions and therefore more prestigious than the manual trades were also accessible through institutions whose doors opened readily to young applicants regardless of preparation. The diploma she earned from the United States School of Embalming qualified Minnie Edwards Atwood of New Hampshire to share her husband's duties as funeral director. Special courses also led to careers of varying levels of prestige in dentistry, pharmacy, nursing, social work, veterinary medicine and accountancy. Columbia's School of Mines offered high school graduates instruction in civil, mechanical, electrical and sanitary engineering and in architecture. Alfred Sloan and Godfrey Cabot went to M.I.T. to acquire command of practical techniques as quickly as possible. The most desirable law and medical schools were more selective but down to 1900 only a few seriously insisted on the previous completion of a college course; William Carlos Williams got into the Pennsylvania Medical School without a bachelor's degree and Louis D. Brandeis also lacked that qualification when he entered the Harvard Law School.

The array of opportunities through apprenticeship and schooling was amplest in variety in the largest cities. The magnetic pull the metropolis exerted upon youth from the country owed some of its force to the options it offered for finding a place, regardless of tracks.

Education in, rather than away from the world, involved rather than isolated the student who observed numerous models of behavior and felt the influence of classmates and playmates, of employers and teachers, of fellow travelers on the trolley or subway and fellow workers in the shop, as well as of parents. Those who lived at home while they learned maintained a continuing relationship with the family and with neighbors, extending thus the anxieties and tensions as well as the dependence of adolescence. Coming back from the classroom or job the boys and girls picked up the continuity of an earlier life and felt some measure of the former obligations and discipline. Those who arrived from elsewhere and lived in lodging houses missed that sense of connection unless they planted themselves in a family or established relations through church, Y or club. Whether they lived with their parents or not, youths could earn while they learned, could study part-time at their own pace or drop and resume their schooling as circumstances dictated. They were in the world.

For all such people school was just one aspect of life, not the whole of it. No matter how boys and girls performed for the teacher they found satisfactions and esteemed themselves as persons in a round of activities entirely unconnected with the classroom or even with the institution of which it was a part.

They shared the life, the pleasures and the pains of other urban youth. The play of the sandlot or the street, the roles a person could perform in the gang or the club, the freedom of the loner to walk and dream by himself offered each individual multifarious opportunities to evolve his own personality and to draw a circle of friends that eased dependence on the family. Without conscious plan too the city generated outlets for the emotions of the young. It cost nothing to stroll in the park or listen to the band concerts; and a nickel or dime would buy the pictures and stories of the newspapers, a daring novel, admission to the show — vaudeville, theater, movies, and the burlygirlicue. To belong to a group — church or club — brought opportunities to act or sing or dance, to be on or for a team, to take excursions on the river, to march in or cheer a parade. The occasions were not frequent, but they were exciting enough in anticipation, in actuality and in recollection to justify postponement of the gratification of the sexual impulses that stirred boys and girls growing toward adulthood.

They did not however escape the problems of family

life. Far from it. The physical difficulties — lack of space and privacy in urban homes, the daily crush of public transportation, the summer heat and winter cold in close but drafty quarters — kept tempers on edge. Straitened incomes called for awkward decisions on every expenditure — who contributed to the rent, the new coat, the brother's school book. Most difficult, though least readily perceived, was the pressure toward adjusting personal and familial goals — what job the youth took, how long he stayed in school, who his friends were and whom he married concerned him and yet also all the other members of the household so that to act alone was callous, to consult all, frustrating. Often bitterness flavored the satisfactions of growing up in the city.

Life on the sidewalks of New York or Chicago was dangerous. It led some to unremitting poverty, to the saloon and to vice or crime and others to the exhausting routines of purposelessness. Young women alone in the city had the additional problem, as Sister Carrie discovered, of weighing the drabness of virtue against the flash — if only momentary — of temptation in the bar or dance hall. Those who failed were brothers and sisters of those who found a way to make something of themselves and achieved contentment. No retrospective calculus will strike the balance of how many earned happiness and how intensely. But whatever their ultimate destiny, young people growing up under these circumstances learned that they did not exist in isolation. Each knew that he was one — separate, yes — but one among many who were also separate and that the need for living with others called for both the exercise and the occasional renunciation of the will. Their experience caused a thoughtful Harvard dean in 1893 to wonder whether the isolation of well-to-do students was not a mistake, whether boys would not do better *to meet city life by day and meet every night the counteracting influence of their own homes,* rather than live cloistered and apart.

Aspirations for self-improvement, as earlier, led some boys and girls not to the city and not directly to experience but to a rural institute devoted to practical training for a vocation. The emphasis on agriculture dictated the location of some schools; others developed under the wing of expanding state universities. The number and variety of opportunities for such learning grew steadily after 1870.

No group had greater need of skills than the Negroes, 90 per cent of whom still lived in the rural South on the eve of the First World War. There the level of education for all youth was so low as to leave little hope that existing institutions could cope with the problems of the freedmen; and segregation by law extinguished any expectation that the situation would improve. Booker T. Washington's experience at Hampton convinced him that black youth above all required the training to help them rise above the hopeless poverty that was the heritage of generations of slavery. They had to cast down their buckets where they were and learn to add value to their labor as farmers, mechanics and teachers. That was the mission of Tuskegee, which he founded in 1881.

At Tuskegee as at Hampton, the focus of concern was on the average student; the genius could take care of himself elsewhere. Learning was by doing and education covered the whole range of life, aiming to form good habits, to encourage industry and thrift and to develop *intelligent practice and self-restraint* in respect to all things.

Skill and drill would make both money and men. Although Washington's views — and his position of personal power — met increasingly bitter criticism after 1900, they corresponded to the aspirations of the great mass of southern colored men and women and retained their influence until 1930. For hundreds, as for Mary McLeod Bethune, the opportunity to leave home for some rustic institute or seminary was a call *to be an Instrument of the Lord, to help my people rise.*

The critics who suspected that the kind of training Tuskegee offered condemned the Negro to permanent inferiority did not understand that other groups also felt the same need. Indians who wanted to learn the ways of the white man — how to build a house, to make boots and shoes, to do blacksmith work and to farm — persuaded Lieutenant R. H. Pratt that they could be educated in useful trades away from their native environment. He was instrumental in establishing a school at Carlisle Barracks in Pennsylvania which taught boys the principal mechanical arts and farming, and girls, cooking, sewing, laundry and housework. An array of establishments at Doylestown, Pennsylvania, and elsewhere too assisted immigrants toward the same goals.

Young men and women of every ethnic background continued to seek training in the mechanical, agricultural and technical arts in advanced institutions specifically set up for the purpose. They flocked to the land-grant colleges founded under the terms of the Morrill Act. These institutions — segregated in the South, open to all elsewhere — drew their funds from the federal government but were each subject to state authority with the result that each developed a character of its own. Each devoted some attention to agriculture but prospective farmers were almost everywhere a minority among the students, for the colleges early yielded to the temptation to emphasize engineering and other mechanical skills as far as the terms of the law permitted. In some places the mandate was broad enough to encompass many different activities — forestry, journalism, education, engineering, nursing, dairy husbandry, among others. In addition, older establishments, public and private, still prepared youths for specific careers; George C. Marshall emerged from the Virginia Military Institute a soldier, his brother, a chemist. William E. Dodd, raw off a back-country farm, started his schooling late and was already twenty-one when he applied for admission to the University of North Carolina. Turned down for social and intellectual deficiencies, he got into Virginia Agricultural and Mechanical College and there began a career in education.

Students away from home and isolated in detached communities faced some of the problems of the college boys of an earlier generation. They sometimes congregated in dormitories but more generally spread out in boarding houses and clumsily tried to create their own social resources. The want of things to do in a small town and the narrow boundaries of their world often left excess energy unused and the potential for personal growth unrealized. Their course was shorter than that in liberal arts and led neither to the same degree nor to the same esteem.

But they had a purpose. The students at A. & M. or State or Tuskegee or Detroit Teachers came in search of specific skills connected with their future careers. They needed little supervision. Acquisition of the knowledge of how to perform was itself a discipline associated as it was with each individual's work when he entered the world.

Severe penalties awaited those who did not behave. Sixteen-year-old Harlan Fiske Stone, bent on being a farmer, entered Massachusetts Agricultural College in 1888. Studies were not hard but he had trouble achieving the mastery of himself that the required military drill and marching in formation were supposed to impart. A chapel brawl in 1890 led to his expulsion.

Young men and women who could not risk the loss of their chances learned in such schools the same lesson that others learned at home, in the shops and in the streets — the utility of habits of obedience, self-denial and self-restraint as a preparation for life. Old John D. Rockefeller knew what he was talking about when he cautioned young men that too easy indulgence in good cheer and good fellowship could lead to their *downfall.*

The wrong tracks to which modest circumstances consigned most young Americans still opened opportunities to some and occasionally led to riches or distinguished achievement. The one building of a prairie land-grant college was a beacon light to the farm boy whose only preparation had come from an old one-eyed man who taught a little arithmetic and grammar in an abandoned store building; and the immigrant youth who fought his way up from the dense public high school found not only opportunity but also cultural liberation in the institute that equipped him with skill. These students knew that the liberal arts college provided some youths with another way to leave home which enjoyed influence far beyond the small number who traversed it, an influence derived from its place in American culture and American society. But the existence of that other track along which the privileged minority moved in ease and luxury toward gold-coast splendor rarely stirred pangs of envy among the majority occupied in their own affairs — any more than did the picture of the University Club in the *Journal,* passed around among the men at Tom Foley's saloon.

On the Right Track

When Harlan Stone's angry father finally relented, he allowed his wayward son to enroll in Amherst College, in the class of 1894. The course of study there would not fit the lad for any specific vocation. But it would set him upon a track that increasingly seemed right.

Between 1870 and 1930 the number of parents and children who followed that course grew substantially. Enrollment in institutions of higher education soared from 52,000 at the earlier date to more than 1,100,000 at the later one. The numbers are neither exact nor precisely comparable. But certainly there were more colleges in existence and they were larger, less fragile and less poverty-stricken than formerly.

Part of the expansion was the simple product of exuberant boosterism; promoters were sometimes so eager to make *the dirt of learning fly and get the structure up* that they left the question of purpose for later. Their frenetic activity reflected, though often without awareness, the high value that Americans now placed upon possession of the bachelor's degree.

An immense number of colleges awarded the diploma in 1930 — well over a thousand of them, some public, others private, some old, others new, some nominally sectarian, others nominally secular, some vocational in origin, others always liberal arts in orientation. Yet although the measure of success varied widely, all struggled to turn out a common product, the college man.

Stone's career was exemplary. Meekness was by no means the end result of his earlier expulsion. He plunged into trouble at Amherst too, where he led the campaign against compulsory chapel and where he gained prominence in battle with the president over student government. A fraternity member who played football, he won election as class president and at commencement was voted *most likely to succeed.* At what? Well, that was not clear. Nor was it very important. His best subjects were chemistry, biology and physics; but his classmates were not predicting for him a career as a distinguished scientist. Their ballots reflected an imprecise but firm judgment about traits of personality shown in the whole round of activities that seemed an index to the future ability to perform. After earning the B.A., Stone taught school and earned the funds to carry him through Columbia Law School, where Amherst connections helped. Then, surely enough, he found a place in the outstanding firm of Sullivan and Cromwell. Dwight Morrow, one year behind Stone at Amherst, followed an almost identical path to Reed, Simpson, Thacher & Barnum. By contrast, John Calvin Coolidge in Morrow's class, who was a *Barbarian* unpledged by a fraternity, settled for reading law in a local Northampton office.

The college was the crucial switching point on the right track both because it gave access to desirable careers and because it completed the youth's separation from the family.

The best professional schools in the United States, unlike those in Europe, were by now postgraduate and usually admitted applicants on the basis of undergraduate records. Talent still counted enough to earn cooption for some brilliant outsiders. Felix Frankfurter, for instance, gained admission to the Harvard Law School in 1903 and went on to teach there. But the advantage lay with the men from the good colleges — all the way. Others surmounted the obstacles to achievement only by unquestionable excellence; and even so, no Frankfurter found a place with a prestigious firm.

The exceptional value of degrees from Harvard, Yale, Princeton and a few of their rivals increased the enrollments at those institutions and enabled them to choose among applicants. No longer did the presidents each fall anxiously count the arriving freshmen and willingly waive or qualify admission requirements. Entry to the best colleges was a prize and the *abjectly servile* secondary schools set themselves to preparing their graduates for the competition.

The academies of necessity turned into prep schools, offering favored youths an advantage in the race. to a desirable college. The rise of the free public high school had been draining away their students and had forced many to close; the new role saved those agile and candid enough to adopt it. Indeed, demands for college preparation added to the number of select private schools. Groton, established by Endicott Peabody in 1885, and a few institutions of the same sort, promised the would-be American aristocracy an upbringing similar to that which little English gentlemen received at Rugby and Eton — proper behavior, solid studies and the intellectual and moral training to serve as the nation's leaders. Andover, which began to recover from its decline only after 1907, stressed academic performance. Military academies tried to keep under control such boys as Lincoln Steffens, who was already a hard drinker at fifteen. But all in the end aimed to cram enough into their products to move them along the proper track.

The high schools followed the fashion. A Committee of Ten under Charles W. Eliot appointed by the National Education Association in 1892 outlined the desired course of study and the college boards established in 1900 provided the mechanism for testing it.

The college was thus decisive. It selected the raw materials from the lower schools, processed and graded them, and then passed them on for vocational finishing. For aspiring parents and children it had become the only acceptable channel for leaving home.

Furthermore, the college experience now acquired a precise significance for the age group it served. The four years after eighteen were a period of preparation before arriving at a decision about future vocation. Education, explained the father in a story, *knocked all the vagueness out of a young chap*. This mountain ridge on the way to adulthood — an interval without precise purpose — was passed more equably away from than at home. In 1907, a president noted that rich parents sent their sons to college as in summers they sent them to the seashore or to the mountains, that is, as a stage of separation. Aspiring parents who were not wealthy also considered it their duty, by rigid economy, to give their sons what they themselves never had, a college education. Such offspring, George Santayana observed, were often compassionately fond of their families, and home was all the more sacred to them in that they were seldom there.

In college a man acquired not technical or professional

competence, but culture, command of a pattern of manners and a body of knowledge — generally classical in antecedents — which since the eighteenth century had been the mark of distinction of the gentlemanly elite. The role of the college as custodian of culture gained strength, after 1870, from English and German influences and from the incorporation of science, with all its prestige, into the roster of subjects taught. The function of the college was to *draw out, stimulate, and strengthen the intellectual powers,* cultivate *taste and sensibility for the finest art and literature* and impart a *thoroughly scientific acquaintance* with all the branches of learning. By *breathing the atmosphere of culture,* the student became a *whole man,* fit for the battle of life.

Culture replaced religion as the guide to thought, behavior and emotion. The battle over evolution led to an adjustment which plastered together professions of loyalty to the old morality and the objective knowledge of the new science. The American universities did not become anti-religious or unchristian; and there was still much concern for the teaching of ethics, the top-work of man's structure. But, except for the surviving sectarian institutions, the college, though required by public opinion to have religion in a general way, somehow was nevertheless forbidden to have it in any particular way. Instead the college tried to *incorporate the spirit of the times in the spirit of the fathers* by producing the type of man that the world most needed, *the cultured citizen in command of scientific methods.*

To attain that goal in the United States where things intellectual had characteristically remained apart from the rough business and passions of life, the college had to resist the prevailing tendencies toward materialism and mercantile morality; it took into its keeping many of the most susceptible and most promising of the nation's youth, to impart to them *better tastes, higher aims, and, above all, to teach them to despise all sorts of shams.* Charles Eliot Norton warned young men against hastening on to professions without first thus arming themselves as undergraduates.

The would-be aristocrats of the gilded age, who sought social recognition through the possession of culture, regarded the proper college as an institution to validate their claim to superiority. Their support enriched endowments and gave prestige and power to the few leading schools which shaped the styles for the whole country. But American society was too fluid to permit the wealthy permanently to dominate the culture. Every mom in the western hick town who sent her son off to college had visions of him returning *in an English ulster and a velour hat, carrying a sleek bag — very dignified, a bit pompous and yet extremely gracious, sweeping her into his arms with the exclamation, "Little Mother!" then sitting down to outline to her the colossal schemes of his big business in the East.*

Negroes, Catholics and Jews, who were victims of prejudice and discrimination, had a hard time of it but nevertheless some among them also valued the chance to get on the right track. Eighteen-year-old Herbert H. Lehman, who came to Williams in 1895, insecure and worried about his status, tried to join every available club — drama, orchestra, chess, newspaper, magazine, debating, athletics. He knew better than to aim for a fraternity but as a sophomore he became assistant manager of the track team and as a junior, the first Jewish manager of the Gargoyle Society. Henry O. Flipper, a colored cadet, met greater frustrations in his eagerness to conform at West Point. At Harvard, William Lewis and W. E. B. DuBois did well at open activities but faced a blank wall in social encounters; and that, Joseph P. Kennedy believed, was also the bitter experience of an Irish Catholic, although he may have exaggerated.

The increase in the number of colleges and their success in imitating one another offset the discriminatory practices of the most sought-after schools. Restriction of higher education to the rich, proclaimed President James B. Angell of Michigan, was hateful, repugnant to natural instincts, calamitous to learning and to the people, unrepublican, undemocratic and unchristian. Every young man and woman at eighteen could pursue culture and attain the distinction conveyed by the bachelor's degree.

The situation of the college at the point of access to the right career track gave it the power to expand remorselessly despite many-pronged attacks by outsiders. Critics who insisted that all forms of expression be native, manly and down-to-earth reacted with instinctive aversion to institutions in the East, which they considered but an extension of Europe, and to gentility, which they considered but another name for effete, dudish snobbery. Suspicion of the foreign, aristocratic influences gained force from the Populist strain, not unmixed with envy, that entered the thinking of professors like V. L. Parrington, J. Allen Smith or Thorstein Veblen, as well as from the writers, Mark Twain to Theodore Dreiser, who challenged conventional academic standards. The college's dedication to its own definition of culture also ran counter to the century-old conviction that education had to be immediately useful and practical, a conviction expressed in the Morrill Act, the new institutes of technology and the state universities.

Yet imitation of the eastern colleges insidiously altered the purest intentions. President Andrew D. White of Cornell placed the emphasis just a little differently from his principal benefactor — on the training of the captains in the army of industry rather than of the rank and file. Soon after Ezra Cornell's death in 1874, Ithaca became another haven of the children of the rich, although never limited to them.

The state universities also shifted their aims to the training of distinguished leaders rather than of plain farmers or mechanics. When the Illinois Industrial University in 1885 changed its name to the University of Illinois, it was well on the way to becoming a *dude factory* in the opinion of its critics. Deans and presidents, of course, assured grumbling legislators that the public funds thus expended would teach youth to prefer the farm to the city. But these institutions, like the older colleges, recruited their students from families which did not want their offspring to remain on the farm. However strong the rural agrarian ideal remained, higher education was an avenue upward into the professions or business; and increasingly Ann Arbor and Iowa City promised to deliver the same skills and polish — the same evidences of culture — that Cambridge or Princeton did; and students in the practical, vocational courses were low in campus esteem compared with those in the arts. In time, the state universities acquitted themselves of their debt to the taxpaying farmers, less by course instruction for youth than by the services of associated agricultural stations made possible by the Hatch Act of

1887, by the spread of extension work, and by the supply of a pool of experts and a body of expertise useful to progressives in government. Despite the association of all these functions in a single institution, the central educational service the state university performed came more and more to approximate that of the old liberal arts college.

The function of the college as custodian of culture also affected its receptivity to science. The day of the learned amateur was all but over; mastery of a subject now called for highly technical skills, for access to extensive libraries and laboratories, and for close communication with peers throughout the world. Science developed an organization by disciplines, set up internal standards for the accreditation of practitioners and for the validation of results, and claimed recognition of its competence by society at large.

Scholarship did not however become an activity of autonomous academies, museums, technical schools, institutes or state agencies, as had been the earlier American expectation. An altogether new kind of setting seemed necessary to its promoters. Daniel C. Gilman, first at Berkeley and then at Johns Hopkins, and William Rainey Harper at Chicago each sought to create an agency *to advance the arts and sciences and train young men as scholars for all the intellectual callings of life*. The center of research and investigation into all the problems of the age would expose error and reveal truth, a law unto itself, *indifferent alike to plaudits or reproaches* and divorced from considerations of immediate utility.

The term applied to the new institutions was "university," in imitation of their German, but not of their American, predecessors. Walter Hines Page, one of the first Johns Hopkins fellows, envisioned himself carrying a torch of learning through life, not engaged in disciplining unruly and uninterested youth, often the preponderant task of the old-time college. The mere suggestion that the chemist John U. Nef offer a general course for non-scientists in 1894 at Chicago evoked a threat of resignation. The founders of the new institutions determined decisively to remove the scientific researchers from undergraduate instruction. It was essential to maintain a clear distinction between *collegiate* and *university* work. The old colleges would have to turn into universities of the new sort, or sink to the level of secondary schools, or lose all reason for existence.

However logical that clear-cut resolution seemed in anticipation, it was not implemented. Instead, undergraduate instruction almost everywhere remained intertwined with the scholarly activities of the university. This outcome was partly the result of the situation of the state institutions which grew not selectively but through the agglomeration of functions and therefore simply thrust graduate teaching upon the same faculty already responsible for undergraduates. The university — private as well as public — became a holding company incorporating a variety of institutes and faculties, some of which had formerly been separate, some of which still received students directly from high school, and some of which had only remote links to other units in the conglomerate. But the central element with which the whole was identified was the undergraduate college.

The outcome also represented the triumph of the concept of the university-college as custodian of culture.

Charles W. Eliot, among others, wished higher education to bring together the future leaders of society and the best attainable instruction in those studies which increased knowledge, elevated the level of intellectual life, and secured the moral improvement of the community. Graduate research, ever refining and redefining the correct answers to the problems of art, literature, the social order and the material world, would certify to the college students the valid views of all the issues they would later face.

The association between the general culture communicated in the college and the scholarship pursued in the university was so compelling — attractive to faculties and persuasive to alumni and donors — that Johns Hopkins, Clark, Stanford and Chicago, which began with the opposite intentions, found themselves pulled in the same direction. Meanwhile parents who mistrusted the consequences of such massive expansion and who believed that undergraduate work was better in a small, rural college than in a great cosmopolitan university, sent their sons to Amherst, Dartmouth, Oberlin or Wabash. But even the institutions which prided themselves on their intimate liberal arts character were transformed by the influence of the universities from which they increasingly drew their teaching staffs.

The role of the college as custodian of culture influenced the schools formed to serve women, Negroes and Catholics, who were the victims of exclusion or discrimination in many existing institutions.

There was no European counterpart of the separate female colleges such as appeared in the United States after the Civil War. Vassar, Smith, Radcliffe, Wellesley, Mills, and Bryn Mawr did not meet a purely academic need;

coeducation in many state and private universities offered ample opportunity to those who sought vocations. Nor did the segregated ladies' college appear in response to arguments for the desirability of special instruction in hygiene or physiology directed toward *matrimony and motherhood* rather than *independence and self-support;* numerous seminaries and finishing schools already offered such training. Scholarly women like Maria Mitchell and Martha Carey Thomas regarded the development of separate women's colleges as regrettable though inevitable because the primary impulse in the establishment of these institutions was the desire to provide women with a counterpart of the social and cultural life of Harvard, Yale or Amherst.

Young ladies could not penetrate those exclusively masculine premises. Nor were they full and equal participants in the curricular or extracurricular activities of the coeducational schools which generally shunted them to secondary roles even in literary and cultural organizations. In the arrangement of the social calender and in joint affairs the sororities invariably followed the lead of the fraternities.

Yet the considerations which swayed girls in the choice of a college were not unlike those that influenced boys. The intellectually minded of both sexes had clear cultural and even scholarly goals; and some considered the degree an aid toward teaching and toward professional careers. But the specific selection of a campus on which to live turned about vaguer considerations, not vocational or even academic in character — where high school chums registered, the desire to make Pi Omega or Pi Delta, the quality of the promised experience outside the classroom, in sum, *the spirit of the place.*

Smith, Wellesley, Radcliffe, and Barnard each, though in different ways, provided women an equivalent of the social life normal to college men. The prospects of marriage exempted most girls from the obligation to strive for success. But they, like boys, said President Alice Freeman Palmer of Wellesley, had a right to the unequaled opportunities the campus offered *merely for good times, for romance, for society*. They had a right, that is, to May Day fêtes, Elizabethan dances and literary societies and to *the little contraction of the heart, the sudden hot tightening of the eyelids, the confused, excited desire to be worthy of the admiration* bestowed on the basketball team. *Lots of the girls here have boys' nicknames,* wrote a Bryn Mawr freshman in 1899 who wanted awfully to be called Dick or Jack but had to settle for Henry because so many sophs and juniors had preempted the more desirable identities. A dandy Cornell flag consoled her. *It's a beaut. Billy has a Yale one over her door. I wish we knew some one in Harvard.*

Wealthy parents who at first thought it preposterous to send off a girl who did not have her own living to make increasingly enrolled their daughters in college, as they did their sons, in the interest of cultural, social and intellectual refinement.

The trickle of colored young men and women who passed through the northern colleges and universities did not satisfy the needs of Negroes who wished to go beyond the practical training of Hampton or Tuskegee. President Horace Bumstead of Atlanta denied that the race was homogeneous and hoped to educate an elite which could make the masses rise by proxy; and W. E. B. DuBois's call for the training of the talented tenth had the same intent. Yet only a few small colleges in the South, like Berea in Kentucky, offered opportunities to Negroes. The establishment of segregation by law extinguished any expectation that the situation might change for the better. After the turn of the century, the spread of racist doctrines northward actually lessened the prospects for the higher education of colored youth. Most could work toward degrees only in separate colleges, some private, others created by the states in order to preserve the lily-white character of existing institutions. The Negro colleges made persistent efforts to follow the model of curricular and extracurricular activity accepted as normal in the United States. Starved for funds, they labored under heartbreaking difficulties to provide their students with liberal and professional educations. Measured by the usual academic standards, the results were meager; yet there was ordinarily no alternative for the ill-prepared, poverty-stricken products of segregated elementary and secondary schools. Nevertheless at Fisk, DuBois studied Latin, Greek and philosophy as if he had been at Harvard and thus kept alive aspirations to do more than manual labor. Wilberforce offered Mary Church Terrell her first opportunity to teach; and Howard gave Zora Neale Hurston an escape from domestic service.

Catholics met no such formal barriers to college admission as did women or Negroes. Indeed, their presence was rather welcome as a means of converting or Americanizing the members of what many still regarded as a foreign faith. Catholic students, however, were not fully accepted in college life and parents and pastors suspected that the secular university, and certainly the sectarian one, was a menace to faith. Some social separateness was a self-imposed safeguard against that danger.

The fears, both of rejection and conversion, encouraged the spread of a Catholic system of higher education which aimed not only to recruit potential seminarians but also to supply an acceptable environment for the lay leaders of the future. Operating under the supervision of the clergy, these colleges taught without departing from orthodox doctrine and trained the young men and women who passed through them in the behavior appropriate to their faith. Nevertheless, the common American collegiate model exerted some pressure upon the Catholic schools. The authority of science raised the thorny issues of modernism. There was a gradual shift to the elective system. Student life in social organization, residences, intercollegiate athletics and fashions acquired features similar to those of the secular universities.

There remained exceedingly important differences among American institutions of higher education. Regional variations were striking as were the distinctive characteristics of the old schools with colonial origins, of the great state universities, of the small sectarian colleges, of institutions with numerous commuting students, and of those with a specialized clientele of Negroes, Catholics or women. Yet there were also significant similarities among all these types. Despite the tremendous diversity in origin, control, and ostensible purpose, the common elements were more consequential. This great variety of institutions, whatever else they did, sooner or later aimed to produce a single product — the college man, his personality rounded by contact with culture, and like Harlan Stone on the right track to success.

College Days

The college endowed its students with the cultural equipment that would distinguish them in the future not so much through formal courses as through participation in the way of life of a community. The model college was therefore residential; the experience was incomplete if it did not take the student away from home. Administrators still shied away from the responsibility of managing dormitories, but as in the past had to take on the burden, for the supply of housing was otherwise inadequate.

Some students lodged in boarding houses, but the general preference was for fraternities, which grew rapidly because they offered their members a large measure of self-government and because they recognized the actual differences in background, interests and tastes among the students. Like the secret societies in some places, or the Harvard and Yale clubs with their links to Boston and New York society, the fraternities everywhere were selective and exclusive as the college as a whole was not; and they provided a means for organizing within the university autonomous subgroups of young men and women drawn from the same station in life and made mutually agreeable by similarity of past associations and experiences.

In the pleasant interlude of independence that the college bestowed before youths settled down into the routine of affairs, they sowed their wild oats or instructed themselves, or they educated one another after their own fashions. The train to New Haven carried Stover to *man's estate and man's freedom.* He was about to become *his own master at last,* at liberty to choose his own way through *that strange guarded mystery — life.*

Stover's friends romped and made fun, had their private brainstorms like *little supermen* in a haphazard existence without much form other than that which was self-created. Some were active in literary and debating societies; others staffed the newspapers and periodicals. A few earnest or ambitious types took part in politics, in reform, in socialist clubs, or in the settlement houses. Others responded to the exhortations of Dwight L. Moody. But by and large, activity focused within the campus rather than spread out to the world about it, and the tone was never too serious but rather playful, even in John Reed who wished to shake the earth.

The rules left a good deal of freedom within which individuals could learn what they liked, either from one another or from their teachers. A sympathetic dean at Yale encouraged Stephen Benét to go on with poetry and it was not difficult for aspiring writers anywhere to find advice and assistance from members of the faculty. William James and his colleagues in the Harvard philosophy department attracted a sizable following both among young people professionally interested in the subject and among those who simply hoped to advance their personal understanding of life. And gifted teachers everywhere — in geology or history, fine arts or economics — left a permanent impress upon the minds of interested pupils.

Although some administrators desired to eliminate special students by stiff entrance requirements, the college generally offered enough latitude to allow almost every type to go his own way, so that off-beat characters — Robert Frost or Margaret Bourke-White, for instance — could drop in for a year and find what they wanted. But the college was also consciously a whole community — *one family, socially considered,* as William Rainey Harper put it — and it made an effort to express its wholeness physically, intellectually and ceremoniously. The plant therefore acquired a novel significance. Endowments were now sufficiently large so that considerations of economy no longer restrained the builders. Architecture acquired an aesthetic and social purpose; the halls and quadrangles — preferably Gothic or Georgian — were to stand away from the structures in which other men did their work and, like churches, were to leave an impression of a society apart, with values and loyalties of its own.

Other features of college life also fixed upon students the awareness that they were members of a distinctive community, in which a sense of common interest and common emotion subdued all latent antipathies. *Jolly youths, arms linked and bawling out a cheery song* — that was the romantic impression Eugene Gant gained from his boyish reading. The class of entry remained the individual's basic identifying unit; the regulations sought to keep the freshmen together in order to establish a unifying spirit, however much they might divide later. The harbor was full of splendid yachts in 1911 when Averell Harriman rowed against Harvard and his mother came down on the *Sultana* and his sister on the *Electra*. Yale lost. It did not matter. The race was one of the social events that studded the year, involving parents and alumni and strengthening the impression of institutional permanence. Through hazing and initiation rituals one undergraduate generation imposed upon another a code of conduct which sometimes also governed examinations and classwork. The code rested on the boy's *honor as a gentleman* or the girl's quality as a lady and thus had vaguely chivalric antecedents. Yet it was not snobbish.

The student brought up always to dine in a dinner coat was cautioned that he might have for his table companions men who had *never owned a dress coat* and had no immediate prospect of needing one. The boys and girls who worked their way through even at menial tasks like waiting on table deserved respect for their display of independence. If college life produced a tendency to uniformity in fashions of clothing, tastes and behavior, as Santayana perceived, it also established an order that the otherwise unruly youths imposed on themselves.

Imperceptibly, acceptance of that order eased the ancient problem of discipline. The quasi-parental oversight of an earlier period was neither to the taste of faculties composed of men with scholarly interests nor in accord with the wishes of undergraduates. Freedom was *the native air and vital breath of student life.* Yet picked youths and maidens protected from the necessities of self-support, exempted from competition, from business and social restraint, could not simply be left free to follow their own wills, for impulses repressed at home might now erupt excessively and aggressively. But a code voluntarily accepted by the students made the choice between chaos and bondage unnecessary. Harvard boasted that it subjected its men to the severe test of making them at once masters of their own lives. Some failed as did William Prescott Frost, a boy from a marginal family who acquired in Cambridge a ruinous taste for poker, whiskey and brothels. But the effect of personal responsibility in developing moral character was, the university believed, unquestionably beneficial to a great majority. Parents who wished their sons constrained to virtue by external observances and formal penalties were told to send them elsewhere.

In practice, not even Harvard was as permissive as it made out; and most institutions insisted that students needed some sort of oversight away from home. Instructors were not hired simply to teach Latin or mathematics, but also to kindle spiritual aspirations and regulate the conduct of the young men and women under them. Presidents certainly kept that dual role in mind in making appointments. Furthermore, fathers continued to believe that the discipline they themselves could not apply ought — though benevolently — to be administered by the faculty. Above all, since students were not a privileged class beyond criminal prosecution, punishment by the college generally fended off more severe action by the civic authorities.

Humor helped dull the edge of conflict; nothing was really that important or decisive, as the self-mockery of the *Lampoon* and its counterparts made clear. The undergraduates who did not deceive themselves could find a laugh, if nothing else, in the life about them. The bogus commencement program of a midwestern college compared the graduates to a drove of hogs crammed with the corn of knowledge and the slop of accomplishment. *Here they stand before you — sleek and well fed: their keepers ready to palm them off for good stock on an unsuspecting public, and to dispose of them clad in the skin of a sheep to make you imagine they are as innocent as lambs.*

Athletics also helped dissolve potential resentment. For many students after 1870 the playing field became the center of college life. Certainly this was the impression the lads who read about Stover or Merriwell brought to Yale, or even to *Good Old Siwash*. Intercollegiate football gained steadily in prominence despite distasteful professionalism already evident in the 1890's and despite a temporary loss of esteem after the heavy toll of injuries in 1905.

The initial impetus to athletic programs had come from the desire to provide a harmless means of expending youthful energies; and some presidents continued to believe that a *thorough fatiguing* of the body kept students out of trouble. In addition competitive team sports developed qualities important to advocates of the strenuous life; rough play, President Theodore Roosevelt explained, prevented the colleges from turning out mollycoddles instead of men. Football tempered character and diminished drinking; it demonstrated the usefulness of both cooperation and individualism; *it taught us hard endurance and fairness — what it meant to be men.* Indeed, its numerous virtues seemed to the president of Williams in 1908 well on the way toward obliterating the difference between a college and an institute of physical culture.

Young ladies also learned the lessons of hard endurance and fairness from basketball; or at least they thought so, though sometimes in a tone of gentle self-mockery. In a contest of 1900, the girls' newspaper reported, a Barnard center *seized the skirt of a Bryn Mawr forward, and though dragged across the field, pluckily held on till carried off on a stretcher.* In the second half one of the Quaker Queens, gowned like her teammates in yellow velveteen skirt, white sash and broad lace collar, burst into tears at the discovery of a rip in her costume, but was comforted by making a goal. When the score was 22–0, everyone was so tired and hot that they agreed amicably to stop playing.

The athletic contest was a great ritual event which

drew together students and alumni and, in the zest of the effort to beat the other side, developed a consciousness of group identity. The sacrifices of the selfless sufferers straining to do or die for the sake of all took hold of the emotions and made internal distinctions relatively unimportant. On the football field, real men recognized each other's prowess, formed true friendships, and showed their essential character. Here was an occasion for a display of loyalty akin to patriotism. The massed crowds in the stadium, the show of winning colors, the songs, were evidences of an attachment to the college which it was not ludicrous to juxtapose with that to God and country. Young men, here away from home, discovered themselves as sons of an alma mater.

Harold Lloyd's *The Freshman,* the popular fiction of the period — of which Charles M. Flandrau's *Diary of a Freshman* and Owen Wister's *Philosophy 4* were representative — and the reminiscences and biographies of the graduates of these years all emphasized the importance of immersion in the activities of a self-contained community. The bookish types who devoted themselves exclusively to their studies missed the chief value ascribed to the experience.

The formal curriculum was far less significant in the eyes of the student than in those of the faculty. Year by year the size of the catalogue grew — at Princeton it trebled in the decade of the 1870's and that institution was not as subject to Teutonic influences as others. But no ordering principle governed the relationship of various offerings to one another.

The hope that the lecture system would transform the teacher from a drillmaster into a creative scholar depended upon giving the professor enough latitude to present a subject he knew thoroughly and yet relieving him of students for whom attendance was an unwelcome task. The solution, popularized as the elective system, clearly made scholarship possible among college teachers. But its proponents also argued that it was beneficial to the pupils. The attempt to give mental discipline by studies which the mind did not desire was as unwise as to give physical nourishment by food the body did not desire, President White of Cornell had explained in 1866. A college man, President Eliot pointed out a little later, knew what he liked best and therefore would find his own way to *happy, enthusiastic work* through the free play of *natural preferences and inborn aptitudes.*

Despite the high praise heaped on the new elective system, few institutions adopted it without qualification. Compromises attained by mediating among the claims of contending departments set up requirements for majors and minors and for survey courses to guarantee that *no window into the scientific palace of delight was darkened for the man of culture.* Some faculty members also envied Oxford and Cambridge where, they believed, daily social intercourse between teachers and students provided an ideal context for instruction.

In the United States, however, the social and the academic aspects of college were separate, though related; and most students preferred it that way. They insisted on respect of the fine line separating instructor from instructed and resented intrusions by older men seeking to recapture a lost youth. The students also accepted the fact that knowledge was divided into segments called courses, a quota of which was the price of four years of relative freedom. Tutoring schools and purchased trots or ponies eased the boredom or pain of compulsory attendance at class and of prescribed reading and examinations. Meanwhile the undergraduate with genuine intellectual interests browsed where he wished with a loose tether.

The modest role of the faculty members was to display in their lives and work the attributes instructive to their charges. Occasional professors won popularity by their eccentricities or performing skills. More generally, the prestige of scholarship earned the "prof" the respect, or at least the tolerance of the undergraduates, so that he became part of the good old days later to be recalled with affection and amusement. Boys in small rural schools still hid his buggy or hanged him in effigy but usually college sentiment condemned as *unmanly and indecent* the tricks of the past, such as locking an instructor in his room or throwing water upon him, stealing his swallowtails, upsetting his chair in recitation or tripping him up outside. The faculty seemed to the student body like clergymen without a church, woodenly sober and slim as their pay, droning away about some forgotten truth but maintaining the standards of virtue and honor in a money-getting nation. Their willingness to devote themselves to the truth which made them content with less remuneration than could be obtained in ordinary business was evidence of their disinterested defense of the modern community against its own material prosperity. They pursued their studies primarily for the sake of pure learning and not for a livelihood and were therefore the appropriate custodians of the nation's culture and of its youth.

Faith in its scholarly temper gained the university the indulgence to extend *open-handed hospitality to all truth.* Within very wide limits, it could assemble for mutual confrontation all sorts of ideas and encourage a sort of *happy insecurity* in intellectual matters. Dink Stover came to Yale for good times, good fellowship, and the opportunity to become a leader, but in adjusting to the place he not only tamed his own wild impulses but even learned about Tolstoy and Strindberg. Imperceptibly and often unintentionally he and others like him absorbed an awareness of the value of ideas, of books, of pictures and of music not so much from instruction in the classroom as from a general sense of the importance the community ascribed to them.

Scholarship did not seem incongruous with, but rather conducive to, the production of a college man, because its unifying themes gave him direction in life. At the University of Wisconsin, President Bascom met the seniors daily in a philosophy course which became living gospel for Robert La Follette — nothing metaphysical, but a continuing discussion of the rationality of human existence. At Amherst Harlan Stone heard Professor Charles Edward Garman argue that dependence on authority made people *Pharisaical* and unable to discriminate the essential from the accidental; men who did not wish to be fossilized, heartless, selfish, cynical, had to develop *self-possession and self-direction so that they could meet the obligations of life with the spirit of self-reliance.* While at the Harvard Law School, Louis D. Brandeis copied the same sort of precepts into his notebook from his favorite author, Emerson: *They can conquer who think they can; & The great man is he who in the midst of a crowd keeps with perfect sweetness the independence of solitude.* It was a reading of William James's *Will to Believe* that sent twenty-three-year-old Robert Frost off to be a special student in Cambridge.

There were strains in a system which drew together scholars, intent upon the pursuit of knowledge, and students without a clear sense of purpose, preparing to prepare for careers. External foes also attacked the university. Muckrakers criticized it as an instrument of special privilege designed to keep America capitalist, and zealots exposed it as a den of iniquity. After a local minister alleged that 2,000 whores battened on the boys in New Haven, a detective sent privately to investigate conditions at Harvard discovered details *too disgusting to publish* but fully as bad as those at Yale.

The tensions reached a crescendo in the decade after the end of the First World War. The universities then suffered because of a worldwide *lapse from culture.* The postwar breakdown of the European sources of authority to which Americans had formerly appealed for support, and the widespread questioning within the United States of accepted canons in the sciences, philosophy, the arts and literature undermined the role of the college as transmitter of durable values, tastes, beliefs and traditions. Nor did training in genteel manners hold much attraction at a time when aristocrats of ancient lineage were in exile or in debt and when the children of the putative moneyed aristocracy showed scant interest in their parents' aspirations.

Rebellion therefore became a conventional student posture. Intellectually, it took the form of a call for liberation from the entanglement of *mere traditional authority* and for the discard of the millstones of *dead formalism* in religion and in social relations. The demands were peremptory: *saccharine Sunday-school religion, blatant Fourth-of-July Patriotism, inherited class bias — all must fall.* Personal behavior expressed the same impatience with institutional restraints. The lost generation — self-proclaimed — flaunted its interest in sex and whiskey in defiance of the Puritans and of the prohibition laws and provided a compelling model for college youth. Jazz, rouge, and frank novels troubled the Dean of Women, who knew that her charges were violating the *six inches apart* edict she had issued when the shimmy dances had come down straight from the black and tan cabarets of Chicago. By the 1920's the movies had exposed boys and girls to outside influences; and the automobile had liberated joy-riding youngsters from whatever restraints operated within the campus and the town. The prof himself, having doffed the silk hat and frock coat, drove a wicked car and was an expert radio ham, although he needed a dictionary to translate his diploma.

Relaxed restraints gave troublemakers an opportunity. Albion in Michigan and St. Stephens in New York rebelled against their presidents; protests against military training at Ohio State, against compulsory chapel at Oberlin and against physical education at Howard led to major crises; and the *Harvard Crimson* launched an anti-football campaign. Underground student newspapers — *Gadfly* at Harvard, *Critic* at Oberlin, *Proletarian* at Wisconsin, *Saturday Evening Pest* at Yale, and *Tempest* at Michigan — demanded not only the right to ask critical questions but also the right to give the answers. Trustees and administrators, suspicious of their faculties and sympathetic to the boys-will-be-boys students, sought to avoid unfavorable publicity by buying off the young. Experiment became fashionable: Antioch revived the work-study idea; Alexander Meiklejohn went to Wisconsin to launch an altogether new kind of college; Brookwood in New York and Commonwealth in Arkansas were to serve labor; and undergraduates formed a free-floating Student University in Connecticut.

Furthermore, some contradictions theretofore implicit came to the surface in the 1920's. It was desirable to have all freshmen live in the same dormitories, but it was not fair to force a white to share his room with a Negro; better to provide otherwise for colored students! Some colleges could no longer admit every applicant and yet were unwilling to adopt a single standard for the selection of the future leaders of society; better to set quotas for Jews and other alien types who might not fit fully into the whole life of the institution! Awkward controversies followed.

Daydreaming rebels, campus beauty queens and flask-toting men followed a standard rather different from that of the genteel culture formerly entrusted to the custody of the college. But in 1930 there was no expectation that the college would control behavior or draw young people back to the old code, for it had long since become reconciled to the autonomy of student life within very broad limits. It exerted influence only through the creation of an environment within which the students found the proper guidelines. If they were unable or unwilling to do so, or if there were doubts about the guidelines themselves, then educators would have to reexamine the purpose of the four years thus expended, a task few wished to undertake.

The bold promoters of the 1870's had hoped to end an earlier uncertainty about purpose by shifting the orientation of higher education from traditional religion to scientific knowledge. For a time faith in a unifying culture, reaching out to the whole society through its future leaders, had made feasible an improbable junction between the socializing function of the college and the scholarly activities of the university and had provided the most fortunate youth a pleasant and advantageous way of leaving home.

Gilbert Patten never went to college, but Burt L. Standish (which was his pen name) wrote more than two hundred novels of which well over 25,000,000 copies found purchasers and unnumbered readers. Through his pages other Americans, who had never crossed a campus, came to know Harvard and Yale and absorbed a respect for the values of college life in those institutions.

DOWN THE RIVER FLOATS A CRAFT SO GREAT THAT HUNDREDS TRAVEL ON IT IN COMFORT, SOME OFF IN THEIR CORNERS READING AND WRITING, OTHERS DISPORTING THEMSELVES IN GAMES AND STILL OTHERS IDLY DRIFTING ALONG FOR THE RIDE. FROM THE STEEP BANKS THAT LINE THE SHORE, THOUSANDS OF ONLOOKERS TAKE TIME FROM THEIR OWN TOIL TO ADMIRE THE ELEGANCE OF THE VESSEL, THE SKILL OF THE HELMSMAN WHO MANAGES IT AND THE STRENGTH OF THE CREW WHO KEEP IT GOING. NO ONE, ASHORE OR AFLOAT, IS AWARE THAT THIS IS A RUDDERLESS RAFT. IT MOVES BECAUSE THE CURRENT IS POWERFUL AND THE CHANNEL DEEP. AND IT DOES NOT SINK BECAUSE THERE IS SPACE ENOUGH SO THAT THE TRAVELERS DO NOT INTERFERE WITH ONE ANOTHER.

5
THE CHALLENGES OF AN OPEN SOCIETY, 1930–1960

NOW THE THOUSANDS OF SPECTATORS TOO DECIDE TO RIDE THE RAFT. AND JUST AT THIS TIME THE CREW DETERMINES TO ESTABLISH ORDER AMONG THE PASSENGERS IN THE INTEREST OF A SWIFTER JOURNEY. THEY SPEED UNKNOWINGLY TOWARD A WHIRLPOOL AROUND THE BEND.

THE three decades after 1930 were rich in paradox. The consistent developments perceptible in retrospect were not evident from year to year, so that events appeared to unfold erratically in response to unpredictable impulses. Often what seemed to be a move in one direction proved in reality an adjustment in course toward quite a different destination.

It was difficult to distinguish long-term from short-term trends. A decade of worldwide depression in the 1930's led into a long era of active and cold war. Both the economic and military disasters had cataclysmic social effects. But the influence of those dramatic events was not as deep as that of other changes which altered the situation of youth, of the family, and of the home in the United States.

Despite the unemployment of the 1930's, this proved to be a time of sustained economic growth. Output returned to its prosperity levels by 1937 and was further stimulated by the war. The postwar depression that many observers anticipated in 1945 failed to materialize. Instead, growth continued through the 1950's, although not at a consistent rate. Expansion, involving as it did technological innovation at every stage of production and distribution, favored large, impersonally organized corporate enterprise. During the years between 1930 and 1960 the size of the bureaucracy increased at all levels of government and in many non-political agencies, including those devoted to health, social welfare and education. By contrast, the numbers occupied in agriculture and in the handicrafts declined. After 1930, still more than earlier, therefore, opportunity lay not in independent entrepreneurship but in a strategic place in some great organization — government, university, or business.

War too required the enlistment of people in large units. The struggle against the fascist powers and the disorderly situation of the world after 1945 demanded that many youths sacrifice the best part of their lives for the preservation of the state. The young men went with few illusions but also with little bitterness. The self-evident need for their services and the clarity of the cause for which they fought, together with the awareness that everyone shared the burden, stilled the inevitable gripes about the brass, the snafus and the rigidities of the military. But also, coming as it did after a decade of disorientation during the depression, the conflict with the fascist powers supplied the nation with a sense of common purpose particularly important to adolescents on the verge of choosing a career. The future, which in the 1930's had seemed a blind alley, now stretched out into a promising open. What lay beyond the hurdle of war was uncertain; but the hardships of the conflict nurtured the certainty that something was there, worth fighting for.

Economic growth and war demanded innovation and made room for new people. Power shifted, fortunes changed hands, commands passed to new men. Entrenched habits, ancient prejudices, procedures, and traditional modes of thought yielded in the crisis to the pressure of necessity. In the continuing emergency of the battle or the production front, efficient performance counted more than family or ethnic background. Gradually the old preferences and associations weakened in favor of the decisive criterion of who could best do the job.

Access to the most desirable places became open and competitive. The tendency was far from complete in 1960; inherited wealth and connections then still brought advantages to some while poverty and prejudice still handicapped others. But the direction of change was unmistakable and the pace accelerated steadily after 1940. More than ever before men and women entered the occupations through which they performed society's work and through which they earned varying rewards and satisfactions by a sorting-out process which tested their abilities.

Other consequences of economic and social expansion increased the importance of the selective procedure. High technology set a value on skills as other earlier forms of mechanization had not. The man on the assembly line had been a replaceable part, trained to perform a simple task with slight margin for judgment; the number of such jobs ceased to grow and their percentage in the labor force declined. Now the man at the console watched the gauges and pressed the buttons, making the decisions that could not be predicted and that could not therefore be previously programmed. His task called for discretion and ability. He was not simply a replaceable part. Ability counted.

A change in the setting within which much of the economy functioned added to the emphasis on personal skill. The shift of industry to the city had been in progress since the nineteenth century; but after 1930 the development acquired a new meaning. In effect the distinction between country and city dissolved; swift communication by automobile, plane and telephone tied plants and offices together wherever they were. From headquarters concentrated in a few metropolitan centers, management directed the operations of enterprises that were national or even international in scope; and the military service, the civilian branches of government and educational institutions took on some of the same characteristics.

The movement of people and plants accelerated. Industrialization transformed whole regions — the borders of the Gulf of Mexico, for instance, or the Pacific Coast. Immense shifts of population, during the war and after, created fresh demands for schools, churches, hospitals and other services and loosened up the procedures for supplying them. Moreover, mobility within and among organizations became characteristic; a transfer from Seattle to Atlanta was as regular an incident in the career of an engineer as of a professor and a flight from one end of the country to another for a conference, consultation or just for lunch ceased to be exceptional.

The new circumstances demanded in successful men and women traits somewhat different from those of the past. Fixed ties to a place, a family known in the community, and a personal reputation among neighbors were not as helpful as the readiness to move, an adaptability to new circumstances and new people, and a sensitivity to the opinion of colleagues, collaborators and customers. In a period of economic growth, of war and of science, the primary demand upon the individual was the ability to work in large groups, not as a mechanical cog, but as a responsive participant. Generally the individual functioned as part of a team and the aggressive, assertive personality was effective only when it was also pliable enough to take account of others.

An increasingly complex, technological productive system met the needs of the society dependent on it by drawing upon an open pool of talent which included a large part of the whole population. The economy competed for personnel in every sector — in industry, education, medicine, welfare, communications; and the millions of young people who annually sought careers sorted themselves out for one calling or another by an intricate pattern of decisions which reached back to their early childhood.

No centralized control directed the flow to jobs. The process of appraisal and selection consisted of myriads of decisions shaped by employer and family preferences, by resources and social values, all weighted in one direction or another by the differences in rewards attached to various occupations. The combinations which determined the individual's calling were as numerous as the individuals.

But there was a growing belief, backed by some evidence, that quality of schooling from early childhood to maturity had a determining effect upon life's chances. Increasingly, therefore, the process of leaving home became one of preparing for competition against the host of rivals in an open race.

To some extent, the change after 1930 was one of degree; society in the United States had always been fluid and competitive. But there was also a subtle difference in kind between the early and the middle decades of the twentieth century. Gone at the uppermost ranks was the expectation of building an aristocratic line upon the foundation of a great fortune; gone in the middling groups was the hope of securing a professional or business refuge against the danger of falling behind; and gone in the lower sectors was the willingness to find contentment in modest gains. The depression and the common experience of war together with the thinning out of the ranks of the immigrants contributed to a mounting insistence that the competition really be open to all.

Shifts in intellectual emphasis reinforced the economic and social pressures toward education aimed at preparing men and women to compete for places. Increasingly after 1930, Americans stressed the value of egalitarianism. The ideal of equality was certainly in accord with the felt needs of a social system, both for a rational allocation of talents among producers and for the distribution of income among a wide consuming population. But the ideal also had spiritual roots deep in the nineteenth century; and the depression, the New Deal, the war and the general reaction against all aristocratic trends discredited by the failures of 1914 and 1929 strengthened it.

Many Americans moreover were willing to explore novel implications of the ideal. Political and legal equality at the ballot box or in the courtroom required a neutral posture of the state and those objectives were hardly fully attained in 1960. But by then, citizens faced the claim that the government had to play a positive role in furthering equality among the people. The society which assumed responsibility for aiding each individual to become self-supporting could not evade the obligation to help young people along the steps necessary to establish them in careers.

That education was an appropriate means for furthering equality and for preparing youth for life was by now so thoroughly taken for granted as hardly to merit discussion. Teachers and administrators expressed a heady confidence in the ability of their institutions to reform the whole society. *Dare the Schools Build a New Social Order?* was the title of a widely read book of the 1930's; that they could do so seemed obvious in a decade when business and most professions were in disarray. The brain trust and its successors during the war and after acquired power by crossing over from the academy to government and confidently prescribed remedies for the ills of society. Their activity was evidence of the importance of learning.

The schools were critical because they commanded the knowledge vital to all and because they transmitted the skills essential to the operations of modern technology. In addition, they molded their products for appropriate places in life. The graduates emerged sound in body, trained to read and drive cars, expected to vote and to marry, and directed toward congenial careers. The claims on behalf of the school gained force with expansion of the corps of teachers and the administrative bureaucracy.

The education industry grew, resistant as it was to the effects of both depression and war, and with it grew its demands for support.

The four-tier system was now complete, each level locked into its predecessor and essential to the next step upward. Elementary to secondary school to college to professional school; six, fourteen, eighteen, twenty-two— the ages were also fixed and the product was not ready to peep at practice until well on to thirty. AND EVERYONE, the expectation ran, WOULD FOLLOW THE SAME COURSE.

The reality was not quite there yet. Substantial numbers, by choice or necessity, were not in the race; and a significant number of winners ran by paths of their own choosing. Aggressive types, impatient with the prescribed course, broke away and some of them prospered, especially if they enjoyed the lead of inherited wealth. Walter Annenberg, for instance, never bothered to finish school but moved early into his father's publishing ventures. At the other extreme, the mass of Negro children and the children of other poor families started with such heavy handicaps that they could rarely catch up. And between the very rich and the hopelessly disadvantaged there lived blocks upon blocks of solid craftsmen, proud of their skills, protected by unions, situated in comfortable neighborhoods, and satisfied with the gains of the post-depression years; often their sons aspired only to take up the same trades.

Despite these substantial exceptions, the norm of the society was open competition. The schools into which the whole population passed sedulously nurtured the expectation that everyone would run the same race, and the more open the terms of entry, the more intense was the expectation that all would take part. Universal education meant universal competition.

In the haste to enroll every young person in some school, educators rather tended to overlook the implications of their own discussions of the content of instruction. Certainly the meetings and journals devoted ample time and space to controversy over curriculum and methods. But the awkward subject of purpose received less attention. Why? Why should the system be able to ingest all the six-year-olds of the nation, pass them through its digestive mechanism and send them forth ten to twenty years later happily fit to distribute themselves among the tasks the world wished performed?

To the extent that there were any efforts to deal with the question at all, they drew upon the concept of a unifying culture inherited from an earlier period. The schools, it was asserted, administered to all a common body of knowledge and values in addition to or preparatory to the specific technical skill each individual acquired for his particular role in life. The blithe reiteration of that assumption in manifesto after manifesto skirted the inconvenient problem presented in these decades by the dissolution of established cultural standards. The schoolmen in the 1890's had known what was correct in art, literature, philosophy and science and, their confidence buttressed by support from European authority and from social acceptance, had unhesitatingly conveyed the right answers to their charges. There were no such certainties after 1930: all authority was open to question. In the arts the wall between academics and avant-garde finally collapsed and a disquieting relativism permeated every organized body of knowledge.

The change in science should have been most disquieting, but was not. Few teachers as yet absorbed the implications of discoveries within the cell and the atom or out in space or in the very structure of logic. The scholars now stressed tentatively formulated probabilities rather than firm natural laws, relativities rather than universalities, flux rather than certainty, and endless progressions rather than clear beginnings and ends. They raised more questions than they gave answers. But it was the business of the school to outfit its products with answers; otherwise they would not compete effectively in the contests of life.

For the time being, practical engineering achievements were more important than abstract scholarly doubts. The schools had only to prepare people for the proper places; teamwork would tie all particular expertises together.

Know how!

Why?

Later . . .

The formal structure of American education grew rigid out of the necessity for accommodating a vast population drawn into it by the prospect of preparation for the pursuit of happiness, so rigid that teachers lost contact either with the student or with the subject matter they taught. And the young people who flocked into the imposing edifice wandered through it in some confusion as they searched its lecture halls and laboratories for understanding of their personal and social problems.

Social and Personal Change

The pressure on young people to delay the transition to adulthood was enormous, despite evidence that they arrived at physical maturity earlier than in the past. Every prudent consideration pointed in the same direction; it was better to wait, to prolong education and postpone the transition to independence. In an open society everyone had to compete; each therefore sought as good a start as possible. The family and the society both conspired to preserve an attachment to home, and both obscured the emotional and social consequences.

The educational system, formal and inflexible, did feel the effects, first at the secondary level and then in the colleges. But few Americans appraised the problem correctly. Most preferred to consider the prolonged crisis in terms of the ways and means of financing schooling. More boys and girls attended school longer than ever before. The question asked was, how to find the money to pay the cost. The question not asked was, why were they there.

The high schools felt the impact most. The number of pupils rose steadily, although mostly without the stimulus of the postwar baby boom, the effects of which would be felt later. The age group fifteen to nineteen grew from about ten million in 1930 to more than twelve million in 1960. An ever-larger percentage of the group demanded a secondary education; their desire to stay on raised the high school population from six and a half million in 1950 to over ten million in 1960.

The dominant economic trends of the period literally drove young people into the schools. The depression hit youth hard and mechanization and automation during and after the war reduced the range of unskilled jobs formerly open to boys and girls. Social legislation and the minimum wage law completed the process. Meanwhile the high school diploma became the prerequisite of the growing number of white-collar jobs. Those who lacked it suffered. Increasingly all the ways up led through the high school so that only the misfits and the children of the very poor and underprivileged were left to drift into idleness or into the narrowing roster of employments which required no skill and from which there could be no exit.

The high school tried to meet the oncoming tide of new students simply by expanding existing facilities. Yet its established forms were inadequate not only because of lack of space and personnel but also because methods and goals originally devised for a rather select group did not meet the needs of a much larger aggregate totally unselected as to ability.

The situation of the talented boys and girls was clear. The old curriculum, made for them, led ahead to college and the professional school. Habituated to the idea of selection by competition, they learned that success consisted of managing to extricate themselves from the average of the mass about them.

But the high school had less experience in dealing with the rising percentage of students who, lacking competence or motivation, were euphemistically called the *academically untalented.* The labor market had no room for them and the imperatives of a democratic society demanded that they have their chance. Formerly, the vocational educational programs of some states had conveniently gotten these youths out of the way of the more able. But this expedient was no longer satisfying and grew at a far lower rate than other forms of secondary education. The very same economic changes that drove more students into the schools also undervalued the handicraft skills taught there. A large part of the high school population consequently found itself enmeshed in an institution with little relevance to present or future needs. These boys and girls drifted on into the ninth grade because it followed after the eighth.

The transition occurred at adolescence. Growing into maturity, feeling the need to test their powers and assert their individuality, they were now told to study subjects they could not grasp and to acquire skills they might never use. Confined to a round of purposeless tasks — on which their future depended — some became utterly apathetic. Others sought escape from total boredom in athletics, marching bands and a self-contained social life. Still others diverted their vitality into the rebellion of juvenile delinquency.

The collapse of the firm culture defined in the universities, which the high school earlier had undertaken to transmit, complicated efforts to deal with the expanding and increasingly heterogeneous student body. The curriculum had swelled, for the high school adjusted to pressures primarily by adding courses to its offerings. Communities demanded that it assume new functions as the price of support and educators rarely refused to accede. The only standard of judgment was that of immediate utility so that the case for drivers' education or etiquette was as plausible as that for history or geometry. To add a subject it was necessary only to appease the guardians of the earlier ones by leaving their cultural domains untouched. Expansion made room for everyone in a live-and-let-live atmosphere.

The labyrinthine bureaucracies that were also a side effect of growth deliberately or unconsciously tended to blur all issues. It was not true, as was often charged, that they resisted all change. The bureaucracies consisted of teachers and the teachers of teachers, of administrators of schools, and of professional associations, of government officials and the staffs of foundations. Education was a big enterprise and its operations complex. The devoted men and women who gave their lives to it had fought a long and bitter battle to win professional status and in the 1950's were still a long way from their goals. They could not be expected lightly to sacrifice their own interests and they generally interpreted policy in terms of those interests. Compromise, adjustment and mutual accommodation were expedient and perhaps, under the circumstances, least likely to lead to conflict. The drawback was the development of the habit of evading choices and a preference for avoiding crises by the insistence that the high school could do everything for everyone. By 1960, the bills had not yet come due, but they were accumulating ominously.

Meanwhile the high school grew, not because its purpose was clear, but because it occupied the time of boys and girls as old as eighteen who had still not left home.

The pressure that kept young people home extended their dependence upon the family; and the sense of helplessness, the fear of inadequacy in fending for themselves, fed back into a reluctance to depart. The delay in separation was the outcome of developments in the relations of parents to children as well as in the economy.

The end of immigration from abroad and the continued movement within the country, the influence of the popular press, movies and radio, and the consequences of the war exerted an evening-out effect upon American families. Peculiarities of region, ethnic background and social class lost their sharpness as common problems bent all to common patterns.

The depression began to break the crust of tradition that had controlled the lives of foreign-born laborers, and of the impoverished rural population — white and colored. In the cities economic stagnation made millions unemployed; in the country, it ousted thousands of marginal farmers from the soil. Restless young people hit the road and the rails, not only the Okies, not only the sons and daughters of black sharecroppers in Mississippi, of Polish, Jewish and Italian workers in Detroit, New York and Chicago, but also the children of hitherto securely established native whites. Some of the boys went off to the Civilian Conservation Corps, most of them in time served in the armed forces. After 1945, they settled down, those who had gone away as well as those who were left, but the ties with tradition had been severed. Meanwhile the end of immigration had cut off the arrival of newcomers who had formerly strengthened ethnic communities; and Americanization — in the sense of conformity to prevailing manners — advanced rapidly. To the extent that society opened up, barriers among its members fell and the same family type became the model for all.

The groups cut off from the general trend suffered from isolation. Migration out of the rural South brought ill-prepared Negroes in growing numbers to northern and western cities at a time when the demand for their unskilled labor shrank, when high costs prevented expansion of the housing supply, and when municipalities groaned under the burden of costly urban services. Moving directly to the crowded slums and handicapped by persistent prejudice against them, many merely exchanged one kind of poverty for another. Their culture and disordered family life reflected their deprivations.

The painfully hesitant steps toward desegregation and toward equality of opportunity helped the most fortunate but left others enmired. Similar though less visible clusters of the poor appeared among the Puerto Ricans, the Mexican-Americans and white migrants from the South. The problems of all these people were similar; their children could not compete on equal terms in a race which stressed educational attainments. Yet concerned individuals, Negro and white, retained the hope that the deprived might be able to break into the mainstream of American life. The line of judicial decisions that culminated in the Brown case of 1954 showed that Jim Crow was dying. A properly organized family might help studious children move ahead despite their color. Even in the least privileged groups, the high school became an oasis of hope; its halls opened the way to chances in life for those with a home to give them support. Only try — the plaintive request of fathers and mothers who had never had a chance.

After 1930 going to high school was routine for the offspring of professional, business and managerial parents — the middle-class majority of American society by the 1950's. In these families doubt never intruded about the value of education; the only anxiety was about which decisions would most enhance the advantages of their children in competition for careers.

Earlier tendencies toward a shrinkage in family size continued, so that the norm declined to about three offspring. The spread of information about the techniques of birth control helped, as did the growing candor about sexual relations in general. Since the first decade of the twentieth century there had been a general loosening up of manners, and a relaxation of restraints that culminated in the roaring Twenties. The heads of most families after 1930 had matured and married in an environment that frowned on inhibitions and various diluted versions of Freudianism seemed to sanction the throwing off of old restraints.

New times, new customs. The church was the setting of the marriage ceremony, but the concept of the union as a sacrament or as a contract joined under the eyes of God faded away. Marriage instead was the means of gratifying individual desires. Since the beginning of the century, naturalistic writers had been hinting with increasing boldness at the brutal source of passion — at root a desire of the flesh. Yet the preference endured to locate those desires among the animal types of *Tobacco Road* or the rich bitches who moved through John O'Hara's novels. The popular media continued to envelop sex in the gauzy veil of romantic love — an incomprehensible flash that passed between two individuals to make both better. Not rational, not physical in inception, though in consummation. Spiritual? Soulful? Not quite; the religious intonations of those terms were not appropriate. Love was a need, a personal need reaching out all the time waiting for fulfillment; the flash came at the magic moment of recognition, when the need of one meshed with and fulfilled the need of the other. The end result was the union in marriage.

And if the personal gratification which was the object did not come or grew dull; or if, sooner or later, another affection promised greater satisfaction, then persistence in a worn-out liaison was cruel and pointless in its frustrations. A steadily mounting divorce rate revealed the way out.

The way in was easier too. A steady drop in the average age of marriage showed the effects of relaxation of earlier restraints. Hesitation about a career, concern about the future problems of sustaining a household dissolved. Why wait for fulfillment? Whatever turn external events took justified the decision to go ahead. During the depression there was nothing to lose —

Potatoes 'er cheaper
Tomatoes 'er cheaper
Nowza time terfall in love —

radio advice from Eddie Cantor. During the war, might as well, who could tell — there might be no future. And after the war, there was a lot of making up for lost time. And if it didn't work, no harm done; separate and try again.

The family was incidental to unions entered upon as a casual means of satisfying personal impulses. Matrimony had ceased to be a rite holy in intention and administered with the approbation of the community for the purpose of generation. That a family resulted from marriage now seemed an unavoidable side effect rather than an end in itself and the children within it were by-products, likable, a source often of expense, also of pleasure and interest, but not the purpose of the marriage. The home as a whole was measured by the same standard, its contribution to the happiness of those in it.

The perspective of the parents and their attitudes toward one another and toward the family were the dominant influences upon the changing pattern of child-rearing after 1930. Certainly, middle-class people turned more readily to Gesell and Spock than to traditional sources of information. They sought advice from the doctors because the important problems seemed medical, that is, involved with physical well-being; and if the family had enough income it could certainly provide that. The infant kept cozy would grow through the expected stages of childhood to attain maturity. Development was an unfolding according to impulses from within; and to further it, the parent had only to furnish comfort and security and to refrain from frustrating the natural demands of the child.

Mothers and fathers could be both possessive and permissive in good conscience. They thus escaped the burden of painful decisions, of troubled encounters with headstrong youth; and life in the family was relatively pleasant when no disagreeable negatives produced painful conflicts. The home became a resource upon which youth drew at will, a credit card with no monthly payments and no expiration date.

From *GEE WHIZ!* to *SO WHAT!* From Henry Aldrich to Holden Caulfield. From the unspoiled boy, for whom small sums counted but who knew where he was going, to the youth who had everything, who checked casually in and out of good hotels but had no sense of direction. Decade by decade, the children of comfortable families cushioned by solicitous parents against the shock of deprivation (of *any*thing you want) grew more dependent; even early marriage did not sever the ties of support. During the depression they doubled up; the young couple just moved in with the old. Later, regular checks paid the rent. The expectation faded that gratification of the desire to marry might be postponed until independence. Any more than the gratification of any other demand.

Large numbers of families guided by the same assumptions gave a distinctive character to the community in which they congregated. Suburbia was not new in American life; nor was it all of a piece. People with means had been escaping from the problems of the central city for a century; and their destinations after 1930 differed markedly according to income level and cost of housing, according to ethnic background and according to the region of the country. Newton was not Larchmont or Oak Park or Glenwood or Pasadena. Even Levittown, Pennsylvania, was not quite the same as Levittown, New York.

More important in these places than size of house or spread of lawn or even distance from the slum was the type of family it sheltered — affluent enough to indulge in choices, free of tradition, ready to find guidance in experts, and concerned with satisfying its members. Since the most dependent were the most demanding the focus of activities in the home inevitably centered upon the child, for in the end often this was the sole common possession and interest of the father and mother.

Suburban communities were selective. Even without conscious policies of discrimination and exclusion they drew together like-minded people, sorted out by age, income, educational attainment and ethnic background. Each community therefore found itself composed of similar families swayed by identical interests and tastes and anxious to take the same steps for the welfare of their offspring, counseled by the best opinions.

Their kids grew up in lockstep, but so well cushioned by delight they could not resent the gentle pressure. Together they toddled off to the nursery school and together passed the stages from one birthday to another.

No objective was more important to well-informed parents than to make their children independent as soon as possible. At Peter Pan School the six-year-olds learned to take a train journey by themselves, while their mothers raced in the station wagon to pick them up at the next stop four miles away. No boy or girl could miss the experience of going off to camp, to be with peers of his own age — natural, although with appropriate oversight. When the time came it was correct that dating begin. O such excitement in Philadelphia (December 1940) as Amy dresses for her first formal dance. *Now it won't hurt to lettum kiss yu,* is mother's advice to her thirteen-year-old daughter being helped into the cutest falsies. Time too brought the driver's license and the freedom of the car.

All of growing up was thus being allowed to do what one wanted to, certainly without fear of Pop's authority, diminished as that was by Mom's solicitude. In the broad-minded, conspicuous unobtrusiveness of the parents, there was nothing to break away from or rebel against. Yet the father and mother remained a vague, hovering presence, their intentions undefined — all for the good of the child — but incapable of offering guidance to those who floundered in permissiveness.

The family that played together, prayed together. The institutions of the suburban community focused upon the upbringing of the young. Much of the postwar revival of religion emanated from concern with providing roots for offspring who lacked dependable places in new and unstable surroundings. Detached from relatives, boys and girls needed some organizing environment to identify them with their parents' antecedents and to involve them in activities that had an ethical base. Theology and even the moral content of a particular faith were less important than the social opportunities they afforded and the links they provided with others in the church. Affiliation often expressed the desire of the family to pray together, so that it would have something to do together.

The church was then primarily a variant of the club, existing to satisfy the member's desire to belong. Unlike most associations which drew together people of a specific age group, this one had room for young and old and indeed its purpose was, in part at least, to provide a link between the passing and arriving of generations which it marked with the appropriate rites of birth, coming of age, marriage and death. The weight given those ceremonies showed the extent to which it was child-centered; for while men and women rarely gave thought to their own departure from earth, they lavished much attention on the arrival of the baby, on the onset of adolescence, and on the achievement of adulthood.

The most prominent building in the suburb was the high school, for here was the center of life for the children who were the center of the community. Here the boys and girls aged fourteen to eighteen spent much of their time; here they received direction not only in studies but in a broad range of social concerns. The younger kids who all knew that they would someday pass through its doors were already familiar with its imposing structure, with the gymnasium and the natatorium, with the playing fields, and with the asphalt spread of its parking lot. Someday they would also sit in its classrooms.

The high school was important because it was inclusive; virtually everyone in town came. The building was utilized at all hours for the meetings of clubs, for contests of sport, for dances, for starwatching and photography, for orchestra, band and choir practice, for public lectures and concerts. So much was there through which anyone could express himself.

But the building was also the setting of a deadly earnest competition. Repeatedly tested and measured, the boys and girls were running a hard race. They got whatever their hearts desired as long as they remained in training; and before them at the end of the fourth year was the great hurdle — admission to college, the right college.

American life had always been competitive. Now it was a free-for-all. The belief that the society was or shortly would be totally open meant that everyone had a chance. But it also meant that everyone had to fight for his place and that each person's hand was against every other's as all grappled for holds in the climb upward along the single pyramid of success.

The image was not totally accurate even in 1960. Some starts were better than others, and some schools than others. Families which perceived the differences anxiously tried to make the most of them.

A prep school launching was still advantageous. Institutions descended from the old academies and seminaries retained more features of the classical-gentle curriculum than did the public high school; and students selected by them were all prospective college men and women who could be specifically readied for the examinations and work ahead. In addition, informed parents knew that the most prestigious colleges directly or indirectly gave a preference to the graduates of the favored schools. Certainly everyone took the same examinations but the raw results were not the sole criteria; nor were they the best basis for predicting performance. In making the less objective evaluations of personality and potential, interviewers and deans inevitably gave weight to qualities imparted at the prep school — presence, ability to fit in, and familiarity with expected people, places, books and concepts. Then also these applicants were the sons of the best people and most likely to be generous donors as alumni. And there were quotas pure and simple to maintain balance within the college.

Less known were the gradations of preference among private schools; Groton and St. Paul's were select — their boys in a somewhat different category from those who emerged from Exeter and Andover, which in turn were not quite the same as institutions with students less carefully picked over.

Public schools were less readily sorted out, but there were nonetheless immense differences among them in character and therefore in the prospects of their graduates for admission to suitable colleges. The wealthy suburbs on the margins of large cities commanded impressive resources and often housed homogeneous populations since the mere cost of residence was selective and was often buttressed by zoning codes and exclusive gentlemen's agreements. These high schools had ample budgets, bought the services of the best teachers, and trained their students thoroughly for college admission.

Parsimonious in expenditures for educational frills, small towns skimped on building maintenance and teachers' salaries. The tax rate, sensitive to every rise in costs, persuaded the honest citizens that unworthy pupils were better off at work than crowding the class rolls. And there was a tendency to judge the worthiness of the student by the quality of the family to which he belonged.

By contrast, the metropolis offered a confusing variety. New Utrecht High School in Brooklyn in 1930 enrolled 8,000 students; some followed a general or college course, others a commercial or a vocational course; its discipline was military; and the teachers — devoted or apathetic, good or indifferent, old or young — were an anonymous, alien presence. At the same time, Erasmus Hall and Townsend Harris, also public high schools, in the same city, gave their select pupils the academic excellence of the best academy. Informed parents who knew the ropes could locate their children advantageously; but the choice usually depended upon the place of residence, a factor which gave enormous importance to the neighborhood in which the family lived and therefore to income and social group. The public high school thus performed its sorting out and preparatory function not as a single great sieve but through multiple filters; and in the absence of guidance and counseling services much depended upon the chance that landed an individual in one spot rather than another.

Opportunities existed even for boys and girls who got onto the wrong track; there were still second chances and third. But the awareness of the increasingly formal structure of education placed enormous emphasis on the competition to grab a strategic place preparatory to the start of the vital race, which was college.

Meanwhile the goal of college remained attractive to young people, not only because they were all along absorbed in the heat of the contest, but also because it opened to them the prospects of running in a newer, greener part of the field. Once they cleared the hurdle of admission, which was the mark of their previous achievements, they would somehow be really free.

The Discipline of Scholarship

Viewed from the perspective of professors, trustees and legislators the depression of the 1930's long imparted a gloomy aspect to higher education. In that grim decade American colleges misread the potential market for their graduates and worried that they might turn loose a mass of unemployed degree holders as Germany had after the First World War. The outlook seemed to warrant contraction and retrenchment.

The actual development was in the opposite direction. Institutions of higher learning grew in number, in size, in wealth and in power. The count rose from 1,409 in 1930 to 1,850 in 1957 and enrollments soared from 1,101,000 in the earlier year to 3,500,000 in the later one.

The growth came despite the declining birthrates of the 1920's and 1930's, the decades which supplied the students of the 1940's and 1950's. This increase owed nothing to the baby boom that followed the Second World War. Until 1960, it was due not so much to an expansion of the eligible age group as to a rise in the percentage of those who continued their education beyond the high school.

Young people after 1930 proceeded to college as a normal incident of life between the ages of eighteen and twenty-two. They ran where the track led. Certainly the degree had economic value. Opportunity, they believed, lay not in independent entrepreneurship but up the steps of a large organization. Only medicine still emphasized the individual practitioner; the other professions, including business, operated in formal structures best entered through an institution of higher education. Moreover, alternative modes of launching a career were unattractive.

The depression was particularly hard upon job-seeking youth and, when the end of the war relieved the acute manpower shortage, the casual employments that had once provided stepping stones tended to disappear; bureaucratic organizations required credentials of those they hired; unions set tight requirements around valuable positions; and mechanization eased the need for hands. The college kept the unwanted high school graduates off the labor market, as the WPA had in harder days. Fortunately the general rise in incomes after 1940 increased the number of families that could thus assist their children.

The widespread assumption that college would follow high school as a matter of course owed something also to the egalitarianism of the period after 1930. Everyone could expect to be one of the *diploma elite* Vance Packard described. The universities were no longer to be merely the instruments for producing an intellectual aristocracy, insisted a presidential commission in 1947. They were to enable and encourage every citizen, youth and adult, to carry his education as far as his native capacities permitted.

Although there was some concern about the effects of the oncoming wave of students, the university blithely expressed its eagerness to assume additional responsibilities. To the undertaking to educate everyone, it coupled the assurance, traditionally sanctified in academic oratory and in appeals for funds, that it would perform as a service station to which the general public could bring any problem for solution. Scholars with *a passionate concern for human betterment* would apply at the point of social action what the scientist had discovered regarding the laws of human behavior. Laboratories of inter-race and interfaith fellowship would eliminate all forms of discrimination. The colleges also would offset the handicaps of poor secondary school instruction and they would undertake massive programs of adult education.

These unexceptionable sentiments did not take account of the actualities of the academic situation and therefore complicated the efforts of the universities to absorb the shock of massive growth. The rhetoric, no matter how benevolent the intentions, did not bridge the gap between social and academic reality. The social reality was the existence of a large and growing age group which had no function but attendance at some kind of school. The academic reality was the existence of colleges increasingly staffed by scholars primarily concerned with an array of specialized disciplines rather than with the heterogeneous student body.

The presidential commission of 1947 estimated that to meet the increase it foresaw by 1960, colleges would have to add 250,000 new teachers to their faculties. The whole number of doctorates produced in the 1930's was 20,783, of whom some 65 per cent went on to teach. The commission therefore recommended a speed-up of preparation to increase the supply. Of course, it also counseled the graduate schools to put training in the hands of *men of broad knowledge, men of imagination and understanding, and wisdom.*

Not a professor in the country but would have recognized in those phrases an accurate appraisal of his own qualifications! The faculties, having steadily and successfully fought for recognition of their professional status, brought an exhilarating sense of confidence — even of arrogance — to their work. In occasional small rural colleges, the instructor still cowered beneath the tyranny of president, trustees and community. But that situation was becoming less and less usual; the struggles of the American Association of University Professors since 1915 had won recognition of the principles of tenure; and violations of academic freedom, even during the depression and McCarthy periods, were gratifyingly few.

Moreover, professors had been gaining in popular esteem. Access to their ranks was difficult and therefore of itself a sign of competence. And their abilities, while specialized, were not confined to abstract matters. Practical men of affairs had run the country into a depression; the brain trust and its successors, consulted by government and by business, controlled the knowledge that could save the nation. War service confirmed that impression. Indeed, institutions of higher education often had to compete for personnel against industry and government. True, salaries remained relatively low; but the scholar after 1930 achieved a good deal of autonomy as the value set upon his research grew. Steadily rising contributions to basic science in the universities from federal and state governments, industry and foundations recognized the worth of the work in the laboratories and libraries.

The faculty after 1930 gained the right to choose its own members. Budgetary restraints remained, as did the formal veto of administrators and trustees. But a large and growing percentage of appointments were by the cooption of the professors themselves according to the internal standards of their discipline. The infusion of refugees from communist and fascist regimes in Europe helped diminish parochialism. Discrimination against ethnic and cultural outsiders subsided and it became inappropriate to scrutinize the details of character, attitude, values and personal life that had once been weighty elements in the designation to a college position. The only relevant question was the extent to which the instructor had mastered his body of knowledge and the only relevant answer was that derived from scrutiny of his degrees, publications, and other credentials. The fact that he would also be a teacher of the youth under his charge was secondary.

In the college the growing importance of science, that is, of the systematized body of knowledge, gave control over the most important decisions to the departments organized according to the disciplines of scholarship. Knowledge itself had become so complex and specialized that the faculty as a whole lacked the competence to understand or judge the work of its members and delegated responsibility to smaller groups qualified in their respective subjects. This academic structure, whatever its utility in advancing research, was not on the face of it a plausible device for administering education to the host of students who came to college not to master any discipline but, in some imprecise sense, to span the years between adolescence and adulthood. Yet for a time, at least, the autonomous faculty, divided into departments, proved surprisingly effective, not because it could execute fully the mission society now assigned to it, nor because of the special merit of the curricula over which it wrangled, but rather because professors enjoyed an environment of freedom in which to pursue their scholarship and because they commanded the respect of the young people who grew up in their proximity.

The broad visions of its future role disoriented the university, however. The promise to encourage every citizen to carry his education as far as his native capacities permitted commanded assent as long as it remained general.

Disagreement followed immediately upon efforts at fulfillment. The emphasis could be on opportunity: the college was then a sieve, applying rigid standards to all who passed through it and sorting them out according to ability. Or, the stress could equally well be on common if not identical experience: all Americans aged eighteen to twenty-two were entitled to their college years, in which case it was necessary to provide an even greater variety of institutions and programs in order to accommodate varying aptitudes.

Given this ambiguity, no ready formula was at hand for what to teach or how to occupy the vast body of young people who now moved into the colleges. The disarray of society gradually emptied of meaning the whole notion of preparation for a gentlemanly style of life, particularly since attendance became so general as to lose the cachet of exclusiveness. The conception of an established genteel culture, already in dissolution before 1930, died with the depression and with the victory of the avant-garde in the arts and even in science, to be replaced by painful uncertainties and an open questioning attitude toward the old verities. Frankly experimental institutions like Bard and Bennington and old established ones like Harvard and Columbia willingly tried novel schemes not merely because it was fashionable to do so but also because of genuine dissatisfaction with the existing curriculum and with the earlier pattern of college life.

The scholars within each department took an internal view of their subject, which they pressed upon the faculty as a whole in the usual juggling and balancing operations of university politics. The outcome presented the students with a grab bag of courses, each taught by a specialist and linked by a variety of devices combining elements of compulsion and free election, of concentration and distribution. But however the elements were manipulated, no formal technique could offset the subtle change in the character of the faculty, the members of which had ceased to be custodians of a general culture and had become instead guardians of particular segments of knowledge.

In recurrent and circular efforts at reform, earnest educators shifted about the same intractable materials available to them, just as their predecessors had for more than a century. Since it was easier to launch a new experiment than to appraise the results of an old one, the innovations gladly and frequently trumpeted to alumni and professional associations were repetitious.

The hope of easing the curriculum-devising task lay behind some efforts to sort the students out in advance. Junior and community colleges, which in effect provided thirteenth and fourteenth high school grades, were encouraged to divert less prepared or less interested youths away from the senior institutions. But since no one wished to close the doors to further education, the two-year college usually offered a *well-integrated single program* that was both general and vocational and thus prepared some of its pupils to go on for two years more.

The full-fledged college flatly rejected the suggestion of a pass degree after the English style; every baccalaureate was to be earned, somehow. But it did not seem invidious to set unprepared or unmotivated students apart from the ablest who could profit from special attention. Even before 1930, experiments such as honors at Swarthmore, tutorial and the house system at Harvard, preceptorial at Princeton had aimed at establishing intimacy with the instructors; and imitation multiplied in the years that followed. The desire to cultivate the brainiest culminated in the 1950's in a widespread hunt for excellence — as if that were a discrete, definable attribute. The surge of applicants for admission in that decade permitted the most prestigious institutions to raise requirements and, in effect, to devote themselves to a select group of undergraduates.

But numbers had a way of catching up with the elite programs. After 1930, as for more than a century earlier, the pressure to make distinction available to all, ran only a little behind the pressure to admit everyone; and only the financially secure private institutions could resist. Those who argued for a wider view objected to the orientation of higher education toward verbal skills and intellectual interests and, by implication at least, demanded accommodations for the unskilled and unintellectual. The university had to provide enough variety so that everyone could do well in something. The number of new course offerings therefore continued to mount at an accelerating pace, in a process that conformed to the elaboration and fragmentation of scholarship.

The remorseless thickening of the course catalogues dismayed even the proponents of diversification. The same report which counseled the colleges to avoid excessive orientation to intellectual interests went on to complain that overspecialization had splintered the unity of liberal education.

What was to be done? The question had reechoed through the decades since the abandonment of the classical curriculum. Some *community of values, ideas, and attitudes* was essential as a cohesive force in an age of *minute division of labor and intense conflict of special interests.* The cluster of surveys, which in most places constituted the required elements in the degree program, could not transmit a liberal education to the heterogeneous body of students now passing through the college.

The drawbacks of the elective system, even when balanced by some requirements, stimulated interest in new offerings aimed directly and specifically at *general* as against *specialized education*. In 1919, Columbia had devised a course on contemporary civilization out of which grew a sequence intended to define the intellectual and spiritual tradition that a man must experience and understand to be called educated. The College at the University of Chicago made a still more ambitious effort to break down the boundaries of conventional departments and disciplines in undergraduate instruction. The adoption of a program in general education at Harvard in 1945 signaled the apparent victory of this approach.

President Robert M. Hutchins's talent for pushing a good idea to absurdity exposed the limitations of general education. The heart of the curriculum, he announced, was *the same at any time, in any place, under any political, social, or economic conditions* — a dictum which could serve a handful of select students or could promote the great books publishing venture, but was inapplicable to American youth in their vast diversity. Actually, compromise everywhere altered these programs as soon as they were formulated. In some institutions, general education became an alternative to scholarship, both as a route to a teaching career and as a repository for spiritual content to offset the harsh precision of the departments. Elsewhere, the old departmental surveys simply acquired new titles, numbers and budgets. But the most durable and most common effect was unforeseen. General education offerings absolved the remainder of the curriculum of the obligation of taking account of undergraduates. Faculties which voted in the new programs, in effect created, or recognized, a dichotomy between general and specialized courses and thus widened the distance between most of the students and most of the scholars.

That outcome was an ironic counterweight to conscious effort in the same years to pull student and teacher together by involving each in the interests of the other. The expansion of the catalogue made possible formal instruction in areas previously left to voluntary effort. Undergraduate organizations had always drawn upon the advice of interested faculty members. But the incorporation of music, the drama, journalism and athletics into the pattern of course offerings attenuated the distinction between curricular and extracurricular affairs. The tendency was general, although rarely recognized as openly or as boldly as at Bennington.

The personal associations thus created undoubtedly rewarded those involved. But the side effects were ultimately costly. As the catalogue and the academic framework officially assimilated one activity after another, the area within which undergraduates were left alone to manage matters in their own way, by themselves, narrowed. At the same time, the students learned to depend upon the formal university structure for the whole of their college experience rather than, as earlier, for only a part, and not always the most important part, of it. It became difficult for a young man or woman to conceive of reading a book or playing the cymbals or making a movie without somehow receiving credit for it. The reckoning of gains and losses from the change would not come until after 1960 when students, having become totally dependent upon the curriculum, naturally found themselves dissatisfied with it.

Despite the glaring contradictions in its character, the university thrived and, between 1930 and 1960, met less difficulty in managing its students than in any comparable period. The times were uncertain and the juxtaposition of scholarship with the mass of young people without clear aims left the curriculum disorderly and blurred the purposes of the institution. Still, that very lack of precise definition created an environment in which all the participants in the college enterprise had remarkable freedom to do what they wished.

For the time being, the coexistence of scholars and students proved possible. A steady upgrading of academic quality turned normal schools into colleges and technical schools into universities more concerned with basic science than with engineering. Notwithstanding the denigration long directed at the Ph.D., that degree was a useful device for staffing the faculties so long as the numbers involved were relatively low, for a network of personal communication within the disciplines permitted an appraisal of individuals that went beyond the paper credentials. Not every teacher held the degree and not every holder of the degree was a creative scholar; but enough were, to establish the norm and to commit the institutions in which they functioned to the pursuit of knowledge, to objectivity, and to rational procedures in the use of evidence. There were enough also to endow the faculty as a whole with prestige that commanded the respect of students.

In addition, a sense of participation in the transmission, if not the advance, of learning had a stimulating effect upon many worthy teachers who had allowed the personal aspiration toward original scholarship to lapse. Numbers had not yet grown so large as to destroy the unity of a department or professional meeting, despite the inevitable clashes of personality and points of view. Moreover, the rapid expansion of specialized personnel for guidance, religious, psychiatric and health services relieved the faculty of tasks which had once been incidental to the classroom and at the same time interposed a variety of shock absorbers between professors and students.

Above all, the changing composition of the student body eased the problems of dealing with it. Drawn from a wider segment of the whole society than previously, it lacked the common assumptions basic to earlier college life, was more susceptible to the influence of such external events as war and depression and was, therefore, more serious about its studies. Even the offspring of affluent families in the 1950's could not ignore the need to find a career. And the rising percentage of students whose parents had incomes below the national median produced a general consciousness that the years of study had to lay a basis for future security. The return of the veterans brought to the campus older, more mature students, many of them married and burdened with family obligations of their own; they had lost time in life, had experienced much and were totally in earnest about what they were doing. In fact, for such people the tensions of college life were likely to arise out of the competitive desire for getting ahead.

The focus of student concern upon performance in accredited courses and of faculty concern upon scholarship altered the disciplinary relationship. What happened outside the classroom lost importance. The surviving supervisory aspects of the college now decayed almost to the vanishing point. Compulsory chapel slipped into gentle desuetude, despite the renewal of interest in religion in the 1950's and the rising membership of Newman, Hillel and other voluntary church-oriented organizations. While the rules regulating personal behavior sometimes remained unchanged, enforcement was lax unless public scandal or internal conflict forced the authorities to act. The student increasingly was conceded the autonomy to guide his conduct in his own way. The college reluctantly and infrequently invoked the residual right to exercise oversight over its charges.

The fraternities, sororities and other societies which had formerly been so central to the college experience lost much of their importance. Some were tainted by discriminatory and exclusionary practices which ran counter to the egalitarianism of the period. Furthermore, the blurring of the distinction between curricular and extracurricular affairs shifted undergraduate interest to credit-bearing or formal and official activities, especially where there was an effort to draw the whole student body together in unions or in such residential and instructional units as the Harvard and Yale houses. The fraternities which held on did so through inertia, the shortage of alternative living space, the uncertainty about how to change, and the interest of alumni.

Many related college customs — hazing, initiation rituals, contests between classes and distinctive requirements of dress — which students had formerly imposed upon themselves, now seemed boring and faded from memory. There was no end to spontaneous pranks and to maniacal outbursts — swallowing goldfish or crowding into telephone booths. But the institutional patterns which had earlier channeled such impulses were in process of dissolution. The passion was even draining out of intercollegiate athletics.

The spread of the belief among undergraduates that learning was the main business of college also inhibited political activity. Unlike their counterparts in Europe and in Latin America, students in the United States did not become a force of consequence in government. Clubs associated with the national parties occasionally used undergraduate labor in electoral campaigns and radical organizations now and then attained a public notoriety unjustified by their meager numbers. The American Student Union, formed in 1935, never attained the 12,000 members it claimed and became an easy front for the communists, who also guided much of the anti-war movement before 1941. Such groups played a serious role on only a few exceptional campuses; and their conservative counterparts of the 1950's did not gain significant ground.

The reluctance of students to participate in radical movements sprang partly from the activity of the communists, who on the one hand were devious, disruptive, and schismatic and on the other, rendered their fellow travelers vulnerable to charges of disloyalty damaging to future careers. But more important inner deterrents also inhibited any involvement, radical or conservative. American college students were not homogeneous in social origins or in values and therefore lacked the common interests and attitudes to provide a basis for national organization. Furthermore, men and women in the United States rarely stretched out their student status long enough to supply durable leadership or continuity within the swiftly changing mass of those who passed through the university gates. Above all, for the overwhelming majority college was an interim period rather than a career; undergraduates were transients on the way toward getting settled in life and their main business was earning the degree. Hence their willingness to accept the discipline of scholarship which, for the time being, permitted the university to encompass and serve a variety of dissimilar objectives.

Negro and Catholic institutions moved more slowly toward a relaxation of disciplinary controls because both types clung to an older view of their function. Catholics still thought of the college as a bulwark to save the faith from the damaging effects of Americanization. Many influential Negroes continued to believe, out of a gnawing need to preserve and foster self-respect, that their own schools would develop the leadership of the future. Neither group regarded integration as a wholly desirable goal; and both stressed segregation as an instrument for inculcating the unique values of their respective traditions. Discipline and the control of student life therefore remained tight. A visitor was astounded at the lack of personal freedom on Negro campuses, which reminded him of mid-Victorian England.

Yet these institutions too had begun to feel the effects of the changes that transformed the majority of American colleges. They too had faith in the capacity of knowledge, reflection and reason to provide serious answers to the serious problems of life.

The belief in the validity of scholarship was the silken band which loosely held the members of the university together. The authority thus voluntarily accepted fostered the peaceful coexistence of professors, administrators, alumni, legislators and staff in large communities so loosely held together that each could pursue his own ends with little interference from others.

The undergraduate enjoyed a liberty particularly without constraint for this was a period of transit during which minimal obligations let him find his own way. Those with very supportive or indulgent parents could take a year off if they desired, return at will, and use what time was necessary for self-discovery.

They were free to do what they wished. Only, they did not know what they wished.

Trained for one purpose — to compete in a race — they could not afford to think, WHY WERE THEY RUNNING?

Yearning for Security

A perceptive college novel of 1933 described an intellectual factory. Images of impersonality, remoteness and detachment recurred in the thinking of youth about its situation in the decades that followed.

Looking back upon the lost generation after the First World War, the young sometimes felt a sense of envy. People in the 1920's were disillusioned too; they had been betrayed, sacrificed for hollow slogans. Aware of reality and of the limits of their own powers, they nevertheless held to a faith in the intrinsic worth of what they were doing. The artists and the novelists, like the teachers and students, like the physicians and the businessmen, then felt no need to justify their callings by extrinsic standards. What they did was worth doing for its own sake, because it expressed their own individuality.

Authenticity seemed to have been the unique quality of that earlier generation. It cherished its own personality, indulged in its eccentricities, trumpeted its ingenuous discovery of sex, was outraged by prohibition — indeed by any sham that derogated from the dignity of the individual. Surface disillusionment and skepticism concealed only dimly an abiding faith. It was no accident that the two books of great meaning for that generation — *Ulysses* and *The Great Gatsby* — both ended with mighty affirmations, which reechoed in the close of *For Whom the Bell Tolls.*

Youth in the 1930's took those affirmations for granted, so much so that it minimized the achievements of its predecessors and was more likely to criticize what was left undone than to value what was achieved. The burden of complaint during the depression was that the men of the 1920's had been too much concerned with the isolated individual, too little with man as a social being. Self-development, free expression and personal dignity were important ends, but in the 1930's the chief impediment to their attainment seemed to be a failure in the social system. Planning was the corrective. Confidence in the power so to mold the social environment as to create an adequate setting for the full realization of personal capacities charged the humanitarian energies on which the New Deal drew. The meaning thus imparted to social justice supplied young people with a drive that made them willing to struggle. They were realistic, believed in economic determinism or dialectical materialism, in behaviorism or Freudianism. Unable to accept the comfortable transcendentalism of the nineteenth century that offered man an easy nobility, they nevertheless wished to be venturesome. During the depression and the war they had little to lose and realism seemed to demand experiment and nonconformity.

The tone changed after 1945. The veterans who returned to college were mature and earnest; they and their successors worked hard and got good grades. But their earnestness and effort pointed toward a limited goal of riskless security, even at the price of a dull conformity. The lad who hoped to be a doctor looked forward to getting onto the staff of some institution, to live without problems and with a salary. On a questionnaire, the graduate students put down what they expected to be after twenty years — their ideal: the administrator-dean. The colleges were muggy with modest ambitions; the little dreams were not of wealth or fame or monumental accomplishment, but of the bureaucrat's office in government or corporation.

The poverty of aspiration was the product of upbringing and of a yearning for security. The desire to avoid risk was not a response to anxiety about the future. Young people in the late 1940's and 1950's married and bore their two or three children without forethought or concern, as the steady drop in the age of marriage and the steady rise in the birthrate showed. They did not regard these undertakings as obligations; somehow someone would provide. Meanwhile, they settled easily into the ruts they dug for themselves, expecting to spend the rest of their lives undisturbed.

Not willing consciously to take chances, the young people avoided deviation from established patterns. Their minds ran to motorcars and suburban bungalows. As students they read thoroughly what was assigned them, but were unadventurous and shied away from heresy. In discussion, they were eminently docile.

Partly they conformed because it was dangerous not to. They believed that those who dealt out the office space in government and industry were not likely to discriminate among types of radicalism, that every heterodox idea reflected a red glow. Still, they did not object against the pressures toward like-mindedness.

On the contrary, youth welcomed the shackles of othodoxy. All the eager faces looking up at the platform waited to be told what to believe. There was a delight in dogma; know the authorities, accept the classics, and wash your problems away. What did the young say when they spoke up to the educators? William Buckley, then chairman of the *Yale Daily News,* bemoaned his instructors' lack of enthusiasm for free enterprise and summoned the trustees to halt the stirring up of nagging doubts.

The swift racer keeps his eyes on the track. He cannot take time to wonder where he is running.

For many competitors, the goals lost all intrinsic value. The educational channels might lead to a government or a corporate office, to a teacher's or a lawyer's desk, to a doctor's or a nurse's uniform. The specific role was less important than the security and income it brought; and personal fulfillment was less often sought on the job than in marriage and the family. Cynicism about the worth of careers grew whether in depression or prosperity for increasingly the competition for place seemed to lead into the bureaucratic labyrinths of great organizations in which the individual counted for little. Men had no socially acceptable alternative to remaining on the treadmill, but a good many women chose to file away their hard-earned credentials and devoted themselves to their suburban homes and the time-absorbing round of communal activities.

The task at hand was adjustment — from early childhood to retirement. People behaved as the situation demanded.

The boys and girls went in and out of uniform with a curious sense of detachment. About war in general, they acquired no strong opinions. They were not convinced that another conflict was avoidable, nor that it was inevitable. They certainly had no feeling that they could do anything about it. They would take it if it came; meanwhile they wished to get as far with their personal lives as possible.

Korea came to them with the uneventfulness of a monthly bill in the mail. Those eligible for the draft or enrolled in the reserves felt more concern than those who had already cleared their obligations. But few expressed any consciousness of the great social and intellectual issues involved or insisted that youth had a special claim to be heard on the matter.

The sheer persistence of international problems after 1930 had no doubt dulled sensitivity toward them. But a serious fault in American thought also contributed toward the apathy. The dominant liberalism of the 1930's had not known how to face up to the challenge of totalitarianism. Japan, Germany, Italy, Spain, the war itself were the evidence; and the peace added the Soviet Union. Every crisis had found the United States unprepared, passively reacting to stimuli rather than actively pursuing positive goals. From the point of view of those who reached maturity in these years the record of foreign affairs, despite military victories, was one of successive defeats.

A fellow who came out of the Army in 1945 thought of liberalism in terms of the struggle for the Democratic vice-presidential nomination of the year before; and he sought to take up the tradition in the pages of the *Nation* and *New Republic*. To chart the course those journals had marked out in the ten years before would not inspire the veteran with enthusiasm; and to trace the eccentric gyrations of Henry Wallace after his displacement by Harry Truman would lead no one to the conviction that in liberalism was any present saving grace.

Nor for the moment did liberal attitudes toward issues at home rouse the excitement or interest of youth. The yearning for security among the young after all echoed the strivings of the New Deal in both domestic and foreign policy. The old spokesmen had insisted that security was a means not an end and they never deliberately surrendered individualism to Herbert Hoover. They hoped that a foundation of stability at the base of the social structure would unloose creative energies through the rest of it. They fought for unemployment insurance or farm relief or industrial unionism, not to plunge a large part of the population into complacency, but to ease destructive fears so that men could turn their energies toward other purposes. But the liberals of the 1930's did not explore those purposes; and the tired, defensive phrases of conservatives evoked no response. Neither bequeathed to the 1950's a heritage that would inform youth that security was an instrument, not an ideal.

The situation of boys and girls who passed through American schools after 1945 encouraged the longing for security. Their parents, having read Gesell and Spock, spared them frustration and taught them the gospel of adjustment. The old frontiers had long since closed, the boys and girls learned. The old chances were gone, the old heroes dead. Life consisted of neatly marked off lanes. Run! Each in his own! All alike!

Only by speed could the individual pull away from the mass. Emerson's America had been the country of young men. A society that believed in inevitable improvement, that judged tomorrow always better than yesterday, ascribed a special virtue to youth, less constricted by the errors of the past, more responsive to the opportunities of the future. Eisenhower's had become a country of old men. A society that shunned risk and feared the future nurtured the caution of old age even in the youths in its schools. It thus neglected, to its later cost, education for the endless insecurity of life.

6

THE GRADUATES, 1960–1970

THREE (bad) popular movies of 1967.

Back and forth from home to college, Benjy-Dustin rushes in the little sports car. (Who pays for the gas? Poppa.) What is Dustin's hurry?

The future is blank. Floating in the swimming pool he nurses his grievance as he nurses his beer. Doomed to the plastics business! Then grow old like the parents who abuse him with gifts and kindness. Make something happen, or in five years he will be like them. Raped by a mom — the indignity: he likes it. So he breaks into the church, steals the girl and rides triumphantly off to nowhere. Poor Benjy.

Poor Paul Newman. He was only drunk and cut the heads off the parking meters (getting back at authority). How they made him suffer. Beatings. Work. But he was cool. Cool Hand Luke. Authority in the dark glasses got him in the end. Poor Luke.

Poor Bonnie. And poor Clyde. They only wanted to make it; and there in the field, just when they do — ALL

THOSE BULLETS AND ALL THAT BLOOD. Violence makes it. Poor Che!

Youth in Affluence

Now that youth extends to age twenty-five, the term refers to more than half the population of the United States.

Affluence: a condition in which the society can assure everyone a subsistence and in which 80 per cent of the population possesses that degree of choice over expenditure formerly characteristic of the middle class alone. Practically everyone of the appropriate age goes to high school; well over 40 per cent to college.

That much was the same, through the decade. Down to the very end of the 1960's the economy continued to expand while enterprise still increased in scale and developing technology called for more skilled technicians. Population streamed into the suburbs, which became more suburban still, linked to the central city by thronged ribbons of concrete. Within the suburban home, the child extended his dependency upon the family, to the concerns of which he was central, and perceived no acceptable way of leaving home except through an educational system, formal, rigid and competitive.

However, the young people of 1970 also differed markedly from those of 1960 — style of hair and clothes, attitudes toward education and careers, unrest instead of passivity, disorientation and destructiveness instead of the desire to conform.

The student movement was ever more prominent in the consciousness of youth and adults. At first its concern was civil rights — the march on Selma, the Mississippi summer, the voting campaign. Then attention shifted to the underprivileged, the poor at home and the Peace Corps beneficiaries abroad. And finally the focus came to rest on the elite universities — Berkeley, Wisconsin, Columbia and Harvard.

What caused the change? The bomb, Vietnam? Certainly. A remote war, difficult to justify, fought for imprecise purposes and bearing unequally upon some while leaving others untouched, triggered much of the discontent of the last three years of the decade — as other issues did among youth in France, Italy, Germany, Britain, Norway or Turkey. But the underlying causes in the United States were deeper than the involvement in Southeast Asia and had already manifested their effect while Saigon was just a hard one on the geography test.

The velocity of the transformation was not surprising; that was the general pattern in American life of the diffusion of styles. High hemlines, low; yo-yo, frisbee; crewcut, sideburns. Consumers, among whom the ability for making conscious, critical decisions atrophied through disuse, bought goods — and ideas — under the influence not of need or utility but of fashion. The habit of *camp* which taught audiences to respond not to the good, the true, the beautiful or the comic content, but to the package emphasized the importance of style. Taste was therefore volatile and one year's mode was out-of-date in the next, so that alert merchandisers had to sense potential shifts and push what was likely to go.

The media added momentum to whatever current of taste seemed likely to become dominant. The movies, TV, the large circulation magazines depended upon a mass market. Controlled by impersonal corporations and by the imperative of the balance sheet, of sales, and of ratings, they had to be sensitive to an imperfectly known audience of which youth was an ever-larger component. Success came from riding the crest of a likely wave; and once a trend appeared, all the prime time and space went to it so that its intensity cumulated. Editors, producers and directors who wished to *make it* had to be *with it.*

No one could be certain in advance what turn fashion would take; and a low budget flyer could sometimes clean up the market. Yet the advantage of getting into production early was an inducement to the gamble on the long shot, the extreme, the sensational, the shocker that might sweep in the whole pot. Often the player himself did not know what he was doing. *My feelings,* wrote Mike Nichols about "The Graduate," *are just my feelings, and my opinion really doesn't have much more validity than anybody else's. Who's to say I'm right and somebody else is wrong?* He was merely the producer of the movie.

In 1965 student radicals were a tiny minority. A study that year revealed none at all in 74 per cent of American colleges and fewer than 5 per cent among the pupils of the remaining institutions. By 1970 book publishers and movie producers had discovered *there's big money in revolution.* M-G-M was making *Revolution for the Hell of It* and the works of Abbie Hoffman and Jerry Rubin had sold hundreds of thousands of copies. Rebellion was in; even General Patton was a rebel. A little trend went a long way.

The origins of the trend and youth's receptivity to it reach back before the Harvard bust of 1969 or Columbia in 1968 or even Berkeley in 1964.

In 1955 of the Eisenhower era Jimmy Dean lost his life in the flaming wreck of his Porsche. For years thereafter the letters came in from fans who refused to believe him dead. His black leather jacket, blue jeans and riding boots became the uniform of a generation, for whom he was the *Rebel Without a Cause* — a symbol of inchoate discontent. More than a decade later, Dennis Hopper, who made *Easy Rider,* still looked to Dean as a model.

By 1960 masses of teen-agers (the next decade's youth) had succumbed to rock 'n' roll therapy — relief from the ordeal of reflection in the sensuous monotony of the strummed guitar, in the plaintive reiterations of the pseudo-ballad. Loss of self, a balm for those who could not find themselves, was another form of rebellion, against a world that demanded rational, consistent competitive performance.

Then the Beatniks copped out. And the Hippies. Signs of where the wind blew.

Rebellion had many ostensible goals but its essence was rebellion for its own sake. Unconsciously echoing Jimmy Dean, James K. Glassman wrote fourteen years later of *the absurdity of dying* FOR *something — it is useless if you are dead.* Man rebelled because he could not be man without doing so.

For the hard revolutionary core, not even power was a goal, as it was for the manipulative political types who talked of participation and structural reform. Tear it down! Pure destructiveness was the aim, revenge against the parents who loaded the Benjys with goods, protected them against want, and stifled desire. Howie Filbert winced at the memories — of Riverdale where the kids always picked on him and Mom was ever after him to play like the other boys, so that when he saw the Continental turn up the driveway he would run madly about the field in a pretense of participation; or of the graduation party when with everyone listening, SHE warned Pop to open the bottles in the kitchen lest the champagne get onto the wall-to-wall living room.

Bred in well-to-do suburban families, having always consumed and never produced, they could not imagine what life would be like without the mountains of goods they casually denounced. Tear it down; burn it; blow it up. The slogans were cheap for those who never felt want.

Their flaming zeal put the revolutionaries at the center of disturbance no matter how few were their numbers. They needed no majorities and rarely got them. But in the crisis they could depend upon the support grudgingly given, but given nevertheless by their classmates of the same background, who responded to the same grievances, although unwilling to go the whole way to rebellion.

They all felt Cool Hand Luke's instinctive mistrust of authority. Any rumor was credible if it discredited the government — of the nation or college. Raised in the utmost security by permissive parents, assured since babyhood that they knew best, they had early learned to denigrate the achievements and standards of their parents and regarded any restraint as an affront. Keep off the grass, no parking, overdue books — the world was full of prohibitory signs, which they casually disregarded. No punishment; amnesty was their due and the more often they received it, the firmer the conviction that they deserved it. Frequently enough there were warnings, as by John W. Gardner in 1969, against sweeping aside *rules, manners, formalities and standards of taste*. So what? Warnings never hurt anyone.

Spasmodic resistance to any control erupted in many institutions. In March 1968 a Barnard College sophomore's claim that she had a right to lie in order to live unmarried with a Columbia junior was still newsworthy. Two years later concealment was rarely necessary.

Yet underlying the compulsive need for self-assertion was a persistent fear of inadequacy. In a life that had been one test after another, the cost of failure was incalculable, for education had given the young people little more than the ability to check the right little squares. One poor performance could lose them all past gains. *No grades, no failures* became the campus cry.

Beautyrest U.
Glide right through!

The concern with not doing well, in class or in bed, oozes out of college literature. What if he did something stupid? Should he see the shrink at the health service? Was he really a goddamned freak? GO FUCK YOURSELF!!! — so runs the plot of a story in the *Harvard Crimson*. A plaintive wail rises from the fiction of sensitive young writers like Jonathan Strong and Fanny Howe. They have lost faith in traditional values, are unsure of themselves, lonely, bored, and have no inner resources on which to rely. James S. Kunen publishes the notes of a college revolutionary: he does not like school, but what else is there to do for someone who has never done anything but go to class? *I'll do anything to feel like I'm doing something.*

Blame THEM. Whom? The unspecified powers that envelop a person, prevent US — sad Alice standing in the doorway, the easy riders and midnight cowboys — from being natural, good in feel and touch. The confining restraints of THEIR civilization win in the end. Poor US!

Lower-class people, without supportive parents, who drifted into a similar state of purposelessness in this period became loners; James Earl Ray or Lee Harvey Oswald, lacking either the discipline of job or family, broke out in the desire to be somebody through dramatic acts of violence heedless of consequences. More generally, the deprived children of the poor, black or white, did have a purpose; one way or another, they reached for a share of the affluence about them.

The reaction of kids with means was more subtle. People like Jane Lauren Alpert, out of Forest Hills and Swarthmore, a gentle, soft-spoken and educated young woman, had been raised with warmth and affection all about them and expected the same relationship in their dealings with school, the authorities and police. Not finding it, they judged everything about them corrupt, demanding destruction. The need for love unbalanced both extremes, those who had suffered too much from want and those who had enjoyed too little the abundance they had. The culture provided few means of channeling their emotions.

What was all that with Anna Karenina? asks Cynthia Field, who has been on the Pill since her second year in high school. The needs of those who define love as a glandular spasm are insatiable.

Full of shit — Jenny Cavilleri's response (very softly) to a declaration of love. Having lost the vocabulary through which earlier generations expressed emotion, she and her peers lacked the words in which to speak with authenticity and sputtered obscenity, being dirty to be taken seriously.

The cry for attention was most bitter among those who considered themselves most deserving. They got 800's on the college boards and were the elite among thousands of applicants. They could not stand to be blank faces in the lecture hall, numbers in the draft-game lottery; their special ME, ME, ME, called for recognition. And now! Accustomed through youth to the immediate gratification of all demands, they had never learned the need for deferment of any desire.

Totally unaware of their own egocentricity, they generated no spark of empathy for the sentiments of others. The movie house in Berkeley rocked with laughter when Clyde shot the other fellow and the blood poured over the car window. How did the people feel in church when Benjy busted in? What emotion moved Anna Karenina? Or their own parents behind the split-level, thermopane picture window?

NO, BOB, NOT YOU. NOT ROBERT J. PILLAR, nice boy in torn sweater from Glencove, California — NOT, HOW WOULD YOU FEEL WITH A GUN IN YOUR FACE? BUT THE COP — stiff in blue serge — HOW WOULD HE FEEL: OR CALHOUN DEFENDING SLAVERY OR GARRISON ATTACKING IT? HOW WOULD THEY FEEL?

Blank.

The ritualistic expressions of regard for the welfare of an ideal humanity concealed a profound indifference to the suffering of the actual masses — the squares absorbed in the pursuit of petty happinesses, the hardhats occupied in accumulating possessions.

Standards of judgment were internal.

Debby Doffer pouts in petulance. *I can't stand it, all those fors and againsts. We've got to* DO *something and not just discuss and discuss. We* KNOW *what's right.*

When I get this feeling right here (hand to stomach), *I* KNOW *what's right. My Conscience tells me.*

What if my conscience tells me to do something absolutely opposite to yours? Debby refuses to acknowledge the question. She believes that all stomachs palpitate to a universal rhythm.

Paul Meadlo is exactly the same age as Debby, but in a different place, at Pinkville. *Why did I do it? Because I felt like I was ordered to do it, and it seemed like that, at the time I felt like I was doing the right thing, because like I said I lost buddies and it was on my conscience.*

Pascal: Evil is never done so thoroughly and so well as when it is done with a good conscience. But they didn't read Pascal in Debby's Basic Civ course.

The only trustworthy judgments are internal because none other are real. Beyond the TV screen Matt Dillon takes the gang on; there is shooting; the bodies fall. Then it's nine o'clock and you know they all get up to take off the makeup. Two hours later on the same screen the gunsmoke hangs over a street in Santo Domingo or Hue; the bodies fall. Do they also get up when the program is over? In Scarsdale High School, the boys and girls get course credits for playing at guerrilla warfare; they run through Butler Woods making like El Fatah or VC. *Anyone shot above the waist with a water pistol is considered dead.* Do they know what happens when the bombs are not aerosol?

Impenetrable, opaque institutions blocked off the sight and sound of experience. Death, birth, serious illness were events that transpired beyond the antiseptic walls of funeral parlors or hospitals so that it was rare for a well-brought-up child to know at first hand the stillness of a corpse or the pains of an invalid. Where Batman was a hero, emotions were *camp,* turned on for the sake of having them rather than out of the depth of feeling. Laughter and tears were not responses to external comic or tragic stimuli; they welled up out of an inner need to feel something. Boys and girls who never discovered who they themselves were (hence their anxiety about *identity*) looked out upon a world that seemed all chaos. The only reality, according to Abbie Hoffman, is *what I experience myself.*

The valedictorian at the Brown University commencement of 1969 sums up: *Society right now has very few realities for me. They exist, but they are not real. When I watch the news every night, it's not real to me. These can't be realities to me. I acknowledge that they exist but I can't allow myself to see them in my real world because, if I do that, then I am willing to accept them. The way things should be has got to be the way things are or none of us should be able to sleep well at night.*

It is not likely that the young man ever encountered Kant's meticulous explanation of why it is first necessary to recognize the way things are in order to be able to make them the way they should be. It wasn't in paperback and anyway, thick books clogged with rationality were not to the taste of the 1960's. The stylish volumes dripping conceits and studded with clever aphorisms did not present structured arguments so much as camp-type paradoxes of which the reader could make what he wished. A summons to experience nothingness, to return to the original innocence of children of nature, liberation by destruction, assertion of the radical will, that sweet feeling of benevolence without firm principles or sense of reality. That was the stuff. *The best and most creative people,* wrote Peter D. Kramer (by confession one of them), were radical romantics. *That had something to do with rock music, mysticism, the carpe diem motif, and the notion that "things aren't caused, they just happen — then we react or categorize." It had a lot to do with self-expression.*

And what was so enjoyable as the act of violent rebellion? ISN'T-IT-WONDERFUL-LOOK-AT-THE-ART-AND-MUSIC-IT'S-INSPIRING-O-HEAR-PEOPLE-COMMUNICATE-O-DAMMIT-I-FEEL-FREE.

Free — of meaning like the colors in *2001,* so that you spin away in sensation to a vague, wonderful, dizzy ambiguity. Sensation, sought in the orgy of the flesh without purpose but its own gratification, sought in the jab of a needle or puff of a joint, sought in the forbidden boy-boy postures, sought in thinking about, seeing, reading, doing; sensation endlessly, repetitively sought, dulls. And the more so when sensuality ceases to be covert. Manuals sold in hundreds of thousands of copies enabled anyone with $6.00 to go into training for sexual acrobatics; so who wants to be an athlete! The thrill that once the peep of an ankle brought, a knee, a thigh recedes from reach even with frequent increases of the dosage. Only the rates of venereal disease and drug addiction rise.

Some seekers after liberation turned to a guru who could supply answers to all inquiries; a flurry of interest in Herbert Marcuse's theories led to the inference that destruction of the old society was the only remedy for alienation. There was a synthetic passion just in reading Frantz Fanon or Régis Debray, who made revolution an end in itself and violence an occasion for a heroic display of determination. Nice boys and girls, destitute of other values, formed little cults for devotion to Mao, Che, or the Panthers and others turned to the togetherness of a commune as Theodore Gold did, who was thus cured of *bourgeois hangups like privacy and monogamy* and whose body was later found in a dynamite-blasted townhouse.

The violence which yielded the big thrill also escalated. The insatiable desire moved from petty acts of impoliteness to obstruction to occupation and then to dynamite. The dramatic gestures, cloaked in self-sacrifice and altruism, attracted an audience and involved the innocent bystanders, who were often the chief victims.

The pretext did not matter. The failure to give tenure to an instructor as at Santa Barbara, free speech at Berkeley, the gymnasium at Columbia, R.O.T.C. at Harvard — all the time administrators spent in discussion was time wasted. The radicals who sought violent confrontation found it, one way or another. Since the demands were utopian and unlimited, an excuse was always at hand; and since the demands were peremptory — NOW — no lesser means would do.

From Barry Goldwater fan to post-Weatherman: or the education of Richard E. Hyland. One big bang all the way. Sunny boy from golden California arrived in Harvard having, he said, read six books in his whole life (accuracy not being his strong point, it may have been sixteen or sixty; no matter). Four years in Cambridge, Massachusetts, taught him that an equally intelligent, rational and valid argument could be made on all sides of any question. Arguments therefore did not matter. *It is the feeling I have in my stomach that matters.* The feeling told him to blow up buildings, only he might get caught; and when the riots came, he could not decide: to throw the brick or not to throw; that was the question. But he ran with the mob.

Yes indeed, only a tiny minority obstructed, rioted, bombed. Less than 1 per cent. But they were the fashion setters. They influenced a large group who ran with the mob, and the much larger body of students who stayed apart from the trouble.

The structure of college life gave an active minority disproportionate weight in the 1960's. The great majority of young men and women in school, uncertain as they were about the ultimate purpose of their attendance, nevertheless believed that they were there to study. Earnest, occupied in the library and the lab, concerned with their careers, anxious to learn, they left college politics to the eager-beaver, glad-hand types, who spoke to everyone but spoke for no one, the kind who loved committees and were good at making arrangements. *Let them run it.* A typical election in an eastern institution in 1968 found fewer than 300 of 4,000 eligible bothering to vote. So that when Charles Palmer, president in 1969 of the National Student Association, spoke he spoke for Charles Palmer and for no one else really.

In the crisis, the radicals ruthlessly shoved the knee-pants politicians aside. There was a debate and a vote and a point of order; meanwhile the radicals acted, disregarding all the little fine points as the TV cameras came into focus, the headlines flared and the moderates ran with the mob. Not in one single case down to June 1970 did the student politicos have the guts to condemn the radicals. When the crisis came the moderate student leaders were busy reaching for a twist of power or signing up to write their memoirs.

In the showdown, too, many more students sympathized with the radicals than sympathized with radical ideas or actions. They should not have done it, but give them another chance. Amnesty.

In part, the reaction expressed an instinctive aversion towards any kind of punishment on the part of children accustomed to permissive treatment. In part it reflected the solidarity of classmates against authority, of youth against their elders.

But another element entered into the response. The S.D.S.ers said, *They are trying to squeeze the life out of you*. Few among their listeners believed the diatribes about imperialism and capitalism; but many felt a surge of long-hidden resentment. THEY were parents, schools, system — the whole apparatus that had cushioned American youngsters since infancy, that through the teens and beyond had denied them any role other than that of competitors. Protest welled up from those who had long been mute. The target was wrong and the mindless mob did itself more harm than good. But the unrecognized grievance was there: fear that the life was being squeezed out of them.

Why did their elders not recognize the lonely cry of children who did not know how to leave home?

The Vulnerability of the University

No one listened while there was yet time. The colleges were growing bigger and richer. Who would notice that they were stifling education?

The numbers were certainly impressive. By 1970 there were somewhat more than 2,500 institutions of higher education in the United States. They accommodated about seven million students, enrollments having doubled in a single decade, as the harvest of the baby boom of the 1940's came in. These enterprises expended some sixteen billion dollars, well over 2 per cent of the Gross National Product. Buildings, endowments, budgets all zoomed upward. Only the students — and particularly the undergraduates — were in trouble; and the faculties which felt a glow of satisfying warmth did not realize that the source was a dangerous fever.

The American college functioned in the 1960's with a time-encrusted mechanism, much of it valuable for the experience, tradition and wisdom built into it, some of it designed for purposes long forgotten. The curriculum divided into blocks of courses each worth a quota of points, and the grade that was evidence of the amount of learning deposited to the credit of each student in a central accounting system, originated more than a century earlier as disciplinary devices for the fourteen-year-old boys who often formed the freshman class. The pattern, no longer appropriate, survived through inertia and the mass of students thoroughly harnessed to the treadmill of examinations accepted servitude as a normal if strenuous condition of life.

The most highly motivated students of the best high schools knew they were in a close race in which only the fleetest would enter the most desirable colleges. Judgments came in the spring of the fourth year and rested on performance in tests taken a good deal earlier. In addition schemes for early admission and early appraisal pushed some of the examinations back into the middle of the third year so that the secondary school often was an extended cram.

Entry into college revealed new hurdles while the pace

quickened. The brightest and best in high school were now in a mass in which all had been brightest and best. Some who had always been winners discovered that they now had to be losers. No matter how hard they worked, one half of the class would always fall below the average. Meanwhile the goal was the same — a high score to open the way to the next competition, graduate or professional school.

Pressure fed anxiety. Dependent young people had to do well lest they jeopardize the love and affection of the parents who had hopefully groomed them for the race. Good grades, scholarships and jobs immediately affected the income of the whole family, the chances for a new car, the little sister's prospects for an expensive education. No one wanted to let down those who had invested in them. The boys and girls of the 1960's never knew that success in tests was not the only way to achievement, that the careers of great men did not always begin with a ranking in the uppermost tenth percentile, that there were other than competitive values to education.

The losses were tremendous. The reconciled mass somehow made their peace with the system. But the ablest, who secured admirable training in the techniques of the correct answer, were rarely called on to use their ability autonomously or speculatively, to deal with situations in which the answers were not known but had to be discovered. Nor could they afford the sense of the tentativeness of knowledge. Writing against the clock, they always put the cross in the right box and rounded out the essay with a solid conclusion. They missed the experience of education — that experience which, by the exposure of one mind to the thinking of others, created not answers but a lifetime of questions. Therefore they remained as uncritical in the rejection of all authority as in its acceptance. Richard Hyland, post-Weatherman, was no more thinking for himself in 1970 than when he had been pro-Goldwater in 1964.

I am so — I am critical, insists the girl who believes everything she reads in the *New York Review of Books. I know if Nixon says it, it's not true.* Only she can't understand about *MacBird,* which is still a snickery in-book on her dorm floor, and why it should be so nasty about Bobby Kennedy, who was on the right side.

The habits of dependency fostered at home and at school further stifled the capacity for originality. Sure, the freshman settled into his room on his own — sometimes armed with a credit card. He asserted himself not by seeking a distinctive personal style but by debating changes in the dormitory rules; and the competitive calculus of course-credit advantages blinded him to the possibility of learning outside the measured blocks and units of formal instruction.

Any blast of awareness could throw off course the youths who had never learned to locate themselves by their own standards. Yet the increasingly rigid educational system made no room for the variant patterns of the maverick. Many sensitive youngsters simply threw up their hands, turned their backs on the whole process, and rejected the values attached to the college. They hastened into marriage, or refused to stick it out for the sheepskin, or broke down, or, preferring the guidance of the stomach feeling to that of the mind, turned rebel.

American educators failed in their appraisal of the problem and failed therefore to cope with it. The fear of inundation by a tidal wave of pupils fixed their attention on budgets and buildings. But they devoted little thought to the means of occupying students who were in the university because it was the reservoir that withheld unneeded hands from the labor market while it sorted them out for ultimate places in a technical economy. A beefed-up psychiatric, counseling and guidance service would take care of the youths who arrived without knowing why they came.

The colleges followed no single model; history made them private or state, large or small, municipal or sectarian. That diversity enabled them to make room for students who differed widely among themselves in social background, in intellectual ability and interest, and in preparation. Variety was the strength of the system which could take account of those differences while preserving the fiction that the degrees awarded were all identical.

The weaknesses emanated from the pretense that all institutions of higher education were essentially the same. Only rarely did a university recognize its own position clearly enough to use its resources effectively. Most aimed, as they had in the past, for the same paraphernalia — campus, professors, library, laboratory, alumni association, color, song and stadium — just as they bestowed the same degrees, whatever the appropriateness to the job they actually did. The faculties too — wherever they were — aspired to the same privileges of tenure, limited teaching load, and aid to research. And the students everywhere regarded the admission certificate as the badge of transition from adolescence to maturity.

The frustration of conforming to standards beyond reach left administrators, students and teachers irritably aggrieved. No one measured up: there simply were not that many good colleges, teachers and students; and primitive selection procedures usually failed to bring the three together.

Faculty resentments were particularly important because they deepened with time. The turnover of students and administrators was relatively rapid. The professors, even when they moved from one institution to another, lived with their problems permanently. There were not enough books in the library or machines in the lab; or if there were, there was not enough time for research; or if there was, there were not enough secretaries or programmers! And if everything was at hand, then there remained the necessity of finding something to say. The pretense that all teachers were creative scholars led to an impasse, particularly since the increase in the size of faculties in the 1960's had sadly diluted their quality.

Teaching on the college as on the school level had been slow to earn esteem in the United States. Signs of professionalism had first appeared in the 1870's; and the next half-century had witnessed the grudging growth of respect for science and learning. Professors therefore were instinctively defensive, disposed to regard their students and society at large as hostile. The dominant concern was to fend off attack. Tenure, the vested right to a teaching post, and immunity to dismissal, became the primary — indeed often the sole — concern of the profession. There was no significant effort to develop standards of competence or of malpractice; the Ph.D. degree which for a time seemed likely to become the test of qualification was never completely reliable and became less so after 1960.

An informal system of personal evaluation was adequate when numbers were small enough so that all the scholars in a discipline knew each other personally. In the 1960's when hundreds of institutions granted advanced degrees, and thousands taught the common subjects, the department which made an appointment could act only on the basis of letters of recommendation, the writers of which it did not know. Yet once hired, the new colleague could be fired only with the greatest difficulty and unpleasantness.

Nevertheless, neither the academic profession as a whole nor any of its constituent organizations defined the obligations of a professor, a task which the founders of the American Association of University Professors had assumed would have an early claim of attention. The task remained unperformed. In 1967, for instance, while enumerating the rights of students, the Association warned that disruptions by physical force and denial of the right to speak were destructive of the pursuit of learning and of a free society. But it was unwilling to affirm that it was improper for faculty members to condone disruptive student action. The absence of an agreed-on code immobilized administrators and colleagues when a problem professor turned up; everyone then sought above all to avoid public exposure, conflict or scandal.

Deep, unhealed scars that were the products of decades of neglect prevented faculties from dealing with their problems in a manner that was not manifestly self-defeating. The thrill — post-Sputnik — of suddenly being desired had a heady effect. As the federal money poured in, salaries spiraled upward; the goodies of American society which had long been counted not worth having now were within reach and the professors, jostling at the same trough with the journalist, the press agent and the businessman, despised themselves for doing so.

Specialization within increasingly narrow fields justified expansion and high salaries and fitted in with the whole process by which knowledge was everywhere organized. The disadvantage, not so evident at first, grew out of the neglect to inquire whether the uniquely qualified individual, the scholar who knew all about fish eyes or metal stress, knew anything else. The drawback was particularly important in institutions the function of which was not only the advancement of knowledge but the custody of youth.

The manic excitement of the 1960's, coming after a much longer period of depression, had a paradoxically frightening effect upon faculty members. Rapid promotion and quick access to high incomes deprived many of any sense of having earned their status or of any confidence that reliable professional norms would protect them against mistreatment or the loss of esteem. The response to the escalating student abuse and violence after 1964 was defensive, either a panicky withdrawal to the lab or an effort to win over the young by pandering to their prejudiced and uninformed views. A desperate will to be liked produced a frolicky imitation of student tastes in dress and opinions, a palsy eagerness to deny the generation gap by disregarding all differences including those of depth of knowledge, and a flaccid acceptance of verbal and physical attack under the guise of accommodation.

For the time being, the willingness to be guided by student views nurtured the infantile leftism also fashionable among other newly affluent groups. Insofar as it contained any common elements apart from the desire to escape student fury by anticipating demands, faculty leftism generally boiled down to aversion of the use of police power. A *New York Times Magazine* symposium of May 1969 was representative. The learned participants shuddered at the prospect of a uniform on campus. Never? Not quite! But, one professor explained, only as a last resort, if for instance a building was about to be blown up with the probability of loss of life — and even then only after all other expedients had failed.

The serene assumption that the police would be willing to wait that long and to go in under those conditions revealed the detachment of the professor from the world of reality. But the moral consequences of the nonviolent posture were more significant. The argument against potential violence by the police called to protect the university became a defense of the violence of the extremists bent on destroying the university. Certainly committees deplored and administrators sternly warned — about next times; but these gentle admonitions did not deter the tiny minority of determined extremists and left helpless the much larger numbers who wished to pursue their studies without interruption as well as the vast majority uncertain about their purpose in college.

The nonviolent argument also contained the glib, self-satisfied claim that it chose life over property. The property, of course, consisted of libraries, museums, laboratories and the apparatus that made learning possible — the repositories, that is, of man's spiritual heritage, assembled through generations of effort. The buildings of the university were property, devoted to diverse and even contradictory purposes; but they were also temples of the intellect, dedicated to rationality and truth and, by some standards, worth fighting for, dying for.

The turtlenecked worshipers of the young, avid for popularity, preferred to evade such issues, to cover up fires in the libraries, vandalism in the museums, damage to research. They saw love in the eyes of the Visigoths who stormed through their offices. Accommodate! Better to yield a little here, give away a little there. It couldn't be rape when the victim yelled that he liked it.

One result was emphasis upon the manipulative skill of administrators. The cardinal rule was: avoid trouble. Presidents and deans who could not depend upon their faculties could not afford to hold to principle. They courted popularity or at least tolerance by the elaborate fiction that violence was the product of a failure to respond to the student demand. GIVE THEM ANYTHING TO KEEP THE PEACE.

The further result therefore was to deprive undergraduates of what they most needed, a sense of standards worth sustaining, of guidelines worth following, of scholarly values worth respecting.

The disorientation of thoughtful undergraduates owed a good deal also to an ancient failing of the American university — the protestations of immediate utility by which it justified itself to an unintellectual public.

The reverend chaplain of Yale University, writing appropriately for *Playboy,* in 1968 criticized professors in ivory cellars who spent endless hours shedding light on what was not worth illuminating. He equated scholarship with a refusal to be ethically responsive, a refusal that in turn he linked to the nation's rapid progress down the road to moral oblivion.

This barbaric yawp had reverberated through the centuries with no foundation in fact. Far from being cloistered or remote from everyday life, the universities of the United States always suffered from the need to demonstrate their utility to taxpayers or donors. Rarely could a professor escape the compulsion of proving that his work was instrumental to some comprehensible utilitarian purpose. Administrators invited society to bring all its problems to the university for solution and the response in the 1960's was a vast, incoherent mushrooming of activities.

The universities had survived until then and had even managed to preserve a humane and scholarly ingredient in their operations. But additional burdens after 1960 strained already attenuated intellectual resources and already weakened faculties. The puddling out of activity in every direction swept into the ranks of the professoriate a variety of types with little sense of identity other than the common source of their salaries. The complex array of faculties, departments and research institutes assembled in a single organization teachers of gymnastics and of Greek, of domestic science, nursing and particle physics, of animal husbandry, neurosurgery and Sanskrit, along with politicians out of office, journalists in search of a live audience, and bureaucrats and technicians between posts. The development blurred altogether the students' sense of the university as a unique undertaking dedicated to scholarly ends and values of its own.

As the percentage of the age group hastening toward degrees of some sort increased, the need for providing some activity for all of them crowded scholarship and learning to the periphery. Diverted from the tasks it could perform to those beyond its capacity, the university was hard put to find residual space for academic concerns, for the effort to uncover the truth and make it known.

Meanwhile decades of wildly extravagant rhetoric had left outstanding an imposing array of promissory notes — the university would solve the problems of disease and poverty, of scarcity and war, of race and old age, that is, it would advance American man toward his birthright of happiness. In the 1960's, to the extent that people ceased to think of happiness as a pursuit and began to demand it as a prize, the university assumed much of the burden of making the world perfect.

Black Studies — a tragic consequence of shortsightedness among students, of moral cowardice or ineptitude among professors, and of the demand on the university that it remedy at once an old and painful illness.

A contrast. In October 1962 James Meredith entered the University of Mississippi, a Negro student in Ole Miss, stronghold of segregation. Ability earned him his place, the full power of the federal government assured it to him, and his personal bearing recalled the dignity of the Greensboro student sit-in, of Martin Luther King's gospel of nonviolence and of the long, steady opening of the right to education since 1945. In April 1969 Tom Jones made his threat at Ithaca, New York. *We put our lives on the line,* with just one proviso, *that along with our lives on the line, everybody else's life was on the line.* A peremptory demand, defiance of the rules, and violence forced Cornell to surrender. Other universities did the same or forestalled the indignity by concessions before the confrontation.

O yes, behind the anger was an experience of frustration. The blacks in college in 1969 had just entered school in 1954, the year of the Brown decision, and the promise of desegregation had been only imperfectly fulfilled so that many had never received the equal schooling that was their due. Many too had moved in the northward migration that carried their families out of the rural South into the urban slums and left them desperate in the search to find themselves, to move upward.

And behind the fear of the whites was guilt, a gnawing belief that they should have done more, and awareness of the contrast between their own affluence and the deprivation of others. The shame reached a peak of intensity in April 1968 with the assassination of Martin Luther King, so that some universities in the agonized wish to expiate hastened to enroll black youths without considering whether they were prepared or what they would do. All along the colleges floundered, for the effort to do what they could not do increased the guilt of having failed, which in turn drove them on to further acts of futile desperation.

Enshrouding the frustration and the fear was an enveloping shadow — the consciousness that the bands of authority no longer held. The faculties that would not punish affluent white students would certainly not discipline poor blacks.

After each capitulation followed the rationalizations. The university had done so many diverse things for others, why could it not do this for those who most deserved attention, whose needs for help were greatest, etc., etc., etc.

Perhaps the costs will never be paid; lucky circumstances in the American past have often turned liabilities into assets and by obscuring causes produced unexpected desirable results. So much for hope.

But many bills are outstanding:

Item, the unfounded imputation that black students cannot do the work of whites and require special courses of study.

Item, the appointment of inferior teachers because of their color.

Item, the assignment of quotas and discrimination by race, contrary to the law of many states and very likely to the federal constitution.

Item, the corruption of standards of admission and graduation and therefore the debasement of all credentials by differential grading and evaluating practices.

Item, the threat of making segregation a permanent feature of college life.

Above all, at least for those who believe in the universality of truth and the common humanity of man, exclusion of black youth from part of its heritage. From a conference on Black Studies, May 1968: *Why should somebody be teaching Shakespeare today with his "thee" and "thou"? People don't talk that way any more. I'm not saying white people can't learn it — they like that sort of stuff. But it's not real world to us, tight pants and funny hats.*

Weep for the university incapable of answering. Mourn for the ideal of men in all their splendid differences united in the love of truth and beauty. Or, grasp at the chance the answer will yet be given, the ideal revived. But be aware of the past negligence of the custodians.

THE TIME — JUNE 1970 — IS NOT PROPITIOUS FOR SUMMING UP THE RECORD. EVIDENTLY A FEVER RAGES; EVERYONE AGREES THAT THE TEMPERATURE RISES. BUT THE PHYSICIANS, POMPOUS IN THEIR WHITE DECORUM, REFUSE TO

RENDER A JUDGMENT. THE CONSULTATION DISSOLVES WITH A REQUEST FOR MORE DATA PENDING A NEW DIAGNOSIS AND RESEARCH CONTINUES IN THE LABORATORY. MEANWHILE QUACKS CHARGE THROUGH THE ROOMS, PEDDLING EACH HIS OWN NOSTRUM. *Rub your troubles away. Try a little this* and *Take a little that. Make a little peace* and *Clear an urban blot. Poverty. Pollution. Population. Crisis. Crisis. Rah Rah Rah.*

AND DOWN BELOW THE RANTERS RUB THEIR LITTLE STICKS, MAKING FIRE TO BURN THE BUILDING DOWN SO THAT THE INMATES RESTORED TO PRISTINE NAKEDNESS WILL HEAL THEMSELVES IN THE FAITH (OR BLOOD) OF THE INNOCENT.

Perhaps a hundred years is as long a life span as any modern institution can expect in a world under stress. It is just about a century since Charles W. Eliot entered upon the presidency of Harvard and began to transform a boys' institution of clerical antecedents into a center of scholarship the influence of which would radiate through the whole culture. His vision was imperfect and never attained fulfillment. But he and his contemporaries who founded the other great American universities created little enclaves of learning, to which families entrusted youths at the crucial moment of leaving home. Whatever reasons of prudence or hope of advantage entered into the decision, it associated maturity with the life of the mind and created durable links to learning among hundreds of thousands of men and women, the alumni otherwise totally occupied with the work of the material world. Growing up, preparing to face life, for many Americans thus acquired an intellectual dimension.

The effort to accommodate in a single institution young people preparing to face life and scholars pursuing knowledge was never wholly successful and from the start called for compromise between the aspirations of educators and the needs of their clientele. But the increase in numbers after 1960 immensely magnified the pull away from the kind of university conceived by Eliot and his contemporaries.

Growth and change will no doubt continue in the years to come so that the universities of the foreseeable future are scarcely likely to resemble those of the past. As long as the labor market makes no place for people under twenty-two they will seek to pass the time in schools of some sort, perhaps 70 per cent of them in the 1980's. The institutions of higher education able to serve those numbers will not be identical with those which once served a small social and intellectual elite group. To cling to the forms of the past will be neither possible nor desirable, but the quality of the transformation ahead may depend on the assessment of the possible consequences for freedom, for learning and for society, as well as for youth.

For freedom. Whereof did the freedom of the university consist? Of the ability of each of its members to do his own thing, of the students to learn and play, of the professors to teach and study, of alumni to provide funds, each confident that his own interests would stand in satisfactory balance with the others. When the funds dry up and all depend upon the government, when committees of committees make decisions about everything, when all participate in determining what each shall do, where is then the freedom of the individual?

For learning. Where in the university did scholarship reside? Not in any building or in the books or retorts, but in the hearts of men for whom the pursuit of truth, generation after generation, was an end in itself and for whom the service of rearing the young was the price paid for the tolerance to do their own work. Shall they now flee to research posts, leaving the teaching to specialists in conciliation and mediation?

For society. How did chances open for those who neither inherited places nor possessed established connections to attain them? By recognizing general standards of competence and defining justice as a condition in which each person did that for which his own personality and ability made him most fit. Competition through education was a necessary, though painful, step in the selection process. Every privilege for one diminished the right of another. How will society fare, with the assignment of places by quota, thus favoring some at the expense of others?

And for youth. Of what did leaving home consist? Of entering the world, insecure and alone and thus severing the ties of childish dependence. For most Americans through most of their past, the plunge came through work and the discipline of a job that provided the instruction in how to govern the self and live in civility with others. First for a few, then for almost all, the school was an alternative, teaching the lesson in different ways. But the object was to become a man — not angelic, not heroic — human, one with others, yet separate. And if the school fails and the work is not there, will they grow up who remain dependent, hanging on to home even while away, never quite ready to face life?

In the final analysis the problem is one of facing life. The pressure on the university is only one manifestation of the intense needs of youth bewildered by a world that has ceased to be a village. A mass society, sustained by an impersonal economy, no longer operates according to precepts verified by the experience of generations and does not expose its youth to life.

The children cannot follow when the parents do not lead.

The parents cannot lead when the path has vanished and the destination is not known.

And the school does not supply the deficiencies of parents, for its numerous, incoherent and conflicting elements offer no dependable guide to the proper direction.

For the young, the years pass and life recedes. Out of the fear of being lost, of losing touch, of nothingness, springs the wish to act, no matter how — if only to prove the fact of being. For the yearning, compassion.

But also a caution. Is it emptiness or openness about us? The absence of familiar paths may be the opportunity for discovery; and the destination unknown may only demonstrate the limits of our vision.

PERSONAE

THIS list supplies the date of birth where known, a brief identification, and a source of reference for most of the persons mentioned in the book.

ABBOTT, BERENICE (1898), photographer.
172

ACKLEY, MARY E. (1842), housewife, born in Missouri, who migrated to California. Mary E. Ackley, *Crossing the Plains and Early Days in California* (San Francisco, 1928).
93

ADAMS, CHARLES FRANCIS (1807), lawyer and diplomat, son of John Q., father of Charles F., Jr., and Henry. Martin Duberman, *Charles Francis Adams, 1807–1886* (Stanford, 1960); C. F. Adams, *Charles Francis Adams* (Boston, 1900) .
80

ADAMS, CHARLES FRANCIS, JR. (1835), lawyer, business executive, and historian, son of Charles Francis and brother of Henry. Edward C. Kirkland, *Charles Francis Adams, Jr. 1835–1915* (Cambridge, 1965).
151

ADAMS, HANNAH (1755), author of historical works. Hannah Adams, *A Memoir* (Boston, 1832).
93

ADAMS, HENRY (1838), historian, son of Charles Francis, brother of Charles Francis, Jr. Henry Adams, *Education of Henry Adams* (Boston, 1918); Ernest Samuels, *Henry Adams,* Volume I (Cambridge, 1965).
129

Personae

ADAMS, JOHN (1735), lawyer, second President of the United States, father of John Quincy. Page Smith, *John Adams, Volume I, 1735–1784* (Garden City, New York, 1962).
57

ADAMS, JOHN QUINCY (1767), diplomat, sixth President of the United States, Congressman, son of John, father of Charles Francis. Samuel F. Bemis, *John Quincy Adams and the Foundations of American Foreign Policy* (New York, 1949).
125

AGASSIZ, LOUIS (1807), naturalist, founder of the Museum of Comparative Zoology and professor of natural history at Harvard University. Edward Lurie, *Louis Agassiz, A Life in Science* (Chicago, 1960).
108

ALCOTT, AMOS BRONSON (1799), transcendentalist, educational reformer and father of Louisa May. Odell Shepard, *Pedlar's Progress* (Boston, 1937); Charles Strickland, "A Transcendentalist Father," *Perspectives in American History,* Volume III (Cambridge, 1969), 5 ff.
86

ALCOTT, LOUISA MAY (1832), novelist, daughter of Amos Bronson. Her more important works are *Little Women* (1868), *Little Men* (1871), and *Under the Lilacs* (1878).
91, 159

ALDRICH, HENRY (1922), central character in *What a Life,* a play by Clifford Goldsmith, which opened in New York on April 13, 1938.
229

ALGER, HORATIO, JR. (1832), minister and author of popular fiction. Frank Gruber, *Horatio Alger, Jr.* (West Los Angeles, 1961).
151

ALLEN, ETHAN (1737), deist revolutionary hero, active in Vermont speculation and politics. John Pell, *Ethan Allen* (Boston, 1929).
20, 50, 150

ALOYS. *See* Grubler, Aloys

ALPERT, JANE LAUREN (1947), graduate of Swarthmore, writer for *The Rat,* concerned with abortion reform, women's liberation and the transforming of American culture, accused of bomb conspiracy. *New York Times,* November 13, 14, 1969.
265

ANDERSON, JAMES (1748), student at Andover Academy from Londonderry, New Hampshire. Claude M. Fuess, *An Old New England School* (Boston, 1917).
104

ANGELL, JAMES B. (1829), journalist, president of the universities of Vermont (1866–1871) and Michigan (1871–1909), diplomat.

188

ANNENBERG, WALTER (1908), editor and newspaper publisher. United States Ambassador to the United Kingdom (1968—). A. J. Reichley, "Moe's Boy Walter," *Fortune,* LXXXI (June 1970), 88 ff.

218

ATWOOD, MINNIE EDWARDS (c. 1860), funeral director in Lisbon, New Hampshire.

174

AUSTIN, JAMES W. (1829), native of Charlestown, Massachusetts, graduate of Harvard College, 1849, of Harvard Law School, 1851, migrated to Hawaii and became a member of Parliament and judge there.

83

BACON, JABEZ (1731), tanner, peddler, became richest merchant in Woodbury, Connecticut.

35

BALDWIN, LOAMMI (1744/5), soldier and civil engineer, builder of the Middlesex Canal and discoverer of the Baldwin apple.

107

BARBOUR, RALPH HENRY (pseud. Richard S. Powell) (1870), author of numerous books and stories for boys.

164

BARNARD, FREDERICK A. P. (1809), teacher and president of Columbia University (1864–1889). John Fulton, *Memoirs of Frederick A. P. Barnard* (New York, 1896).

129

BARUCH, BERNARD (1870), financier and presidential adviser. Margaret L. Coit, *Mr. Baruch* (Boston, 1957).

160

BASCOM, JOHN (1827), philosopher, president of the University of Wisconsin (1874–1887).

206

BEECHER, CATHARINE ESTHER (1800), sister of Henry Ward Beecher and of Harriet Beecher Stowe, teacher and author of *Educational Reminiscences and Suggestions* (New York, 1874).

95

BEECHER, HENRY WARD (1813), clergyman and author, brother of Catharine Beecher and of Harriet Beecher Stowe. William G. McLoughlin, *The Meaning of Henry Ward Beecher* (New York, 1970); Joseph Howard, Jr., *Life of Henry Ward Beecher* (Philadelphia, 1887).

103

BENÉT, STEPHEN VINCENT (1898), poet and author of *Young Adventure* (New Haven, 1918); and *Ballads and Poems* (New York, 1931). *145, 165, 198*

BENJY. *See* Braddock, Benjamin

BENTON, THOMAS HART (1782), lawyer and United States Senator from Missouri (1821–1851). William N. Chambers, *Old Bullion Benton* (Boston, 1956). *129*

BETHUNE, MARY MCLEOD (1875), educator and lecturer, founder of National Council of Negro Women. Rackham Holt, *Mary McLeod Bethune* (Garden City, New York, 1964). *179*

BIGELOW, JOHN (1817), lawyer, editor of *New York Evening Post,* diplomat. Margaret Clapp, *Forgotten First Citizen* (Boston, 1947). *88*

BIRD, MRS. THOMAS (c. 1820), character in Harriet Beecher Stowe's *Uncle Tom's Cabin or, Life among the Lowly* (Boston, 1852). *91, 92*

BLACKWELL, ELIZABETH (1821), teacher, physician, active in the women's rights movements. *110*

BLAINE, AMORY (c. 1900), protagonist in F. Scott Fitzgerald's *This Side of Paradise* (New York, 1920). *143*

BOIT, JOHN, JR. (1774), Boston sea captain. Robert A. Boit, *Chronicles of the Boit Family* (Boston, 1915). *86*

BONNIE (c. 1916), central character in *Bonnie and Clyde,* a movie of 1967 set in the 1930's. *258*

BOONE, DANIEL (1734), pioneer and Indian fighter. John Bakeless, *Daniel Boone* (Harrisburg, Pennsylvania, 1965). *81, 167*

BOOTH, SHIRLEY (1907), actress, radio performer. *171*

BOTTS, ALEXANDER (c. 1900), tractor salesman, hero of a series of short stories by W. H. Upson, published in *Saturday Evening Post,* April 16, 1927 and thereafter. *167*

BOURKE-WHITE, MARGARET (1905), photographer and war correspondent. Margaret Bourke-White, *Portrait of Myself* (New York, 1963). *198*

BOURNE, RANDOLPH (1886), radical critic. Louis Filler, *Randolph Bourne* (Washington, 1943). *163*

BRADDOCK, BENJAMIN (c. 1942), central character in Charles Webb's novel, *The Graduate* (1963) and in the movie of the same name (1967).

258, 262, 266

BRAINERD, DAVID (1718), missionary among the Indians and author of a spiritual journal. Jonathan Edwards, *A Life and Diary of David Brainerd* (Chicago, 1949).

20, 41, 42, 50, 65

BRANDEIS, LOUIS D. (1856), lawyer and justice of United States Supreme Court. Alpheus T. Mason, *Brandeis, A Free Man's Life* (New York, 1956).

175, 206

BRICE, FANNY (1891), singer, entertainer. Norman Katkov, *The Fabulous Fanny* (New York, 1953).

171

BROOKS, PHILLIPS (1835), Episcopal clergyman and pulpit orator. Alexander V. G. Allen, *Life and Letters of Phillips Brooks* (New York, 1900).

79, 99

BROWN, BENNY (c. 1870), character in Louisa May Alcott, *Under the Lilacs* (Boston, 1878).

151

BROWN, BUSTER (c. 1896), comic character drawn (1902 ff.) by Richard F. Outcault, who had earlier created the Yellow Kid.

152

BROWN, CHARLES BROCKDEN (1771), novelist, journalist and editor. David Lee Clark, *Charles Brockden Brown* (Durham, 1952).

92, 111, 121

BROWN, MOSES (1738), cotton manufacturer and Quaker philanthropist, nephew of Obadiah. Mack Thompson, *Moses Brown, Reluctant Reformer* (Chapel Hill, 1962).

36

BROWN, OBADIAH (1712), merchant, uncle of Moses. James B. Hedges, *The Browns of Providence Plantations* (Cambridge, 1952).

36

BRUCE, EMILY A. (c. 1850), teacher and physician in Boston.

174

BRUNOT, FELIX R. (1820), manufacturer and president of the Board of Indian Commissioners. Charles L. Slattery, *Felix Reville Brunot* (New York, 1901).

126

BUCKLEY, WILLIAM F., JR. (1925), editor of *National Review* and author of *God and Man at Yale* (Chicago, 1951). *Time*, November 3, 1967.

254

BUFFALO BILL. *See* Cody, William F.

BUMSTEAD, HORACE (1841), Congregational minister, educator and president of Atlanta University (1888–1907).

194

BUSHNELL, HORACE (1802), Congregational clergyman and author of *Christian Nurture* (1847). Barbara M. Cross, *Horace Bushnell: Minister to a Changing America* (Chicago, 1958).

72

BYRD, WILLIAM II (1674), planter and colonial official, member of Virginia House of Burgesses, author.

40, 54

CABOT, GODFREY LOWELL (1861), manufacturer and aviation enthusiast. Leon Harris, *Only to God* (New York, 1967).

175

CALVIN, JOHN (1509), theologian and reformer, resident of Geneva, author of *Institutes of the Christian Religion* (1559). J. T. McNeill, *The History and Character of Calvinism* (1954).

42

CAMPBELL, ARCHIBALD (c. 1710), Scottish-born minister of Washington parish, Virginia (1754–1774). William Meade, *Old Church Ministers and Families of Virginia* (Baltimore, 1966), Volume II, 158ff.

101

CANTOR, EDDIE (1893), comedian, motion picture actor and radio personality. Eddie Cantor, *My Life Is in Your Hands* (New York, 1928); and *As I Remember Them* (New York, 1963).

228

CARNEGIE, ANDREW (1835), manufacturer and philanthropist, author of *Triumphant Democracy* (1886). *Autobiography of Andrew Carnegie* (Boston, 1920).

87, 174

CARRIE, SISTER (1871), protagonist of Theodore Dreiser, *Sister Carrie* (New York, 1900).

177

CARTER, NICHOLAS (c. 1870), central character in a series of detective stories written from 1889 by various authors, including Frederic Van R. Dey, John R. Coryell and Frederick W. Davies.

152

CARTER, ROBERT (1663), Virginia landholder and government official. Clifford Dowdey, *The Virginia Dynasties* (Boston, 1969).

101

CARTER, ROBERT (1728), Virginia planter. Louis Morton, *Robert Carter of Nomini Hall* (Williamsburg, Virginia, 1941).

101

CARTER, ROBERT (c. 1770), godfather of Robert E. Lee, who gave up agriculture out of dislike for slavery, and became a physician.
109

CASSATT, BARNARD (c. 1790), preacher assisted by Lorenzo Waugh.
90

CAULFIELD, HOLDEN (c. 1935), protagonist of J. D. Salinger, *Catcher in the Rye* (Boston, 1951).
229

CAVILLERI, JENNIFER (c. 1948), heroine in Erich Segal, *Love Story* (New York, 1970).
265

CHANNING, WILLIAM ELLERY (1780), Unitarian minister and writer on ethics. William H. Channing, *Memoir of William Ellery Channing* (Boston, 1848); David P. Edgell, *William Ellery Channing* (Boston, 1955).
99, 101

CHAUNCY, CHARLES (1592), clergyman, president of Harvard College (1654–1672).
54

CHE. *See* Guevara, Ernesto

CLAP, THOMAS (1703), clergyman and president of Yale University (1739–1766). Louis L. Tucker, *Puritan Protagonist* (Chapel Hill, 1962).
56, 63, 65

CLEMENS, SAMUEL L. (1835), humorist and novelist who used the pseudonym Mark Twain. Justin Kaplan, *Mr. Clemens and Mark Twain* (New York, 1966).
188

CLEVELAND, GROVER (1837), lawyer, political leader, twenty-second and twenty-fourth President of the United States (1885–1889, 1893–1897). Allan Nevins, *Grover Cleveland: A Study in Courage* (New York, 1932).
84

CLYDE (c. 1914), character in the 1967 movie, *Bonnie and Clyde,* set in the 1930's.
258, 266

COCKRAN, W. BOURKE (1854), lawyer, orator and United States Congressman from New York. James McGurrin, *Bourke Cockran* (New York, 1948).
172, 173

CODY, WILLIAM F. (1846), known as Buffalo Bill, frontier scout, hunter, hero of dime novels and organizer of Wild West shows. R. J. Walsh, *Making of Buffalo Bill* (Indianapolis, 1928).

152

COLLES, JAMES (1788), successful merchant whose business centered in New Orleans, father of James Colles, Jr.; Emily Johnston De Forest, *James Colles 1788–1883* (New York, 1926).

70, 71

COLLES, JAMES, JR. (1827), merchant in New York City, son of James Colles.

105

CONWAY, MONCURE D. (1832), clergyman, free thinker and author. Moncure D. Conway, *Autobiography, Memories and Experiences* (Boston, 1904).

90

CONWELL, RUSSELL H. (1843), soldier, clergyman, founder of Temple University. A. B. Burr, *Russell H. Conwell and His Work* (Philadelphia, 1917).

172

COOKE, JAY (1821), banker and financier whose interests centered in Philadelphia. Henrietta M. Larson, *Jay Cooke, Private Banker* (Cambridge, 1936).

87

COOLIDGE, JOHN CALVIN (1872), lawyer, Massachusetts politician and thirtieth President of the United States (1923–1929). William A. White, *A Puritan in Babylon: Calvin Coolidge* (New York, 1938); Claude M. Fuess, *Calvin Coolidge* (Boston, 1940).

183

COOPER, THOMAS (1759), lawyer and chemist, professor and then president of South Carolina College (1820–1834). Dumas Malone, *The Public Life of Thomas Cooper, 1783–1839* (New Haven, 1926).

130

COREY, BROMFIELD (c. 1835), character in William D. Howells, *The Rise of Silas Lapham* (Boston, 1884).

142

CORNELL, EZRA (1807), inventor, one of the founders of Western Union Telegraph Company (1855) and patron of Cornell University.

114, 189

CRANE, STEPHEN (1871), novelist and author of *The Red Badge of Courage* (New York, 1895). R. W. Stallman, *Stephen Crane* (New York, 1968).

145, 164

CROCKETT, DAVY (1786), frontiersman and United States Congressman (1827–1831, 1833–1835). Constance Rourke, *Davy Crockett* (New York, 1934).

20, 81

CROWNINSHIELD, GEORGE (c. 1730), head of Salem mercantile family. William T. Whitney, "The Crowninshields of Salem," *Essex Institute Historical Collections,* XCIV (1958).
36

DAN (c. 1858), the wild boy in Louisa May Alcott, *Little Men* (1871).
152

DANA, RICHARD HENRY (1815), lawyer and author of *Two Years Before the Mast* (New York, 1840). Samuel Shapiro, *Richard Henry Dana, Jr., 1815–1882* (East Lansing, 1961); C. F. Adams, *Richard Henry Dana* (Boston, 1891); *Journal of Richard Henry Dana, Jr.* (R. F. Lucid, ed., Cambridge, 1968).
80, 88, 129, 151

DANFORTH, MARY SHEPARD (1853), physician in Manchester, New Hampshire. *New Hampshire Women* (Concord, 1895).
174

DANTE (1265), poet.
114

DAVIDSON, LUCRETIA MOTT (1808), precocious poetess who lived in Plattsburg, New York. Jared Sparks, *Library of American Biography* (Boston, 1837), VII.
94

DEAN, JAMES (1931), movie actor.
261

DEBRAY, RÉGIS (1941), philosophy student and revolutionary, author of *Revolution in the Revolution* (Paris, New York, 1967).
269

DEBS, EUGENE V. (1855), labor leader, frequent Socialist Party candidate for United States President, president of the American Railway Union, and author of *Debs, His Life, Writings and Speeches* (Chicago, 1910).
170

DELANCEY, JAMES (1703), born in the Province of New York, educated in Cambridge, England, Chief Justice and Lieutenant Governor of the colony.
54

DEPEW, CHAUNCEY M. (1834), lawyer, president of New York Central Railroad (1885–1898), and United States Senator from New York (1899–1911).
138

DERHAM, JAMES (1760), Negro physician in New Orleans. Kelly Miller, "Historic Background of the Negro Physician," *Journal of Negro History,* I (1916), 103.
89

DEWEY, JOHN (1859), philosopher and educator.
159

DILLON, MATT (c. 1890), character played by James Arness in the television series, *Gunsmoke*.

267

DODD, WILLIAM E. (1869), historian and diplomat, professor at University of Chicago (1908–1933), Ambassador to Germany (1933–1937). Robert Dallek, *Democrat and Diplomat the Life of William E. Dodd* (New York, 1968).

180

DOFFER, DEBBY (c. 1947), pseudonym of a student in an eastern college.

266, 267

DOUGLAS, STEPHEN A. (1813), lawyer and United States Senator from Illinois (1847–1861), unsuccessful candidate for United States President in 1860. Gerald M. Capers, *Stephen A. Douglas* (Boston, 1959).

70, 71, 86, 88, 111

DOUGLASS, FREDERICK (c. 1817), fugitive slave, abolitionist, politician, author of *Narrative of the Life of an American Slave* (Cambridge, 1960 [first publication, 1845]).

82

DRAPER, JOHN W. (1811), chemist, educator and author. Donald Fleming, *John William Draper and the Religion of Science* (Philadelphia, 1950).

113

DREISER, THEODORE (1871), journalist and author of *Sister Carrie* (New York, 1900); and *An American Tragedy* (1925). W. A. Swanberg, *Dreiser* (New York, 1965).

188

DUBOIS, W. E. B. (1868), historian, editor and Negro leader. W. E. B. DuBois, *The Souls of Black Folk* (New York, 1903); Francis C. Broderick, *W. E. B. DuBois* (Stanford, 1956).

188, 194, 195

DUNBAR, PAUL L. (1872), poet and Negro intellectual. Benjamin Brawley, *Paul Laurence Dunbar* (Chapel Hill, 1936).

172

DUNSTER, HENRY (1609), first president of Harvard College (1640–1654). Samuel E. Morison, *The Founding of Harvard College* (Cambridge, 1935).

58

DUSTIN. *See* Hoffman, Dustin

EARHART, AMELIA (1898), aviatrix.

171

EDISON, THOMAS ALVA (1847), inventor of the phonograph, incandescent lamp and other devices. Matthew Josephson, *Edison* (New

York, 1959); and F. L. Dyer and T. C. Martin, *Edison* (New York, 1929).

90, 91

EDWARDS, JONATHAN (1703), theologian, philosopher, president of the College of New Jersey at Princeton, author of *Freedom of the Will* (1754) and other religious works.

60

EISENHOWER, DWIGHT D. (1890), supreme commander of Allied Expeditionary Forces during World War II and thirty-fourth President of the United States (1953–1961).

139, 140, 257

ELIOT, CHARLES W. (1834), educational leader and president of Harvard University (1869–1909). Henry James, *Charles W. Eliot* (Cambridge, 1935).

90, 110, 123, 137, 185, 192, 204, 286

ELSSLER, FANNY (1810), Austrian dancer who toured the United States in 1842. Ivor Guest, *Fanny Elssler* (Middletown, Connecticut, 1970).

73

ELYOT, SIR THOMAS (c. 1490), English diplomat and author. William H. Woodward, *Studies in Education during the Age of the Renaissance* (Cambridge, 1906).

58

EMERSON, EDWARD BLISS ("NED") (1805), younger brother of Ralph Waldo Emerson, son of William.

76, 77, 96, 103, 165

EMERSON, RALPH WALDO (1803), brother of Edward, son of William, essayist, poet and clergyman. R. L. Rusk, *Life of Ralph Waldo Emerson* (New York, 1949); R. L. Rusk, ed., *Letters of Ralph Waldo Emerson* (New York, 1939).

76, 109, 111, 206, 257

EMERSON, WILLIAM (1769), clergyman, one of the founders of the Anthology Club, father of Ralph Waldo and Edward.

77, 111

FAIRBANKS, DOUGLAS (1883), stage and screen actor, famous in adventure films such as *The Three Musketeers* and *Robin Hood*.

167

FANON, FRANZ (1925), psychiatrist, participant in the Algerian revolution and author of *The Wretched of the Earth* (Paris, 1961, New York, 1963).

269

FARRELL, JAMES T. (1904), novelist, author of the Studs Lonigan trilogy (1932–1935).

172

Fernald, Mark (1784), Baptist pastor in Kittery, Maine, and itinerant preacher. Mark Fernald, *Life of Elder Mark Fernald* (Newburyport, 1852). *80*

Fessenden, Samuel (1784), graduate of Dartmouth, class of 1806, general in the Maine militia, leader of the Cumberland County bar, practicing in Portland. Francis Fessenden, *Life and Public Services of William Pitt Fessenden* (Boston, 1907). *89*

Field, Cynthia (c. 1950), student in a midwestern liberal arts college. *265*

Filbert, Howard (c. 1943), graduate student and strike leader at an eastern university. *262*

Finley, Robert (1772), clergyman, educator. Organizer of the American Colonization Society (1816); president of the University of Georgia. Isaac V. Brown, *Memoirs of Reverend Robert Finley* (New Brunswick, New Jersey, 1819). *122*

Finley, Samuel (1715), clergyman, evangelistic preacher, later president of the College of New Jersey at Princeton (1761–1766). *51*

Finn, Huckleberry (c. 1850), protagonist of Mark Twain's novel, *The Adventures of Huckleberry Finn* (1884). *152*

Fish, Hamilton (1808), lawyer, governor of New York (1849–1851). United States Senator (1851–1857) and Secretary of State (1869–1877). Allan Nevins, *Hamilton Fish: The Inner History of the Grant Administration* (New York, 1936). *98*

Fisher, Jonathan (1768), class of 1792 at Harvard, minister. Mary Ellen Chase, *Jonathan Fisher, Maine Parson* (New York, 1948). *79*

Fitch, James (1622), minister at Saybrook and then at Norwich, Connecticut. *325*

Fitzgerald, F. Scott (1896), novelist, author of *The Beautiful and the Damned* (1921), *The Great Gatsby* (1925), and *Tender Is the Night* (1934). Andrew Turnbull, *Scott Fitzgerald* (New York, 1962). *143*

Flanders, Martha J. (1823), physician in Lynn, Massachusetts. *110*

Flandrau, Charles M. (1871), Harvard B. A. (1895), author. *203*

FLANNER, JANET (1892), *New Yorker* correspondent under the name Genêt.

171

FLEMING, HENRY (c. 1845), Civil War soldier, character in Stephen Crane, *The Red Badge of Courage* (New York, 1895).

151

FLIPPER, HENRY O. (1856), Army officer and frontiersman. Henry O. Flipper, *A Colored Cadet at West Point* (New York, 1878).

188

FLYNT, HENRY (1675), tutor in Harvard College for many years.

64

FOLEY, TOM (c. 1852), New York City saloonkeeper and local political leader.

182

FOLLEN, CHARLES (KARL) (1796), emigrated from Germany in 1824. Professor of literature at Harvard University and active abolitionist.

133

FORD, HENRY (1863) , industrialist, pioneer automobile manufacturer. Allan Nevins, *Ford: The Times, The Man, The Company* (New York, 1954).

38, 160, 172

FORRESTER, CAPTAIN SIMON (1746), native of Waterford, Ireland, became richest merchant of Salem, Massachusetts, brother-in-law of Nathaniel Hawthorne the elder, uncle of the younger.

86

FRANKFURTER, FELIX (1882), lawyer, professor at Harvard Law School, and associate justice of United States Supreme Court. Helen S. Thomas, *Felix Frankfurter Scholar on the Bench* (Baltimore, 1960).

184

FRANKLIN, BENJAMIN (1706), printer, journalist, scientist, statesman, inventor, discoverer of the electrical nature of lightning in 1752, proposer of the one-fluid theory of electricity; member of the Second Continental Congress, 1775, brother of James, son of Josiah. Carl Van Doren, *Benjamin Franklin* (New York, 1938).

33, 34, 49, 57, 59, 65, 85

FRANKLIN, JAMES (1696), printer, journalist, brother of Benjamin, son of Josiah, and publisher of *New England Courant* (1721–1726).

34

FRANKLIN, JOSIAH (1658), Boston artisan, father of Benjamin and James.

34, 57

FROST, ROBERT (1874), poet whose important collections include *A Boy's Will* (London, 1913), *North of Boston* (London, 1914), and *A*

Further Range (1936), son of William P., Jr.; Lawrence Thompson, *Robert Frost the Early Years 1874–1915* (New York, 1966).

163, 198, 206

FROST, WILLIAM PRESCOTT, JR. (1850), teacher and journalist, father of Robert.

200

FULLER, MARGARET (1810), journalist, critic, social reformer and author of *Woman in the Nineteenth Century* (1845). Mason Wade, *Margaret Fuller* (New York, 1940); M. B. Stern, *Life of Margaret Fuller* (New York, 1942).

95

GANT, EUGENE (c. 1900), protagonist in Thomas Wolfe, *Look Homeward, Angel* (New York, 1929), and *Of Time and The River* (New York, 1935).

199

GARDNER, JOHN W. (1912), president of the Carnegie Corporation (1955–1965), Secretary of Health, Education and Welfare (1965–1968), chairman of Urban Coalition (1968) and Common Cause. *Chicago Sun-Times,* April 27, 1969, p. 11.

263

GARMAN, CHARLES EDWARD (1850), graduate of Amherst in 1872 and professor of moral philosophy there, after briefly teaching in high school.

206

GEORGE III (1738), King of England (1760–1820).

55

GESELL, ARNOLD (1880), psychologist and student of infancy and childhood.

229, 256

GILMAN, DANIEL C. (1831), educator, president of University of California (1872–1875), and The Johns Hopkins University (1875–1902). Fabian Franklin, *The Life of Daniel Coit Gilman* (New York, 1910).

190

GLASSMAN, JAMES K. (c. 1947), student, prospective journalist. James K. Glassman, "A History of Our Class," *Harvard Crimson,* June 12, 1969, p. 39.

262

GODDARD, ROBERT H. (1882), physicist and experimenter in rocketry. Milton Lehman, *This High Man* (New York, 1963).

144, 163

GOETHE, JOHANN WOLFGANG VON (1749), German poet and natural philosopher.

114

HANDY, W. C. (1873), musician, composer of "St. Louis Blues," and author of *Father of the Blues* (New York, 1941).

140

HANNAH, HUGH (c. 1750), merchant in Litchfield, Connecticut.

35

HARLOWE, CLARISSA (c. 1730), heroine of *Clarissa, or the Adventures of a Young Lady,* a novel by Samuel Richardson (1749).

92

HARPER, WILLIAM RAINEY (1856), educator, founder and president of University of Chicago (1891–1906). T. W. Goodspeed, *William Rainey Harper* (Chicago, 1928).

190, 198

HARRIMAN, AVERELL (1891), statesman, United States Ambassador, Secretary of Commerce (1946–1948) and governor of New York (1955–1958), son of Edward H.; Persia Campbell, *Mary Williamson Harriman* (New York, 1960).

199

HARRIMAN, EDWARD H. (1848), railroad executive and investor. George Kennan, *E. H. Harriman* (Boston, 1923).

143

HARVARD, JOHN (1607), benefactor of Harvard College.

54

HASKINS, JOHN (1729), seaman, grandfather of R. W. Emerson.

80

HAWTHORNE, NATHANIEL (1775), sea captain, father of Nathaniel.

76, 86

HAWTHORNE, NATHANIEL (1804), novelist, son of Nathaniel. Newton Arvin, *Hawthorne* (Boston, 1929).

76, 101, 123

HAY, JOHN (1838), poet, journalist and Secretary of State (1898–1905). Tyler Dennett, *John Hay* (New York, 1933); W. R. Thayer, *Life and Letters of John Hay* (Boston, 1915).

160

HEINZ, HENRY J. (1844), founder of prepared food firm. E. D. McCafferty, *Henry J. Heinz* (New York, 1923).

143

HEWITT, ABRAM S. (1822), iron manufacturer, statesman and philanthropist. Allan Nevins, *Abram S. Hewitt: With Some Account of Peter Cooper* (New York, 1935).

73

HILDRETH, AZRO B. F. (1816), teacher, printer, publisher and editor. Charles Aldrich, *Life and Times of Azro B. F. Hildreth* (Des Moines, 1891).

103, 111, 113

HITCHCOCK, EDWARD (1793), clergyman, geologist and educator; president of Amherst College (1845–1855).

130

HOFFMAN, ABBIE (1938), professional revolutionary, a founder of The Youth International Party ("Yippies") and author of *Revolution for the Hell of It* (New York, 1968); John J. Goldman, "There's Money in Revolution," *Los Angeles Times,* June 5, 1970.

261, 268

HOFFMAN, DUSTIN (1937), movie actor, star of *The Graduate* (1967).

258

HOLBROOK, ABIAH (1718), master of the South Writing School in Boston. Ray Nash, "Abiah Holbrook and His 'Writing Master's Amusement'," *Harvard Library Bulletin,* VII (1953), 88ff.

46

HOLMES, OLIVER WENDELL (1809), essayist, doctor and poet, father of Oliver Wendell, Jr.; Mark DeWolfe Howe, *Holmes of the Breakfast Table* (New York, 1939).

109

HOLMES, OLIVER WENDELL, JR. (1841), jurist and associate justice of United States Supreme Court (1902–1932). Mark DeWolfe Howe, *Justice Oliver Wendell Holmes* (Cambridge, 1957).

151

HOOVER, HERBERT (1874), mining engineer and thirty-first President of the United States (1929–1933).

256

HOPPER, DENNIS C. (1925), actor and director. *Life,* July 20, 1970.

262

HOWE, FANNY (c. 1942), short story writer. Fanny Howe, *Forty Whacks* (Boston, 1969).

264

HOWE, SAMUEL GRIDLEY (1801), physician and reformer, concerned with the education of the blind. Harold Schwartz, *Samuel Gridley Howe Social Reformer* (Cambridge, 1956).

68

HUNT, FREEMAN (1804), author on economic subjects, editor and publisher of a merchant's magazine.

72

HURSTON, ZORA NEALE (1901), novelist.

195

HUTCHINS, ROBERT M. (1899), lawyer, president of University of Chicago (1929–1945), foundation executive and author of *The Higher Learning in America* (New Haven, 1936).

244

HUTCHINSON, ANNE (1591), Massachusetts pioneer and religious dissenter. U. K. Rugg, *Unafraid: A Life of Anne Hutchinson* (Boston, 1930).

41

HYLAND, RICHARD E. (c. 1948), student in Harvard College and author of "Can We Know the Dancer from the Dance?," *Harvard Crimson* October 22, 1969.

270, 275

JACKSON, ANDREW (1767), soldier and seventh President of the United States (1829–1836). Marquis James, *Andrew Jackson* (Indianapolis, 1933).

68, 82, 84, 86, 88, 136, 167

JACKSON, THOMAS J. ("STONEWALL") (1824), Confederate general. G. F. R. Henderson, *Stonewall Jackson and the American Civil War* (London, 1898).

23, 113

JAMES, HENRY (1843), novelist, brother of William. Leon Edel, *Henry James* (Philadelphia, 1953–).

163

JAMES, JESSE W. (1847), desperado and train robber. Robertus Love, *The Rise and Fall of Jesse James* (New York, 1926).

152

JAMES, WILLIAM (1842), psychologist, philosopher and university professor, brother of Henry. Gay W. Allen, *William James* (New York, 1967).

198, 206

JARRATT, DEVEREUX (1732), minister of the Church of England in Virginia. *The Life of the Reverend Devereux Jarratt* (Baltimore, 1806).

325

JEFFERSON, THOMAS (1743), statesman, third President of the United States (1801–1809), author of the Declaration of Independence, 1776, and founder of the University of Virginia. Dumas Malone, *Jefferson and His Time* (Boston, 1948–1952).

115, 136

JOHNSON, ANDREW (1808), United States Senator from Tennessee (1857–1862), and seventeenth President of the United States (1865–1869). L. P. Stryker, *Andrew Johnson: A Study in Courage* (New York, 1929); Eric L. MacKitrick, *Andrew Johnson and Reconstruction* (Chicago, 1960).

68

JOHNSTON, JOHN (1781), migrated to New York in 1804 and there prospered as a merchant. Emily Johnston DeForest, *John Johnston of New York* (New York, 1909).

87, 325

JONES, JOHN PAUL (1747), American naval officer, hero of the American Revolution. S. E. Morison, *John Paul Jones* (Boston, 1959).

81, 167

JONES, TOM (194–?), black student leader at Cornell University. *New York Times,* April 24, 26, 1969.

283

KANT, IMMANUEL (1724), German philosopher.

268

KELLY, JOHN (1822), New York stonecutter, politician and Congressman. J. Fairfax McLaughlin, *The Life and Times of John Kelly* (New York, 1885).

99

KENNEDY, JOSEPH P. (1888), financier and American Ambassador to Great Britain (1937–1940). Richard J. Whalen, *The Founding Father* (New York, 1964).

188

KENNEDY, ROBERT F. (1925), United States Attorney General and Senator from New York (1965–1968).

275

KEY, FRANCIS SCOTT (1779), lawyer and author of the "Star-Spangled Banner" (1814).

124

KING, MARTIN LUTHER, JR. (1929), civil rights leader and advocate of nonviolence, Nobel Peace Prize winner 1964.

283, 284

KOERNER, GUSTAVE (1809), lawyer, statesman, historian and American Ambassador to Spain (1862–1864). *Memoirs of Gustave Koerner* (Thomas J. McCormack, ed., Cedar Rapids, 1909).

110

KRAMER, PETER D. (1949), member of Harvard class of 1970 and editor of the *Harvard Crimson.*

269

KUNEN, JAMES S. (1943), member of Columbia class of 1970 and author of *The Strawberry Statement* (New York, 1969).

264

LA FOLLETTE, ROBERT M. (1855), governor of Wisconsin (1900–1905), United States Senator (1906–1925) and Progressive Party presidential candidate in 1924. Belle and Fola La Follette, *Robert M. La Follette* (New York, 1953).

78, 95, 206

LANGDELL, CHRISTOPHER C. (1826), lawyer, Dane Professor (1870–1900) and dean of Harvard Law School.

103

LAPHAM, SILAS (c. 1835), central character in William Dean Howells's novel *The Rise of Silas Lapham* (1884).

142

LAWRENCE, ABBOTT (1792), merchant, Congressman, and philanthropist, United States Minister to Great Britain (1849–1852), one of the founders of the town of Lawrence, Massachusetts, in 1845.

118

LAWRENCE, CATHERINE S. (c. 1825), teacher, missionary, anti-slavery and temperance advocate, war nurse. *Autobiography: Sketch of Life and Labors of Miss Catherine S. Lawrence* (Albany, 1893).

111

LEE, ANN CARTER (1773), wife of Henry, mother of Robert E.

75

LEE, HENRY (1756), known as "Light-Horse Harry," revolutionary general, governor of Virginia (1792–1795), husband of Ann C., father of Robert E.; won fame as commander of cavalry known as "Lee's legion." E. M. Boyd, *Light-Horse Harry Lee* (New York, 1931).

69

LEE, MARY C. (1806), wife of Robert E.

92

LEE, ROBERT E. (1807), commander of the Confederate Army of Northern Virginia (1862–1864), son of Henry and Ann C., husband of Mary C.; Douglas S. Freeman, *Robert E. Lee: A Biography* (New York, 1934–1935).

69

LEHMAN, HERBERT H. (1878), banker, governor of New York State and United States Senator. Allan Nevins, *Herbert H. Lehman and His Era* (New York, 1963).

187

LEWIS, ELLIS (1798), lawyer and Chief Justice of Pennsylvania Supreme Court (1851–1857). Burton A. Konkle, *Life of Chief Justice Ellis Lewis* (Philadelphia, 1907).

85, 88

LEWIS, SINCLAIR ("RED") (1884), novelist. Mark Schorer, *Sinclair Lewis An American Life* (New York, 1961).

149

LEWIS, WILLIAM H. (1868), football star at Amherst and Harvard, attorney.

188

LIEBER, FRANCIS (1800), political economist, professor at South Carolina College (1835–1857) and later at Columbia University (1857–1872). Frank Freidel, *Francis Lieber, Nineteenth-Century Liberal* (Baton Rouge, 1947).

129

1964); C. C. James, *The Years of MacArthur* (Boston, 1970); F. T. Miller, *General Douglas MacArthur* (Chicago, 1942).

162

MacArthur, Mary P. H. (1852), mother of Douglas.

162

MacAuley, Jeremiah, ("Jerry") (1839), reformed criminal, evangelist, author of *Transformed, or the History of a River Thief* (New York, 1876).

82

McClellan, George B. (1826), soldier, railway executive, Union commander during Civil War and political figure, Democratic presidential candidate in 1864. *McClellan's Own Story* (New York, 1886).

106

McClure, David (1748), teacher, missionary to the Indians, minister in Connecticut. *Diary of David McClure* (New York, 1899).

32, 47, 52

Macdonough, Thomas (1783), naval officer who led American revolutionary forces to a vital naval victory on Lake Champlain in 1814. Rodney Macdonough, *Life of Commodore Thomas Macdonough* (Boston, 1909).

106

MacDougall, Alice Foote (1867), business woman. *The Autobiography of a Business Woman* (Boston, 1928).

163

M'Ilwaine, Richard (1834), Presbyterian minister and educator; author of *Memories of Three Score Years and Ten* (New York, 1908).

122

Maclean, John (1771), professor of chemistry. John Maclean, *Memoir* (Princeton, 1876).

121

McPherson, Aimee Semple (1890), evangelist.

171

McQuaid, Bernard (1823), Roman Catholic bishop of Rochester. Rick J. Zwierlein, *The Life and Letters of Bishop McQuaid* (Rochester, 1925–1927).

81

Manigault, Pierre (1729), Huguenot, native of France, established a prominent family line in South Carolina.

27

Mann, Horace (1796), lawyer, public school reformer and Congressman, later president of Antioch College (1853–1859). Henry Mann, *Life and Works of Horace Mann* (Boston, 1891).

99

Mao Tse-tung (1893), Chinese revolutionary and theorist.

270

MARCUSE, HERBERT (1898), educator, professor of political philosophy, Brandeis University (1954–1965), University of California, San Diego (1965–). Author of *Reason and Revolution* (Boston, 1941) and *One-Dimensional Man* (Boston, 1965).

269

MARKS, MARILLA (1840), lawyer in Washington, D.C., also United States Commissioner and Examiner in Chancery.

173

MARSH, GEORGE PERKINS (1801), lawyer, diplomat and scholar specializing in Scandinavian languages; Congressman from Vermont (1843–1849), author of *Man and Nature* (New York, 1864). Caroline Marsh, *Life and Letters of George Perkins Marsh* (New York, 1888).

122

MARSHALL, GEORGE C. (1880), United States Army Chief of Staff and Secretary of State and Defense. Forrest C. Pogue, *George C. Marshall* (New York, 1963).

139, 180

MARSHALL, JOHN (1755), lawyer, Chief Justice of the United States Supreme Court (1801–1835). Albert J. Beveridge, *Life of John Marshall* (Boston, 1916–1919).

88, 101

MATHER, INCREASE (1639), Puritan clergyman and educator. Kenneth B. Murdock, *Increase Mather* (Cambridge, 1925).

63

MAYO, WILLIAM W. (1819), physician. Helen B. Clapesattle, *The Doctors Mayo* (Minneapolis, 1941); Charles W. Mayo, *Mayo* (New York, 1968).

89

MEADLO, PAUL (1947), veteran of Vietnam. *New York Times,* November 25, 26, 1969.

267

MEEBER, CAROLINE. *See* Carrie, Sister

MEIKLEJOHN, ALEXANDER (1872), educator and president of Amherst College (1912–1924); chairman of Experimental College, University of Wisconsin (1926–1938).

208

MEREDITH, JAMES (1933), civil rights worker, first Negro admitted to the University of Mississippi in 1962 and author of *Three Years in Mississippi* (Bloomington, Indiana, 1966).

283

MERRIWELL, FRANK (c. 1875), central character in novels of Burt L. Standish, pen name of Gilbert Patten.

201

MILTON, JOHN (1608), English poet.
114

MITCHELL, MARIA (1818), astronomer and educator.
193

MOODY, DWIGHT L. (1837), evangelist and founder of Northfield Seminary and of Mt. Hermon School.
198

MOOR, JOSHUA (c. 1710), landowner in Mansfield, Connecticut, and benefactor of Wheelock's School.
51

MORGAN, J. PIERPONT (1837), merchant banker and financier. Frederick Lewis Allen, *The Great Pierpont Morgan* (New York, 1949).
87

MORROW, DWIGHT (1873), lawyer, banker, diplomat. Harold Nicolson, *Dwight Morrow* (New York, 1935).
183

MORSE, SAMUEL F. B. (1791), painter, inventor of the telegraph in 1835 and of the telegraph code. Carlton Mabie, *The American Leonardo: The Life of Samuel F. B. Morse* (New York, 1943).
103

NED. *See* Emerson, Edward Bliss

NEF, JOHN U. (1862), organic chemist and university professor who organized and headed the Department of Chemistry at the University of Chicago (1892–1915).
191

NEWELL, FANNY (c. 1800). *Fanny Newell's Memoirs* (Springfield, Massachusetts, 1833).
92

NEWMAN, PAUL (1925), movie actor and director.
258

NICHOLS, MIKE (1931), entertainer, movie director. "Mike Nichols Talks about His Films," *Atlantic Monthly,* February 1970.
261

NIXON, RICHARD M. (1913), thirty-seventh President of the United States (1969–).
275

NORTON, CHARLES ELIOT (1827), educator and author.
187

O'FLAHERTY, AL (1885), character in James T. Farrel, *No Star Is Lost* (New York, 1938).
170

O. HENRY. *See* Porter, William Sydney

O'HARA, JOHN (1905), novelist, author of *Ten North Frederick,* winner of National Book Award in 1955.

227

OPHELIA, MISS. *See* St. Clare, Ophelia

OSWALD, LEE HARVEY (1939), assassin of President John F. Kennedy. Albert H. Newman, *The Assassination of John F. Kennedy: The Reasons Why* (New York, 1970).

265

OWENS-ADAIR, B. A. (1840), Oregon pioneer, early female physician and author of *Some of Her Life Experiences* (Portland, n.d.).

94, 173

PACKARD, VANCE O. (1914), author of *The Status Seekers* (New York, 1959), and *The Pyramid Climbers* (New York, 1962).

237

PAGE, WALTER HINES (1855), editor and diplomat. B. J. Hendrick, *Life and Letters of Walter Hines Page* (Garden City, New York, 1922–1925).

191

PAINE, THOMAS (1737), revolutionary author of *Common Sense* (1776) and *The Age of Reason* (1794). M. D. Conway, *The Life of Thomas Paine* (New York, 1892).

131

PALMER, ALICE FREEMAN (1855), educator and president of Wellesley College (1881–1888). H. P. Palmer, *The Life of Alice Freeman Palmer* (Boston, 1908).

94

PALMER, CHARLES (1947), graduate of the University of California at Berkeley, elected president of the National Student Association, September 1969. *San Francisco Chronicle,* September 11, 1969.

271

PARRINGTON, V. L. (1871), professor, historian and author of *Main Currents of American Thought* (New York, 1927–1930).

188

PASCAL, BLAISE (1623), French philosopher.

267

PATTEN, GILBERT (1866), created character of Frank Merriwell, about whom he wrote numerous college stories.

210

PATTON, George Smith, Jr. (1885), United States Army general prominent in Second World War.

261

PEABODY, ENDICOTT (c. 1860), founder and headmaster of the Groton School.

184

PEABODY, GEORGE F. (1852), banker and philanthropist. Louise Ware, *George Foster Peabody* (Boston, 1951).

87

PECK, GEORGE W. (1840), humorist and journalist in Milwaukee, author of *Peck's Bad Boy* (Chicago, 1883).

152

PENROD. *See* Schofield, Penrod

PERKINS, FRANCES (1882), sociologist, government official, United States Secretary of Labor (1933–1945).

160

PERKINS, THOMAS H. (1764), Boston merchant active in trade with China and India, philanthropist.

68

PERRY, OLIVER (1785), naval officer, commander of naval forces on Lake Erie in victory over British, 1813.

81

PHILLIPS, JOHN (1719), land speculator and philanthropist, uncle of Samuel, incorporated and endowed Phillips Exeter Academy in 1781.

102

PHILLIPS, SAMUEL (1752), educator and public official, founder of Phillips Academy at Andover in 1771, nephew of John.

102

Phips, Sir William (1650/1651), colonial merchant and governor of Massachusetts (1692–1694). Cotton Mather, *Pietas in Pietam, The Life of His Excellency Sir William Phips* (London, 1697).

16

PILLAR, ROBERT J. (c. 1949), pseudonym of a college student.

266

PINCHOT, GIFFORD (1865), professional forester and progressive political figure whose dismissal during Taft's administration led to a bitter dispute. M. Nelson McGeary, *Gifford Pinchot* (Princeton, 1960).

164

PORTER, WILLIAM SYDNEY (1862), short story writer who used the pen name of O. Henry. C. A. Smith, *O. Henry* (Garden City, New York, 1916); Gerald Langford, *Alias O. Henry* (New York, 1957).

170, 171

POWELL, RICHARD S. *See* Barbour, Ralph Henry

PRATT, JULIUS H. (1821), Yale graduate, teacher, businessman, and author of *Reminiscences* (n.p., 1910).

73

PRATT, R. H. (1840), soldier and founder of Indian School at Carlisle, Pennsylvania, 1879. Paul E. Zuver, *Short History of Carlisle Barracks* (Carlisle Barracks, 1934); Thomas G. Tousey, *Military History of Carlisle and Carlisle Barracks* (Richmond, 1939).
179

PUPIN, MICHAEL (1858), physicist and inventor. Michael Pupin, *From Immigrant to Inventor* (New York, 1923).
140

QUINCY, JOSIAH (1772), political figure and mayor of Boston. Edmund Quincy, *Life of Josiah Quincy* (Boston, 1867).
103, 104

RAY, JAMES EARL (1928), assassin of Martin Luther King. William B. Huie, *He Slew the Dreamer* (New York, 1970).
265

REED, JOHN (1887), journalist, witness of the Russian Revolution and author of *Ten Days That Shook the World* (1919).
198

RHETT, ROBERT BARNWELL (1800), lawyer, Congressman (1837–1849) and editor of *Charlestown Mercury*. Laura A. White, *Robert Barnwell Rhett: Father of Secession* (New York, 1931).
88

RICE, JOHN HOLT (1777), Presbyterian clergyman and educator.
72

RICHARDSON, MARY. *See* Walker, Mary Richardson

RIIS, JACOB A. (1849), journalist, reformer who effected massive improvements in housing through his writings, and author of *How the Other Half Lives* (1890) and *The Making of an American* (New York, 1902). Louise Ware, *Jacob A. Riis* (New York, 1938).
168

ROCKEFELLER, JOHN D. (1839), industrialist and philanthropist. Allan Nevins, *Study in Power: John D. Rockefeller* (New York, 1953).
83, 87, 143, 181

ROE, EDWARD PAYSAN (1839), Presbyterian clergyman and popular novelist.
151

ROGERS, ROBERT (c. 1800), conducted a classical school in Newport, Rhode Island.
101

ROOSEVELT, THEODORE (1858), statesman, historian and twenty-sixth President of United States (1901–1910).

202

ROYALL, ANNE (1769), traveler and writer.

93

RUBIN, JERRY (1939), revolutionary and business rival of Abbie Hoffman. Jerry Rubin, *Do It* (New York, 1970).

261

RUSH, BENJAMIN (1745), physician and signer of Declaration of Independence. N. G. Goodman, *Benjamin Rush: Physician and Citizen* (Philadelphia, 1934); *Autobiography* (G. W. Corner, ed., Princeton, 1949).

38, 40, 50

RUTGERS, HENRY (1745), landowner, revolutionary officer and philanthropist.

119

RUTH, GEORGE HERMAN ("BABE") (1895), professional baseball player.

167

ST. CLARE, AUGUSTINE (c. 1820), wealthy resident of New Orleans, character in Harriet Beecher Stowe's *Uncle Tom's Cabin*. H. B. Stowe, *A Key to Uncle Tom's Cabin* (Boston, 1853), 35.

72, 92

ST. CLARE, MARIE (c. 1827), wife of Augustine in *Uncle Tom's Cabin*. Stowe, *Key to Uncle Tom's Cabin*, p. 33.

91, 92

ST. CLARE, OPHELIA (c. 1818), Yankee cousin of Augustine in *Uncle Tom's Cabin*.

72, 92

SANTAYANA, GEORGE (1863), philosopher and teacher. George Santayana, *Persons and Places* (New York, 1944); and *Character and Opinion in the United States* (New York, 1934).

185

SCHLATTER, MICHAEL (1716), clergyman, educator and patriot. H. Harbaugh, *Life of Reverend Michael Schlatter* (Philadelphia, 1857).

43

SCHOFIELD, PENROD (c. 1904), central character of Booth Tarkington's novel *Penrod* (New York, 1914).

152

SCOTT, WINFIELD (1786), soldier and statesman. Edward D. Mansfield, *Life and Services of General Winfield Scott* (New York, 1852).

24, 82, 120

SCRIBNER, JOHN M. (1806), minister of the Dutch Reformed Church, Rochester, New York, and author of books on engineering.

113

SEVIER, JOHN (1745), pioneer, soldier and governor of Tennessee; C. S. Driver, *John Sevier: Pioneer of the Old Southwest* (Chapel Hill, 1932).

35

SHEARER, NORMA (1900), movie actress.

171

SHELBY, GEORGE (c. 1840), character in Harriet Beecher Stowe's novel *Uncle Tom's Cabin*.

123

SIBLEY, JOHN L. (1804), minister and librarian of the Harvard College Library.

109

SILLIMAN, BENJAMIN (1779), scientist, professor of chemistry and natural history at Yale University. E. F. Fulton and E. H. Thomson, *Benjamin Silliman* (New York, 1947).

121

SILSBEE, NATHANIEL (1773), Massachusetts mariner, shipowner and merchant.

86

SIMS, J. MARION (1813), gynecologist and author of *The Story of My Life* (New York, 1885).

69

SLATER, SAMUEL (1768), one of the founders of the cotton spinning industry. G. S. White, *Memoir of Samuel Slater, The Father of American Manufacturers* (Philadelphia, 1836).

72, 107

SLOAN, ALFRED P., JR. (1875), industrialist and president of General Motors.

175

SMITH, ALFRED E. (1873), figure in New York politics, governor of the state and unsuccessful candidate for United States presidency in 1928. Oscar Handlin, *Al Smith and His America* (Boston, 1958).

168

SMITH, CATHERINE DUNN (c. 1875), wife of Alfred.

168

SMITH, CATHERINE MULVEHILL (c. 1845), mother of Alfred.

168

SMITH, CHARLES PERRIN (1819), politician, editor and genealogist. Hermann K. Platt, *Charles Perrin Smith* (New Brunswick, 1965).

142

SMITH, J. ALLEN (1860), political scientist and university professor, author of *The Spirit of American Government* (New York, 1907).

188

SMITH, WILLIAM (1726), Scottish-born provost of The College in Philadelphia, orator and patriot.

58, 65

SNYDER, ORA HENRIETTA (1876), business executive.

171

SPARKS, JARED (1789), editor of the *North American Review,* later professor of history and president of Harvard University. H. B. Adams, *Life and Writings of Jared Sparks* (Boston, 1893).

103, 109, 122

SPOCK, BENJAMIN (1903), physician, author. Benjamin Spock, *Decent and Indecent* (New York, 1970).

229, 256

STANDISH, BURT L. *See* Patten, Gilbert

STEFFENS, JOSEPH (c. 1835), migrant to California where he earned a fortune in trade, father of Lincoln.

100

STEFFENS, LINCOLN (1866), reporter and author. *The Autobiography of Lincoln Steffens* (New York, 1931).

185

STEINBECK, JOHN (1902), novelist and Nobel Prize winner in literature.

171

STEWART, A. T. (1803), drygoods merchant whose shop developed into the largest retail store in America.

68

STILES, EZRA (1725), clergyman, educator and author.

65

STONE, HARLAN FISKE (1872), lawyer, professor of law and associate justice of United States Supreme Court. Alpheus T. Mason, *Harlan Fiske Stone, Pillar of the Law* (New York, 1956).

181, 182, 183, 196, 206

STORY, JOSEPH (1779), lawyer, professor of law and associate justice of United States Supreme Court.

68, 69

STOVER, DINK (c. 1890), student at Yale in the stories by Owen Johnson (1878–1952).

197, 198, 201, 206

STOWE, HARRIET BEECHER (1811), author of *Uncle Tom's Cabin* (Boston, 1852), sister of Catharine Beecher and Henry Ward Beecher.

92

STRINDBERG, JOHN AUGUST (1849), Swedish novelist, dramatist and publicist.

206

STRONG, JONATHAN (c. 1940), author of *Tike and Five Stories* (Boston, 1969).

264

STURGIS, WILLIAM (1782), merchant, prominent in the China trade.

86

SUNDAY, WILLIAM A. ("BILLY") (1862), professional baseball player, evangelist and prohibitionist. William G. McLoughlin, *Billy Sunday Was His Real Name* (Chicago, 1955); Thomas Lee, *The Billy Sunday Story* (Grand Rapids, 1961).

170, 171

SUTER, JOHN (1781), orphaned at eight, went to sea, earned fortune as ship captain.

86

TAPPAN, ABRAHAM B. (c. 1830), lawyer who practiced in Fordham, Bronx County, New York; appointed to the state judiciary in 1867.

173

TAPPAN, HENRY P. (1805), clergyman and president of University of Michigan.

120, 125

TARKINGTON, BOOTH (1869), novelist, author of *Penrod* (1914).

152

TAYLOR, SAMUEL HARVEY ("UNCLE SAM") (1807), graduate of Dartmouth, classicist and principal of Phillips Academy, Andover, Massachusetts.

103

TAYLOR-COLE, ANNA B. (c. 1860), physician in Somerville, Massachusetts.

174

TERRELL, MARY CHURCH (c. 1865), graduate of Oberlin, taught at Wilberforce, member of the Board of Education of the District of Columbia, lecturer and writer, author of *A Colored Woman in a White World* (Washington, 1940).

195

THOMAS, MARTHA CAREY (1847), suffragette, educator and president of Bryn Mawr College. Barbara M. Cross, ed., *The Educated Woman in America* (New York, 1965).

193

TOCQUEVILLE, ALEXIS DE (1805), French social analyst, traveler and historian, author of *Democracy in America* (1835).

78

TOLSTOY, LEO (1828), Russian novelist and social reformer, author of *Anna Karenina* (1875–1877).

206

TRUMAN, HARRY S. (1884), thirty-third President of the United States (1945–1953).

256

TRUMBULL, JOHN (1750), lawyer and poet, one of the Hartford wits.

65

TWAIN, MARK, *See* Clemens, Samuel L.

TYLER, TOBY (c. 1871), leading character in James Otis (Kaler), *Toby Tyler; or Ten Weeks with a Circus* (New York, 1881).

151

VEBLEN, THORSTEIN (1857), educator and economist. Author of *The Higher Learning in America* (1918). Joseph Dorfman, *Thorstein Veblen and His America* (New York, 1934).

188

VESEY, DENMARK (c. 1790), Negro carpenter who had gained his freedom and was accused of conspiracy to revolt in Charleston, South Carolina in 1822.

83

VILLARD, HENRY (1835), journalist and railroad executive. *Henry Villard, Memoirs* (Boston, 1904).

83

VINTON, ALEXANDER H. (1807), Episcopal clergyman and pastor of St. Paul's Cathedral, Boston, after 1841.

325

WAEGELIN, PROFESSOR (c. 1690), theologian in St. Gall, Switzerland.

43

WAITE, MORRISON R. (1816), lawyer, and Chief Justice of United States Supreme Court. Bruce R. Trimble, *Chief Justice Waite, Defender of the Public Interest* (Princeton, 1938).

83

WALKER, MARY RICHARDSON (1811), teacher in Maine and missionary among the Spokanes. Clifford M. Drury, *Elkanah and Mary Walker* (Caldwell, Iowa, 1940).

95

WALLACE, HENRY A. (1888), agricultural experimenter, Secretary of Agriculture, Vice-President and third-party candidate for the presidency in 1948. Dwight Macdonald, *Henry Wallace* (New York, 1948).

256

WASHINGTON, BOOKER T. (c. 1859), Negro educator and leader. E. J. Mathew, *Booker T. Washington* (Cambridge, 1948).

140, 178, 179

WILEY, REBECCA WEEKS (1848), homeopathic physician in Laconia, New Hampshire.
174

WILLARD, EMMA HART (1787), teacher and founder of the Troy Female Seminary. Alma Lutz, *Emma Willard* (Boston, 1964).
104

WILLIAMS, ROBERT LEE (1868), governor of Oklahoma and justice in the state and federal courts. Edward Everett Dale and James D. Morrison, *Pioneer Judge* (Cedar Rapids, Iowa, 1958).
162

WILLIAMS, WILLIAM CARLOS (1883), pediatrician and poet. *Autobiography of William Carlos Williams* (New York, 1951).
163, 175

WINTHROP, JOHN (1714), Hollis Professor of mathematics and natural science at Harvard (1738–1779).
65

WISE, JOHN (1652), Congregational clergyman and community leader in Ipswich, Massachusetts.
43

WISTER, OWEN (1860), lawyer and novelist.
203

WITHERSPOON, JOHN (1723), Presbyterian clergyman, member of Continental Congress, signer of Declaration of Independence and college president. E. L. Collins, *President Witherspoon* (Princeton, 1925).
54, 65

WRIGHT, CARROLL D. (1840), statistician, labor expert and bureaucrat. Massachusetts Bureau of the Statistics of Labor, *Sixth Annual Report* (1875), pp. 23, 57; James Leiby, *Carroll Wright* (Cambridge, 1960).
156

WRIGHT, RICHARD (1908), novelist, author of *Black Boy* (1945) and *Native Son* (1940). Constance Webb, *Richard Wright* (New York, 1968).
172

YALE, ELIHU (1649), English official in India, benefactor of the college at New Haven.
55

YOUNG, JACOB (1776), Methodist minister, itinerant preacher in the South and Middle West and author of *Autobiography of a Pioneer* (Cincinnati, 1857).
90

OTHER REFERENCES

We have treated some of the subjects of this book in detail in the following:

The American College and American Culture. New York, 1970.

"Are the Colleges Killing Education?" *Atlantic Monthly,* CCIX (1962), 41 ff.

"College and Community in 1900," *Harvard Library Bulletin,* Spring, 1958.

"Ethnic Factors and Social Mobility," *Explorations in Entrepreneurial History,* IX (1956), 1 ff.

John Dewey's Challenge to Education, New York, 1959.

"Live Students and Dead Education," *Atlantic Monthly,* September, 1961.

"Textbooks that Don't Teach," *Atlantic Monthly,* December, 1957.

"The Vulnerability of the American University," *Encounter,* March, 1970.

"Yearning for Security," *Atlantic Monthly,* January, 1951.

Other References

page:

14 The Puritan was James Fitch.

33 Devereux Jarratt's teaching career was representative.

68 *The Rivulet* (Boston Latin School), June 7, 1848.

77 The father whose son went to Yale was John Johnston.

79 The minister was Alexander H. Vinton.

91 The novel was *Uncle Tom's Cabin.*

126 The boy at Brown was Francis J. Lippitt.

128 Jonathan Fisher observed the puking.

151 The minister was Richard M'Ilwaine.

164 The orator was Phillips Brooks.

168 The estimate is from "The Little Laborers of New York City," *Harper's New Monthly Magazine,* XLVII (August, 1873), 325.

194 *The Fortnightly Philistine* (October 27, 1899), 8ff.

202 "Fatiguing," in Louis G. Geiger, *University of the Northern Plains* (Grand Forks, 1958), 239.

202 *The Fortnightly Philistine* (November 23, 1900), 3ff.

234 Howard M. Bell, *Youth Tell Their Story* (Washington, D.C., 1938), 58 ff.; August B. Hollingshead, *Elmtown's Youth* (New York, 1949).

251 The novel referred to is George A. Weller, *Not to Eat Not for Love* (New York, 1933).

253 "The Careful Young Men," *The Nation,* CLXXXIV (March 4, 1957), 199–214; "The Class of '58 Speaks Up," *The Nation,* CLXXXVI (May 17, 1958), 432–39.

263 The Barnard incident is reported in *New York Times,* March 15, 1968, 42.

264 Samuel Bonder, "For Betty, With No Hard Feelings," *Harvard Crimson,* June 12, 1969.

267 Scarsdale is reported in *New York Times,* August 15, 16, 1969.

268 Ira C. Magaziner, "We Need a Cultural Revolution," *Brown Alumni Monthly* (July, 1969), 30ff.

268 Stylish examples are Susan Sontag, *Styles of Radical Will* (New York, 1969); Michael Novak, *The Experience of Nothingness* (New York, 1970).

269 Dr. Nicholas J. Fiumara of Boston (UPI), IHT, March 4, 1970; Mervin B. Freedman and Harvey Powelson, "Drugs on Campus," *The Nation,* CCII (January 21, 1966), 125–27.

271 On the small numbers of the student radicals, Robert Martinson, "State of the Campus: 1962," *The Nation,* CXCIV (May 19, 1962), 432 ff.; Jeffrey K. Hadden, "The Private Generation," *Psychology Today* (October, 1969); "The New Mood on Campus," *Newsweek,* December 29, 1969, p. 43; James A. and Robert K. Foley, *The College Scene* (New York, 1969), 49 ff., 170 ff.; Kenneth Keniston, "Sources of Student Dissent," *Journal of Social Issues,* XXIII (1967), 109, and "Heads and Seekers," *The American Scholar,* XXXVIII (1968), 97 ff.

281 John R. Seeley provides a particularly fatuous example of such justification in *The Center Magazine,* II (May, 1969), 15.

page:

281 William S. Coffin, "Education," *Playboy,* XVI (January, 1969), 91, 282–84.

285 The tight pants statement is in Armstead L. Robinson, Craig C. Foster, and Donald H. Ogilvie, *Black Studies in the University* (New Haven, 1969), 47.